"The *heartbeat* of this book is vocation—
released, and re-created over the seaso
juxtaposing narratives with theological ai
biblical interludes to yield fresh, fluid pe _ .... w w
dom is penetrating, contributing freshly to the literature on vocation and
to people who deliberate the meaning and purpose of their lives."

— MARY ELIZABETH MOORE
Boston University School of Theology

"Discussions of vocation and calling have typically focused on the experience of young adults—and rightly so, given the pivotal nature of this stage
of life for reflection on questions of meaning and purpose. But Cahalan
and Miller-McLemore invite us to expand our vision, reminding us of the
relevance of vocation throughout the life course."

— DAVID S. CUNNINGHAM
Network for Vocation in Undergraduate
Education Scholarly Resources Project,
Council of Independent Colleges

"Several decades ago now, James Fowler elaborated a typology of the ages
and stages of human development as they related to faith. The criticisms
of Fowler's vision were so severe as to stifle reflection on the theological
significance of human ages and stages. Cahalan, Miller-McLemore, and
their coauthors revive this important conversation by illuminating concrete dynamics of development that hold theological meaning."

— DAVID WHITE
Austin Presbyterian Theological Seminary

"This is a beautiful book that weaves divine and human stories together.
Alternating between pertinent biblical reflection and scholarly inquiry, the
authors provide a generative and thoughtful engagement with the dynamics of life from the earliest moment of childhood through to the challenging
transitions of late adulthood. In the process they make the strongest case
I've read for using vocation as an invitation for discernment."

— MARY E. HESS
University of St. Michael's College,
University of Toronto

Calling All Years Good

Christian Vocation
throughout Life's Seasons

Edited by

Kathleen A. Cahalan
Bonnie J. Miller-McLemore

WILLIAM B. EERDMANS PUBLISHING COMPANY
GRAND RAPIDS, MICHIGAN

Wm. B. Eerdmans Publishing Co.
2140 Oak Industrial Drive NE, Grand Rapids, Michigan 49505
www.eerdmans.com

Published 2017
Printed in the United States of America

26 25 24 23 22 21 20 19 18 17   1 2 3 4 5 6 7 8 9 10

ISBN 978-0-8028-7424-5

Library of Congress Cataloging-in-Publication Data

Names: Cahalan, Kathleen A., editor.
Title: Calling all years good : Christian vocation throughout life's seasons /
    edited by Kathleen A. Cahalan, Bonnie J. Miller-McLemore.
Description: Grand Rapids : Eerdmans Publishing Co., 2017. |
    Includes bibliographical references and index.
Identifiers: LCCN 2017010012 | ISBN 9780802874245 (pbk. : alk. paper)
Subjects: LCSH: Vocation—Christianity. | Life cycle, Human—Religious aspects—Christianity.
Classification: LCC BV4740.C3155 2017 | DDC 248.8—dc23
    LC record available at https://lccn.loc.gov/2017010012

Contents

CONTENTS

Introduction

Finding Life's Purposes in God's Purposes

KATHLEEN A. CAHALAN

Do older persons with dementia have a calling? Or newborns? Can children before they walk and talk have a sense of vocation or teenagers as puberty disrupts their bodies, relationships, and sense of self? When I began working on a theology of vocation in 2010 through the Collegeville Institute Seminars, these questions did not occur to me. In fact, I thought I might plan a seminar focused on young adults, particularly as they left college and entered the workforce. But after listening to theologians, pastors, and social scientists—all experts on vocation (and some on young adults) during the first summer of the project—I changed my mind. In fact, retirement emerged as one of the central vocational moments in adult life. As I began to consider the questions and issues that emerge when we leave full-time paid employment, I began to think about the elderly, children, and teens. Where were they in the vocation literature? Clearly young adulthood is pivotal to vocation, but by focusing on this one time of life our research would fail to capture vocation as a lifelong question and experience.[1] Furthermore, it would make the issues of young adulthood central to vocation and thereby obscure the challenges that arise during retirement, childhood, and other life phases. So I decided to launch a seminar devoted to this question: What would a lifelong perspective do to our understanding of vocation?

This volume attempts, then, to offer a perspective quite unique in the literature on vocation as well as in the literature on lifecycle development by examining callings over the span of human life. What does it mean to talk about God's callings in relationship to the duration of our lives, from birth to old age? What difference does it make to understand Christian vocation not only from the experiences of young adulthood but also from the play of children, the transition into assisted living in late adulthood, and the middle years of multiple callings? We have found that engaging vocation across the span of our lives demands a more nuanced theology than previous interpretations of calling offered in the Christian tradition, especially when we consider it outside the framework of speech, rationality, and choice, as with a newborn or a person with dementia. In addition, the pursuit of meaning and purpose in life, which is central to Christian understandings of vocation, is integral to human personhood but is often missing in current social science theories on the lifespan. We believe that a theological understanding of calling, broadly understood as discerning one's life purpose in relationship to God's purposes, has something to offer both theology and lifespan theory.

A Theology of Calling: Lost but Found

At the outset of the Seminars' work on vocation, we decided that rather than reframing the *idea* of vocation and teaching it to people[2] we would first attempt to understand how people, primarily those in churches, understand their life as a calling.[3] What operative notions of vocation exist in the Christian community? Is vocation a meaningful way that people interpret their lives, or is it trapped in outmoded notions from the past? What would be most helpful to people if we invited them to reframe their understanding of vocation, drawing insights from the tradition as well as engaging new frameworks? Or is the idea or very term "vocation" beyond repair and too corrupted by historical interpretations to be of much use to us today?

Over the past five years, under the direction of the Seminars' research associate Laura Kelly Fanucci, we have gathered hundreds of people—Protestants and Catholics—in small groups, primarily in congregations, and asked them to reflect on a series of questions: What is my sense of God's callings in my life? How can I learn to listen to God's call? How do I live out multiple callings in service to others? How have challenges and struggles shaped my callings? How is my vocation changing over my lifetime?[4]

What we heard from these participants shaped our work in profound ways. First, most people in our small groups had limited, mostly nonexistent, experiences and conceptions of God as Caller. Remember, these were people from various churches who volunteered to participate in a six-week program to think about their life as vocation. For example, Jay described his life in terms of multiple commitments and joys: marriage, children, and extended family. He described his skills as a financial analyst and his ability to help others make difficult decisions. He spoke of how he found God in others, especially as a father, husband, leader, and little league coach. Jay felt gratitude for his life, and he wanted to give back to the community. But at the end of our first discussion he concluded: "But I don't know that I've ever been given a calling."[5]

Second, when asked about vocation most people tend to refer to the major commitments clustered in the young adult years pertaining to work and partnering, as I initially did. When we engaged college students they expressed anxiety and fear that they might miss God's one call. They assumed that there is a single answer to the question of vocation and once they find it, discerning callings is mostly over. But framing vocation as decisions made in young adulthood left most other adults, especially as they get older, feeling that figuring out callings did not have much to do with them.

Third, those people who could recount stories of having a sense of calling as a child or a teen tended to discount their religious experiences or lacked a way to talk about or interpret the experience. Operatively, their notion of a calling that comes from God remains rather calculating, too easily imaging God as having a definite plan or will for them. Discernment constituted figuring out this deeply held secret or having direct access to God's wishes. Experiences of hearing or seeing, having a dream, being grasped or drawn to an activity or a place, giving extensively to community or religious organizations, identifying and utilizing particular gifts, or being invited by another to share those gifts—these common experiences were not framed as calling experiences.

If people examine their lives through the lens of calling, they do it primarily through what psychologist and contributor to this volume Matt Bloom calls "retrospective sense-making," looking back and creating a narrative to make sense of their lives and discovering God's hand at work in the past.[6] Few people we talked to either looked inward or forward to consider how God might be calling them now and in the future.

Fourth, most communities are not places of calling—that is, communities whose vocation it is to draw forth each person's callings as well as the vocation of the whole community. We found that congregations, schools, and campus ministries generally do not engage people in the practices of vocation. For instance, many people reported that their small group was the first time they had been asked such questions. In relationship to work, for example, a majority said their pastors and congregations had rarely asked them about their job or profession, what they did, why they did it, what they loved, and what they were good at. Those who were retiring had little opportunity to explore the new horizon of callings in the next part of life. Generally, the key practices of vocation—discernment, prayer, and storytelling—are not fostered in congregations, the most obvious places where one might expect such activities to occur. Religious education, sermons, and sacraments or other celebrations seldom address vocation or foster vocational conversation, especially across the lifespan. We also found that most people did not pray about their callings or seek guidance and direction from the Spirit or from others, especially when they were younger and deciding what to do, where to do it, and for whom. The majority of people did not have a listening practice to hear God's guidance, such as regular prayer with scripture or a silent meditation practice. Most significantly, they had not learned to foster a relationship with God who is understood as the "Caller."

Finally, the language of vocation was not compelling for most people. When we began we suspected that we would find outmoded Protestant and Catholic theologies—that vocation is equated with work (Protestants) or has to do with states of life (Catholics) or with a call to ministry (both)—and we did to some extent. But what we mostly found is that people had no idea what the word "vocation" means. The term almost always fell flat: people did not know what it referred to in greater depth. As a central doctrine and vocabulary of the Christian faith, vocation is nearly gone.

However, when we heard people's stories we began to see that what traditionally would be referred to as the "language of callings" was everywhere: meaningful relationships; powerful experiences of being given something to do; purposeful work, skills, and abilities experienced as gifts; confirmation about who one is; a sense of gratitude; struggles through transitions and painful loss; aspirations to serve others; and a desire to give themselves to God's people for God's purposes. In fact, people have a deep sense of calling in their lives but they often lack ways to make sense of it.

Recovering the Language of Vocation

What, then, happened to the language of vocation, a language that was once rich in the Christian vocabulary? In modernity, many Christians held

4

narrow views of divine power and purpose that portrayed a provident all-powerful deity who makes blueprints for human lives. Such an image proved untenable, and by the twentieth century many had tossed it into the dustbin of useless religious concepts. Furthermore, vocation became a doctrine to be believed in rather than a lived practice. It functioned primarily as a noun—*what is my vocation?*—rather than as a relationship, a process, or a creative endeavor. The language of calling became static and fixed rather than dynamic and fluid, something church and academic theologians might talk about but not something everyday people needed to consider.

And yet the language of calling is everywhere. What Christians have largely lost, others have discovered. The titles of several books about "calling" demonstrate the way in which it has become the language of the secular age: *Callings: Finding and Following an Authentic Life; Your Personal Renaissance: 12 Steps to Finding Your Life's True Calling; The Path to Purpose: How Young People Find Their Calling in Life; Let Your Life Speak: Listening for the Voice of Vocation.*[7] *The New York Times* featured a series entitled "Vocations" in the business section for a short time; it is now called "What I Love."[8] And the evangelical pastor Rick Warren, whose book *The Purpose Driven Life* has sold millions of copies, prefers the language of "purpose" over that of "vocation" or "calling," but he is essentially talking about the same reality.[9]

The search engine Google Ngram Viewer tabulates the frequency of words, now covering about five million books. Terms such as "purpose" and "meaning" have grown in usage since the 1900s, rising steadily up to today; "calling" also has had steady usage. But the term "vocation," the least used of the four terms, gained some steam around the 1920s, but dropped considerably by 2000. While not a scientific study, word usage reveals that the language of "purpose" and "meaning" has gained ground as the culture has become more secular. The term "calling" certainly leans more in a nonreligious direction despite the fact that "calling" and "vocation" are nearly synonymous terms.

What secular writers on calling have discovered is that vocation is a deeply human quest. What is the purpose of my life? To what shall I give myself? Whom shall I serve? Such questions are at the same time both frightening and exhilarating. They press for an answer. Terms like "purpose" and "meaning" also seem like they offer a greater avenue than the term "vocation" for considering change and development across the lifespan. However, these secular understandings of calling have deep roots in the Christian tradition's claim, whether these authors recognize this heritage or not, that each person is made in the image of God, has inherent dignity and worth, and lives with a purpose shaped by divine initiative. Moreover, our culture's "expressive individualism" prizes the notion that each person has an inner nature, truth, or self that drives toward expression.[10] Such common or popular notions of calling in the broader culture are influenced by an unnecessarily singular focus on human well-being at the expense of community, the animal world, and the environment as well as divine life and its purposes. In large part, theological sources for vocation have been severed from its broader cultural meaning today. But as we reframe vocation in this book, we see that the Christian tradition gives us a much broader framework that honors the deeply personal and individual character of calling but claims this human quest as fundamentally communal and divine.

A Practical Theological Consideration of Vocation

Why, then, pursue a theology of vocation? What difference does a practical theological understanding of vocation make? Our approach to vocation across the lifespan takes account of several ways in which theology is rendered as practical.[11] First, we begin with the stories and experiences of calling—we listened to people in churches, and when the Seminar participants gathered over the past four years, we told stories of our own callings as children, teens, young adults, and adults. When we were learning about phases of the lifespan we had not yet experienced, such as older adulthood, we interviewed people in our families and communities, and we relied significantly on social science literature that includes empirical study of people's lives.

Vocation, we contend, is inherently narrative. Its first language is story. According to personality psychologist Dan McAdams, author of *The Stories We Live By*, "If you want to know me, then you must know my story, for my story defines who I am. And if *I* want to know *myself*, to gain insight into the meaning of my own life, then I, too, must come to know my own story ... a story I continue to revise, and to tell to myself (and sometimes to others) as I go on living."[12] We found McAdams's claim to be true: telling stories about our lives helps each of us to reframe our identity and purposes. But beyond self-insight, we found that telling stories about our callings forged strong bonds of friendship. Once you hear other people's stories about their callings, you know them in a more full and integral way and can honor and support their discernments and choices.

In our work with people in congregations and during our Seminar, the practice of storytelling captured the contextual, embodied, and temporal character of callings. Stories reveal most clearly that calling is not one thing. We heard powerful and illuminating stories, in fact, too many to be included here. We especially felt that stories that don't fit expected patterns helped us qualify our claims about vocation—the grandmother who has to parent small children; the teen who cares for a sick parent; the executive laid off from work. Narrative approaches to vocation are one way that we can invite readers to tell their stories and thereby expand our awareness of the multiplicity of vocation experiences.

Second, in addition to lived experience and narrative, we turn to a variety of sources to help us understand both vocation and the span or course of human lives. In terms of theology, there has recently been important retrieval work done by a Protestant, Douglas Schuurman, and a Catholic, Edward Hahnenberg. Each explores his tradition's interpretations of biblical narratives as well as the doctrines of creation, providence, and salvation as they relate to vocation.[13] Each historically situates theological insights from the past and critically assesses what about vocation became distorted, even destructive, over time.

Despite the fact that a theology of vocation became marginalized, even lost, for many Christians, its critical retrieval is imperative.[14] As we learned from people's stories and analysis of popular culture, many have a deep desire to grapple with the meaning of their lives and may need more help now than ever navigating the multiple and complex vocational transitions that occur across the lifespan. Consequently, people fail to grasp the potential of deliberation on vocation that can enhance everyday decisions, commitments, and obligations in fresh ways. As Schuurman notes, vocation has traditionally been related to "all relational spheres—domestic, economic, political, cultural"—as "divinely given avenues through which persons respond obediently to the call of God to serve their neighbor in love."[15] In fact, its reinterpretation might be one way of framing the Christian life that could appeal to many people for whom faith no longer makes much sense. Emil Brunner, nearly a century ago, claimed that "we must not throw it [vocation] away, but we must regain its original meaning," which is "so full of force and so pregnant in meaning, it gathers up so clearly the final meaning of God's acts of grace—the Calling."[16]

Historical and theological analysis demonstrates, however, that the questions we are pressing have not been part of the conversation about vocation until very recently. As theologians and social scientists, then, we turned to one further essential source—social science perspectives that provide a more contextual understanding of callings and their psychological, sociological, economic, and biological dimensions. A book on vocation across the lifespan obviously benefits immensely from theories of human development that have emerged in the past century in the sciences. Each author engages various schools of thought, such as psychoanalytic, constructivist, cognitive, and narrative, as well as faith development theory. From such sources, we gained insight into identity formation; capacities for meaning-making; transitions; and neurological, physical, emotional, and spiritual development that accompanies each age of the lifespan. While we do not advance a particular theory of the lifespan, we want to show the ways in which vocation, as both a human and a religious quest for purpose and meaning, is essential to understanding how persons develop, grow, and mature over time. We believe we have something important to offer from a theological perspective to otherwise secular sources on human development.[17]

We hope to provide a new, even unique, way to approach human development that features or makes central spiritual, ethical, and theological questions, deliberations, and practices at each life phase.

Vocation across the Lifespan

In the following chapters we delve into our claim that callings encompass the entire span of human life. In Chapter 2, I explore a theology of vocation as contextual, embodied, and temporal. In her exploration of children and vocation, Bonnie Miller-McLemore recognizes children's diverse but often overlooked experiences of calling that evolve out of who they are (e.g., small, new, vulnerable) as much as what they do. She points out their multiple callings as involving experimentation and obligations in work, play, learning, and love. Because humans are living longer and theorists are reconstructing adulthood, we explore four periods in adult life: younger, middle, later, and older. Katherine Turpin describes younger adults as being called through the exploration of possible selves, creating friendships and significant relationships, experiencing suffering and loss, and negotiating cultural narratives. Younger adults, Turpin argues, explore calling through performing adult identity, seeking full adult status

8

economically, and facing impermanence and multiple transitions in work and relationships. In the middle adult years, Matt Bloom observes, most adults experience callings as both a joy and a paradox. They face new opportunities (economic, employment) and freedoms (legal) at the same time as increasing responsibilities emerge for the social, spiritual, and economic well-being of others (e.g., children, employees, parents). I explore how callings can end in later adulthood, such as retirement from full-time work or death of a spouse, and new callings emerge, such as grandparenting and caregiving. In older adulthood, Joyce Ann Mercer describes the shift in calling toward accepting the body's demands and limitations and relinquishing past roles for new kinds of relationships such as great-grandparent or care-receiver.

When considering Christian vocation, we recognize how the scriptural narrative informs and shapes our vocational stories. In an effort to draw out that connection, we include scriptural narrative as an essential source for reflection. Between each of the chapters, New Testament scholar Jane Patterson draws on her expertise in biblical study and its role in vocational discernment to reflect creatively on biblical figures, drawing out themes and patterns from our research on the lifespan.

Even though the book has six chapters on particular life phases—childhood, adolescence, younger adulthood, middle adulthood, late adulthood, and older adulthood—we do not view human development as a matter of lockstep movement through a set of chronological stages. Rather, we look at the phases of human life through the crucial experiences of calling that emerge and shape a given time. We unpack what is unique to each life age but also what is enduring to a sense of calling over time. Authors strive to understand common features of a particular life phase while also recognizing the amazing variance and diversity among people and between cultures, an awareness made more acute as we navigate a postmodern age sensitive to and weary of the power and exploitation that often lurks behind essentialist claims about universal experiences. Although as authors we represent a fairly narrow and homogeneous perspective, shaped and limited by our university professions and social location, we do not want the general features of vocation to be misperceived or prescribed as ideals; rather, we try to describe the many realities of each phase in as much complexity as possible.

To accomplish these ends and to aid the reader in making connections between the six chapters on life phases, each chapter is organized around the following template of five themes:

Entering: What signals the transitioning into this phase from another life phase? How do people awaken to the vocational questions at the heart of this age?

Characteristics: What are some of the key vocational characteristics, especially in terms of changes in the body and living through time?

Vocational Experiences: What are some of the key calling experiences (e.g., gifts, skills, decisions, identity, love, work, joys, losses, service)? How is God encountered as Caller?

Communal Dynamics: What are supportive practices for the nurture of vocation, including implications for ministry? What callings does this lifespan age evoke in others (e.g., parents, children, siblings, grandparents, colleagues, mentors, and mentees)?

Ending: What signals the transitioning out of this phase and into another life phase?

The Collegeville Institute Seminar on Vocation across the Lifespan

The book's authors are members of The Collegeville Institute Seminar on Vocation across the Lifespan, a seminar at the Collegeville Institute, which is located at Saint John's Abbey and University in Minnesota. We are a group of educators, professors, pastors, and social scientists. Laura Kelly Fanucci provided research as well as organizational, intellectual, and editorial assistance throughout the project. We began our work in 2011, and over the past several years we have read and studied a variety of perspectives on vocation, on each phase of the lifespan; we have also shared our stories of God's callings in our lives and pondered future callings. We are an ecumenical group, representing diverse streams of the Christian tradition, and we are trained in different disciplines, including New Testament, psychology, practical theology, and leadership studies. There are eight participants in the seminar; six authored this book and the other two contributed to the conceptual work in significant ways.[18]

Many of us are called as theological educators and teachers, and we hope that this book can engage students in ministry studies, at both the outset and the conclusion of theological education as students consider their vocation, as well as in their study of pastoral care, preaching, and religious education, where questions about vocation and the need to address them arise most acutely. We also hope to reach working pastors, chaplains, and spiritual directors in local congregations, church camps, campus ministries, retreat centers, schools, and healthcare facilities, particularly those for older adults. We believe that the vocation of the minister is to call forth, nurture, acknowledge, guide, and support the many callings in people's lives at each age and also regardless of their age. Seminar member Jack Fortin wrote in his book on vocation, *The Centered Life*, that "congregations are the best places for God's people to be inspired and equipped to live out their callings every day . . . in their many vocational settings."[19] Participants in our research expressed a similar desire that congregations (and we would include other places of Christian community) can become communities of calling. We hope that this investigation into vocation across the lifespan opens a new and important door into key theological questions about the nature of our callings and the Caller.

2

Callings over a Lifetime

*In Relationship, through the Body,
over Time, and for Community*

KATHLEEN A. CAHALAN

It is not easy to delineate the term "vocation" today. The *Oxford English Dictionary* defines it as "the fact of being so called," which seems to beg the question.[1] Biblical scholar Walter Brueggemann places being so called in the context of the divine-human relationship: "The dynamic of humanness is in the interaction between the One who *calls* and the one who is *called*. And the agenda between them is a *calling*."[2] But because the One-Who-Calls has been called into question and the experience of being so called may not have its source in the One-Who-Calls as named by the Christian tradition, the source of vocation is often obscured today.

Christians have long wrestled with grasping the agenda between the Caller and the one called, and contemporary theologies of vocation are taking up these questions once again. And yet what they have not wrestled with is how calling is experienced, formed, and lived out across the whole of human life from infancy to old age. We believe that a lifespan perspective on vocation offers new ways of interpreting the Caller, the one called, and callings. For the Protestant Reformers who made vocation a central doctrine of the Christian faith, callings were described as both general and particular, as responsibilities and duties in a role, and as gifts of the Spirit.[3] Catholic theologians have traditionally used the language of inner and outer callings, and some today emphasize the true self and the false self.[4] While the tradition is helpful in exploring calling across the lifespan, these definitions and categories of vocation are insufficient on their own. The issues that the lifespan raises in terms of the body, age, time, and context shed new light on these traditional categories but they also require us to look for additional sources in both theology and the social sciences.

Critically engaging historical and contemporary theological perspectives through a lifespan perspective expands and nuances the way we define vocation in relationship, through the body, in time, and for community. God calls us at the age we are and at every age in our lives.

By taking account of the span of human life, we discovered several insights that receive powerful illustration throughout the book's chapters and that I explore more explicitly in this chapter: callings are discerned through relationships; they evolve over time; they are multiple and changing; they are dependent on the emergent capacities of the body; and, last but not least, they are mutually influencing and responsive to others.

In Relationship

Social scientists and theologians share a common perspective on human life: personhood is essentially relational. We become who we are as unique persons in and through relationship. Many psychologists and narrative theorists have moved away from individualist and autonomous theories of personhood to a relational understanding of identity and development. Where healthy development was once construed as "increasing individuation" from familial relationships, it is now seen as "a process of increasing—and increasingly complex—connections to others."[5] Cognitive psychologist Robert Kegan makes the point even stronger: "Who comes into a person's life may be the single greatest factor of influence to what that life becomes."[6]

What can be said about human persons can also be posited about "Holy Mystery."[7] If relationship is integral to personhood, Christians have also seen it as fundamental to who God is. Personhood as relationship is a central emphasis in contemporary discussions of the Trinity, contextual theologies, missiology, and science and creation. In Trinitarian theology, the Orthodox theologian John Zizioulas argues for a relational ontology, that the "being" of God is not in divine nature or substance but in personhood understood in terms of relationship. Divine personhood is not prior to relationship but exists only in and through relationship; the idea that God is three persons in loving union attempts to explain this strange claim, which is described through the Greek term *perichōrēsis*, a dance of love between persons.[8] Thus, who God is and what God does is relationship. As Catholic theologian Elizabeth Johnson states, "For God 'to be' means 'to be in relation.'"[9] This dance of abundant life that is God is given to the world in an "overflowing communion of self-giving love."[10]

If personhood, divine and human, is essentially relational and if the agenda between the One-Who-Calls and the one called is what we name as a calling, vocation is inherently relational, more a verb or activity than a noun or state of being. We become who we are in and through communion with God and others. Contextual theologians have highlighted the importance of seeing relationality not as a formal or abstract category but through the lens of culture as a social and contextual category. In his discussion of U.S. Hispanic theology, Miguel Diaz notes that "the songs that God sings are not universal songs capable of being heard by a universally conceived hearer. Rather, the songs contain the specific lyrics, rhythms, and melodies associated with concrete human subjects."[11] Vocation, then, is not abstracted from our social and cultural situations. Because personhood is "always *intrinsically* relational," according to Catholic theologian Roberto Goizueta, it means that "I am a particular, concrete, and unique embodiment" of relationships and communities from where I come: "When someone encounters me, they also encounter my parents, relatives, friends, community, my people, as well as the God who created me and the earth which nourishes me."[12] And as Emilie Townes notes, womanist spirituality is a "radical concern for the is-ness in the context of African American life." That is-ness is both physical and spiritual, connecting persons with the "movement of creation itself."[13]

While age is the central focus of our work, it is important to note that there is little reflection on how culture or social location influences vocation. It matters whether we are talking about the calling of an Asian immigrant, a Hispanic x-ray technician, a Caucasian student from Illinois, or a Malaysian civil servant. The particularity of each person's life—family, ethnicity, gender, economic conditions—is unique. Context is not something added to our callings; these conditions comprise the substance of vocation. The story of each person's life takes on a radically particular character given the situated character of existence, and that individual hears God's callings in that place. Some ways of speaking about vocation as authenticity and the true self may appeal to those persons who have a great deal of choice in constructing a life, but for those who do not, a calling may appear to be a luxury they cannot afford. Can an immigrant such as Francois who has an advanced degree from his home country and is forced to take a job washing dishes in a New York restaurant find meaning and purpose in that work?[14] Or a couple who has planned for their retirement but lost that

14

dream because one is diagnosed with Alzheimer's disease?[15] Or persons who are stuck in jobs because they need an income but find little value in their work? If vocation does not make sense in relationship to persons in a variety of social and cultural contexts, it does not have much to contribute to our communities today.[16]

Many Christians, however, if they consider the One-Who-Calls, imagine a God who from a great distance in time and space has determined their vocation. This operative understanding of calling was largely informed by early modern ideas in which callings were understood as part of a divine plan or will for each person. Put simply, God, who has complete control over the world, created each person with a particular calling. A calling required Christians to know God's plan, accept their duty and responsibility for their callings, and respond faithfully. In a positive sense, each person was cooperating in God's provident care for the world. However, this view of divine control over all natural and moral events had unfortunate consequences for the Christian life. It tended to foster virtues that "are mainly passive. Our duty under God's providence is to adjust to the way things are, to accept the order of things and to receive with all humility and gratitude what God sends."[17] This view also assumes that one can easily know God's will through prayer, for instance, or by reading certain signs in the world. For many today, the provident Creator lurks in the cosmic background as a dominant image of the One-Who-Calls, despite the failure of this doctrine to explain the relationship between a highly detailed divine plan and human freedom and suffering.[18]

As with the Trinity and theological anthropologies, theologies of divine providence have shifted from static and determined interpretations to more open, dynamic, and evolving understandings of God's relationship to the world. For all of its limitations, the theology of the divine plan pointed to a profound belief in the interrelationship of all that is, which has its origin in divine life. In considering how God creates, provides, and sustains all created life, Johnson emphasizes divine being as dynamism rather than through traditional categories that emphasized an impersonal, static, and abstract being. Such traditional ontologies of the One-Who-Calls are "unfit to signal the dynamic and inherently relational nature of incomprehensible mystery."[19] Johnson asserts that when we speak of God's "being" we should use verbs or adverbs rather than nouns. This grammatical shift "signifies ultimate reality as pure aliveness in relation, the unoriginated welling up of fullness of life in which the whole universe participates."[20] Such a relational understanding of divine life and purpose is more consonant with contemporary physics, developmental theory, and evolutionary patterns of life on our planet.[21]

Rather than creation as a single event in time, divine power creates and initiates all living things in an ongoing vigorous movement in an evolving and emerging universe. Johnson writes that "the Creator Spirit, as ground, sustaining power, and goal of the evolving world, acts by *empowering* the process from within." God is active *"in, with, and under* cosmic processes. God makes the world, in other words, by empowering the world to make itself."[22] Such a perspective shifts vocation from prearranged details of our lives worked out by God to the One who empowers us from within our creaturely existence. We develop through a complex web of biological, psychological, communal, and social processes within which the divine movement is at work. Calling, then, is in our being and our bones as we work out our salvation in time with the One-Who-Calls.

From a relational perspective, the One-Who-Calls sustains all living beings in their existence and is also drawing them toward fulfillment within the divine life. Thus, to reinterpret the language of God's "plan" is to claim what God is doing on behalf of all living beings toward the same end. Methodist theologian Charles Wood interprets God's providence through a similar framework. God is "providing *in* everything that goes on but relates differently to different elements of what is occurring: empowering creaturely existence and action, allowing creaturely conflict and failing, opposing the consequences of creaturely undoing, and working in and with each situation toward new possibilities for the fulfillment of creation's purpose."[23] Calling becomes participation in God's purposes. God creates and wills all creation to live into its fullness of being-in-relationship and to live ultimately in relationship to Holy Mystery.[24] To be in relationship is to be invited into the conversation about the meaning and purpose of our lives. Vocation, therefore, is the language to describe the lifelong task of figuring out our life purposes in relationship to God's purposes.

Grammatically speaking, "calling," like "being," can be used as a verb—"vocating"—rather than only as a noun—"a vocation" (singular). Prepositions—"in," "through," "over," and "for"—also give us a way of speaking about vocation since grammatically prepositions point to the relationship between words.[25] For example, I have experienced God calling to me *through* my parents to familial love, *in* marriage to my husband, and *for* my students. "Calling" as verb and preposition heightens personal response-ability and freedom as we search to understand and align our lives to God's purposes in the world and to make choices for those purposes rather than others. This added grammatical perspective makes "calling" as a noun more dynamic as well. I am called as daughter, wife, and teacher, each of which points to aspects of my identity and roles as well as the commitments that claim me as so called.

A relational and dialogical theology emphasizes that the One-Who-Calls creates us *for* vocation, a capacity for responding to relationship. As Katherine Turpin notes, "Within a Christian framework, *vocation* expresses the partnering relationship between humans and God that serves as the primary source of direction for constructing a life path or journey."[26] Our callings, rather than being fixed, are something we enact in response to an invitation. As Townes writes in a poem based on Toni Morrison's novel *Beloved*,

> to be called beloved
> is to be called by God
> to be called by the shining moments
> to be called deep within deep . . .
> to be called beloved
> is the marvelous yes to God's what if
> the radical shifting of growth
> mundane agency of active faith[27]

Finally, we need to acknowledge that relationality does not render the divine and the human on equal terms. As Brueggemann notes, "Because God is God, there are purposes to which we belong which are larger than our purposes."[28] Discerning callings across a lifetime will always entail the struggle to understand God's ways and purposes that remain mysterious and hidden from us.

Through the Body

Central to God's purposes, Christians contend, is the life, death, and resurrection of Jesus, the one who called his disciples into a new fellowship and community. The meaning of *ecclēsia*, the Greek word translated as "church" in English, actually contains the verb "to call." Earliest Christians understood themselves to have been *called* into the *community* of the church. Christian callings, from a biblical perspective then, are first of all a call to community. The metaphor of the body is a central symbol for the Christian community and relates to calling in two ways: our common calling as the body of Christ and our callings through our physical bodies.

A Common Calling: The Body of Christ

In the New Testament book of Romans, Paul develops the link between calling and community in his theology of baptism. Through bodily immersion into water, baptism represents a death to sin and a sharing in Christ's death and burial. Rising from the waters, persons share in the "newness of life" as part of Christ's resurrection (Rom. 6:4), a regeneration by the power of God to live according to the gifts of the Spirit (1 Cor. 12:4–11). As Townes writes,

> to be called beloved
> is to answer the question
> we are not dipped
> we are not sprinkled
> we are not immersed
> we are washed in the grace of God[29]

Through the washing of baptism, we become "children of God in Christ Jesus," who are "clothed" with Christ and called to be a community who are "all one in Christ Jesus" (Gal. 3:27–28; 1 Cor. 12:13). The one body has many members but they remain united, joined together in Christ's body (1 Cor. 12:12).

Vocation, then, is not a solo effort. The question of calling has traditionally begun not as my individual vocation, the way it is commonly framed today, but as the common calling Christians share. Vocation is received in community, through community, and for the sake of community. Whatever the particularities of my call might be, from a Christian viewpoint, it can never be separate from my identity and calling as a member of Christ's body. "Community is the birthplace of the self," according to Goizueta, in which the distinctness of each person is allowed to emerge at the same time culture binds the person to a particular community that forms him.[30] The Christian narrative is always told through culture, and it does not exist apart from it; thus the cultural interpretations of the primary narratives of a community will provide the stories through which calling is understood.

Communal calling is rooted in a relational ecology vividly seen by the interrelatedness of generations. As becomes clear in the chapters that follow, we are called by others, and we call others into relationship—the infant calls the woman to be a mother, the mother calls forth the infant; the grandfather calls forth the boy through play, the boy calls the older man to grandparenting; the engaged couple call each other to marriage; the teen calls forth adults to prophetic action, adults call forth the teen's identity; and so forth.

The psychologist Erik Erikson called the intergenerational influence of development "cogwheeling" and "dovetailing." Persons at different life stages connect with and draw forth capacities of those at another stage. For example, the child's need for care draws out the mother's generative need for caregiving. A child, Erikson noted, is itself a lifecycle within "a community of life cycles."[31] A child's abilities and strengths "dovetail" as they interlock with the abilities and strengths of people "arranged around" her. More generally, one age calls forth vocation to those at other moments in the span of life. In and through these connections, the divine life is at work calling us into relationship. In this sense, we are all one body—agents and recipients of God's callings through each other.

Many people first experience a sense of "calling" through another person. Nearly half of the people we gathered in churches shared that they chose a profession because it had been recommended by family members, friends, or mentors; many entered the work of their parents or siblings. Adults had significant influence on helping youth and young adults to identify their gifts, affirm their passions, and hone their skills. It is also the case that these very same people can discourage or deny a calling that a person may hear. Unfortunately, this is a story we heard too many times. The middle-aged man who went into the family business because he felt he had no other choice and hated it; the African American woman whose high school did not acknowledge her desire to become a physician; and the boss who would not let a woman advance in the corporation because "women can't do those jobs." Stories are full of influential people: those who are agents of vocation and those who failed to live out that calling.

German priest and seminal figure in the Protestant Reformation Martin Luther (1483–1546) made a distinction that has remained important in contemporary theologies of vocation. God's callings are first and foremost a general calling that is shared in common among Christians (what he called "spiritual" calling and later was named "general"), and second, callings are particular to each person (what he called "external" and later was referred to as "particular").[32] Calling is communal because it is relational. The individual person does not find a calling on her own but only in the context of community. For Luther, the general calling was by far the most critical aspect of vocation.

In fact, the idea of general calling in community, rather than individual callings, is central for both Jews and Muslims. According to Rabbi Amy Eilberg, even though the specific concept of calling is foreign, Jews have a general rather than a particular sense of the idea as a "direction for life addressed to all Jewish human beings rather than uniquely to any individual Jew" that begins "with the biblical commands that the Israelites are to be 'a kingdom of priests and a holy nation' (Exod. 19:6) and the essential exhortation, 'Be holy, for I the Lord your God am holy' (Lev. 19:2)."[33] The Jewish people are called through the covenant that binds them together to the God of Israel and to a life of holiness.[34] Similarly, the general calling in Islam is to be a Muslim, according to John Kelsay. "The Arabic al-islam 'the submission' begins with God's call to human beings. To be a Muslim— that is, to be 'one who submits'—involves saying to God 'Here I am, at your service'—a statement that opens up to a life of prayer (that is, calling upon God) and good works (including calling other human beings to serve God)."[35] The three traditions share this emphasis on general calling.

Paul offered a similar interpretation through his image of the body of Christ, expanding his metaphor to refer to the interrelationship and interdependence of its various parts—hands, feet, eyes, head. From our lifespan perspective, the metaphor can be stretched further. The body of Christ is made up of young bodies, older bodies, brand-new bodies, as well as sick and healthy ones and a whole host of other variable attributes. Our callings as members of the one body always come to us as particular bodies; we do not experience our callings in any other way than through our age-identified body.

Embodied Callings

Embodiment has recently become an important source of theological insight. As Bonnie Miller-McLemore states, "Our theology is grounded in our bodies. We have no other way to know God than through our bodies."[36] By looking at callings through the lifespan, authors in this book make it clear that our awareness, experience, and response to callings are conditioned by our bodily capacities.

Embodiment, as discussed by spirituality scholar Colleen Griffith, encompasses the biological, the social, and the psychological.[37] As a vital organism, the body consists of biological and physiological processes, some continuous (such as breathing) and some emergent (such as reproductive capacities). Vocation is largely dependent on what the body can and cannot do at a given age and the emergent capacity to do a particular activity (e.g., walking), accomplish work by using that capacity (e.g., be a floor manager at a grocery store), or face relinquishing some or all of that ability (e.g., using a walker or wheelchair).

As sociocultural sites, we embody cultural ideals, norms, and behaviors that are not always positive. For example, Turpin has argued that children and teens are "branded" at an early age by marketing campaigns related to clothes, hair, makeup, and physical size.[38] "How can Christian vocation develop in adolescents in the midst of a strong alternative formation of vocation offered by the cultural-economic system of consumer capitalism?" Similarly the elderly body is shunned as changes in hair, skin, and ability render it diminished and useless.[39] How does an elderly person respond to a calling if he feels a sense of shame or unworthiness because of bodily decline?

The body is also a sociocultural and political site of race, ethnicity, and racism. Many people of color tell stories of migrants, refugees, immigrants, and slaves that challenge theologies of calling. Could vocation be a way of interpreting the betwixt-and-between experience, say of immigrants, who leave one home and must make a life in another place? When a person occupies the precarious place of being on the margins of two dominant groups, according to theologian Peter Phan, identity and community are negotiated over and over again. What could be said about God's calling from this place?[40] Related problems arise around other bodily factors, such as gender, sexuality, and ability. Many people's lives and vocations are constrained by sexism, heterosexism, and able-ism that impede them from actualizing gifts for work, love, and other pursuits.

Bodies shape vocation through both their social construction and their physical materiality, and these two elements stand in complicated relationship to one another. Scholars have searched for fresh ways to talk about the relationship between culture and biology. The psychological body, what Griffith calls the enactment of consciousness and will, highlights persons as agents of their identities and environments. The psychologist Robert Kegan argues that a "person" is "an activity . . . an ever progressive motion engaged in giving itself a new form."[41] He draws from both constructivism ("persons or systems constitute or construct reality") and developmentalism ("organic systems evolve through eras according to regular principles of stability and change").[42] We are agents in constructing our social worlds, and we do so in relationship to both our emergent developmental capacities and the social world in which we live. The central developmental task, according to Kegan, is meaning-making: "It is not that a person makes meaning, but that the activity of being a person is the activity of meaning-making."[43] Such activity forms the capacity to live as so called. Kegan's perspective is akin to a theological relational ontology: "It is not about the doing which a human does; it is about the doing which a human is."[44] The teen or the older adult, then, has the chance to construct a meaningful sense of self if negative views of their bodies are countered by positive narratives.

Despite Christianity's history of "damning the body and its temptations," we are coming to appreciate the body as an important source of theological knowledge and the more positive sources the tradition offers. As Miller-McLemore notes, "incarnation, God's inhabiting a human body, is central. Redemption includes bodily resurrection. Congregations are Christ's body in the world; members are eyes, feet, hands, each with a purpose and gift. Most centrally, every week . . . in many churches God's presence and promise is celebrated through a partaking of Christ's body and blood."[45] If we understand Jesus's teaching that "the kingdom of God is within you" (Luke 17:21), we may be able to construct a sense of meaning and purpose as people called through the bodies we have with all their physical, social, and psychological abilities and limitations.

Over Time

Bodies exist in time and according to age, the number of our days. We think of age in terms of chronological time and aging as growing older or being old. As Protestant theologian K. Brynolf Lyon points out, the aging body is "an expression of our finitude"; some conditions of aging "will be treatable" but aging "is not eradicable."[46] We live with bodies that change through growth as well as degeneration, maturity as well as decline.

The stories we tell about our lives and our callings are framed in temporal categories. As theologian Janet Ruffing notes, "narrative reconstructs a plausible set of events in temporal sequence in order to explain, if not why something happened, at least what happened."[47] Our stories help us to make sense of what happened in the past, what is going on now, and what we hope for or anticipate in the future. Temporal framing is found in our stories of calling, most prominently in looking back. We often fail to see, though, that vocation is very much in the present and looking toward the future.

Our sense of time, like the body, also carries sociocultural meanings. We have inherited modernity's construal of "temporal passage" as positive. Time "opens out possibility, possibility of the new and the achievement of the new in the future," according to Protestant theologian Langdon Gilkey. We are conditioned to believe that time moves *forward*, with "benevolent change, of growth, and so of the magic of unlimited possibility."[48] Our progressive view of history in the West has in fact shaped psychologies of human development. One consequence of this optimistic view of history is the rejection of aging, death, and the loss of eternal time. For Gilkey, our cultural sense of time is one in which "no eternity penetrates easily into time," and thus we "obscure the threat of temporality by hiding . . . the reality of decay involved in passage."[49] We think of aging as unnatural, a condition to be remedied if science would hurry up and discover how to stop it. And, as Catholic studies professor Paul Lakeland asserts, postmodernity has further obscured space and time: "Daylight is unimportant, the climate is controlled, and you can shop furiously at ten o'clock at night. Nothing is old, worn, weather-beaten, mellowed with age; age is the enemy."[50]

Christians have been shaped by another sense of time, however. Early Christians adopted the Greek distinction between *chronos*, time that is measured and sequential, such as the hours of the day, and *kairos*, time that is filled with possibility and decision as in Jesus's declaration that the kingdom of God is "at hand" (Mark 1:15). *Kairos* time heightens the radical nature of calling, breaking into and disrupting *chronos*. It is a time of decision and action in history, according to mid-twentieth-century theologian Paul Tillich. "Time is all-decisive, not empty time, pure expiration; not the mere duration either, but rather qualitatively fulfilled time, the moment that is creation and fate. We call this fulfilled moment, the moment of time approaching us as fate and decision, *kairos*."[51]

Both *chronos* and *kairos* shape our understanding of vocation. Joyce Ann Mercer's claim about youths' callings informs our lifespan perspective. She notes that "God calls youth *as the young people they are*—i.e., Christian youth have life-purposes that exist within the purposes of God not in spite of their young age, but because of it."[52] We too often think of adolescence as the time of preparation for adulthood, diminishing it to a linear *chronos* trajectory: ninth grade prepares you for tenth grade, which prepares you for college entrance exams, which prepares you for college applications, and so on. But *kairos* places the emphasis on the present moment as filled with possibility for responding to God's call: the call of teens is to be teens and to experience God's purposes for them as they are in adolescence. *Chronos*, then, is the context for *kairos*: we experience callings at the age we are, the "appointed" or "crucial" time of decision.

We apply Mercer's claim about youth to every lifespan age: God calls each person as the embodied person he is in the time of life he is, whether he is 2 years of age, or 12, or 64, or 98. Each has an "already" vocation; we fail if we see younger people as living in a time of "not yet" vocation or older adults as having lived out their callings. As we will see in the chapters that follow, this recognition is especially important when it comes to the two ends of the lifecycle that we moderns have conventionally seen as vocationally insignificant—infants and the very old. Religious traditions sometimes surprise us by honoring these positions as especially *kairos*-filled and, thus, central to faith and vocation.

Understanding vocation as embodied and temporal means that it is not singular. In fact, we experience multiple callings, as psychologist and theologian John Neafsey notes. It is possible "to experience different callings at different times of our lives, or to experience multiple callings at any particular time of our life."[53] The multiplicity of callings is particularly evident among adults in the vitality of midlife, as we will see in the chapter on middle adulthood, but this dynamic is not limited to this phase. Similar to the Spirit gifting persons in new ways across the lifespan, we can experience the *kairos* of vocation at any time through the in-breaking of God's invitation to respond to callings in and around us: the child entering school, the teen taking a first job, the young adult leaving college for work, a couple becoming parents, a middle-aged man changing jobs or leaving full-time employment, a woman losing her partner after many years of marriage, or an elderly person entering an assisted living facility.

The temporal dimension of callings also points to their endings. Across the lifespan, callings emerge, shift, and cease, and all callings come to an end with death. Dying relativizes vocation: God's calling is here and now in this place. But theologies of vocation also point to relationship in eternal time, as in Jane Patterson's scriptural reflection that concludes this book.[54] In Christ's eschatological promises, God's call reaches beyond embodied time in history toward the promise of life with the One-Who-Calls. This is why experiencing *kairos* time is important in our everyday *chronos*-filled lives. Our call is eternal in the sense that God's purposes and plan for us are to remain in relationship, in our dying and beyond death, in a new life made manifest in Christ's resurrection. Vocation, according to Mercer, "bears an eschatological fingerprint."[55]

For Community

What, finally, are God's purposes to which our callings find their source, direction, and meaning? Love of God and neighbor was Luther's answer, and few have disputed that the Great Commandment is the foundation of Christian vocation (Matt. 22:35–40). In addition to general calling, Luther emphasized particular callings, expanding both who can be called and to what: all Christians have a calling, he said, and every station constitutes a context for that calling.[56] In the particularity of family and work, roles and responsibilities, a person experiences God's call to love God and serve her neighbor. The particular context is where each person responds to the general calling of neighbor love. As Schuurman notes in his analysis of Luther's view, "the particular shape action was to take within the 'offices' of parent, spouse, judge, lawyer, or farmer was to a significant degree determined by intelligent discernment or obligations germane to the relevant context. 'Faith active in love through one's callings' became the benchmark of Reformation ethics."[57]

But modernity shifted the relationship between the general calling and the particular calling. We live in the age of the particular calling rather than the general calling.[58] Modernity's turn to the subject has meant that a sense of general calling shared with others is secondary to my own pursuit. As philosopher Charles Taylor notes, our understanding of the self has shifted to an "individualism of personal commitment" that undercuts a social ethic.[59] It becomes more difficult to find communities that ground particular callings in a general call shared with others. What keeps vocation from falling into an individualist ethic is the claim that callings are relational and communal and their purpose is to serve the neighbor.

We experience God's callings through others and for others as the way we embody self-giving love in community. Vocation, then, is a way in which God calls persons to be in relationship to and for one another. As Brueggemann says, a biblical anthropology is missional since "vocation means we are called by this One who in calling us to *be* calls us to *service*."[60] Calling as it relates to community can be understood in a number of ways:

as gifts of the Holy Spirit or as service in a variety of forms, such as stewardship, hospitality, compassion, empathy, advocacy, and witness.[61] The communal nature of callings is also experienced as a moral duty.

Callings and Gifts

The particularity of Christian callings is often explored through Paul's theology of charisms.[62] Paul distinguishes the common gifts of faith, hope, and charity—shared by all through baptism—and gifts that are unique to each person, what he calls *charismata*, from the Greek term for "grace." Generally, Christians have emphasized that grace is the total unmerited gift of salvation based on God's love for humanity (Eph. 2:8–9), which is in no way dependent on human persons. But interpreting charism as a free gift "obscures an essential aspect of Paul's perspective on vocation," according to biblical scholars Jane Patterson and John Lewis, rendering persons as passive recipients rather than engaged actors.

> This definition erroneously destroys the integral connection between human action and people's experiences of grace in daily life. When disciples of Jesus Christ "walk worthily of God, the one calling you into his own kingdom and glory" (1 Thessalonians 2:12), they become conduits for God's grace to enter the world. Through their Christ-like actions in service to others, disciples mediate God's generative, life-giving power that enriches the lives of others and builds up communities in Christ. These experiences of grace reflect momentary encounters with the kingdom and glory of God.[63]

Patterson and Lewis argue against the popular conception that a charism is a permanent endowment, ability, or talent that a person possesses. It is misleading to say that I "have" a charism for teaching because grace is always on the move. They are the "particular experiences of God's life-giving grace that continue to take place through people who follow Christ's pattern of living according to God's will for the world."[64] Recognizing charisms is discerning how God uses persons as a means of "God's gracious will for others." It is more accurate to say that as the grandmother tells her grandson about their family history, she experiences the power of grace, God moving through her to help the child to understand. Calling requires a readiness and willingness to be a conduit for God's grace to work through me for others.[65]

In discerning callings, it is common to explore one's abilities, skills, and talents. For example, Catholic theologian Michael Himes asks young adults to consider three questions in their discernment of a college major, a career, or a life commitment: "Is this a source of joy? Is this something that taps into your talents and gifts—engages all of your abilities—and uses them in the fullest way possible? Is this role a genuine service to the people around you, to society at large?"[66] In lifting up the threefold importance of joy, talent, and service in discerning vocation, Himes is pointing to the nature of the Spirit's gifts: they bring life to a person and bear fruit for others.

We might assume from the focus on college students that these three questions do not pertain to all ages. The assumption is that we discover our gifts and make choices for work, service, and life commitments at these ages. It is rarer to find the language of gifts in discussions of the vocation of children or the elderly. However, a lifelong perspective on gifts as God's power moving through our own lives toward others reframes our notion of gifts away from something we possess toward the active power of God regardless of our age, ability, speech, or rationality. Thus, as we will see in the chapter on older adults, the very old woman who feels that she has no purpose may in fact be gifted in such a way that God continues to reach out to others through her. Likewise, the infant, often experienced as a gift, is one through whom God is calling forth others, as explored in the following chapter on children.

Paul's understanding of the Spirit's gifts also points to an important dimension of callings across our lifetime. Callings emerge at certain points, and they can change and even cease. The movement of the Spirit is not bound by human age; its purpose is to sustain, heal, and reconcile persons. Identifying and responding to the Spirit's giftedness in our lives means we are participating in the Spirit renewing all of creation (Ps. 104:30). Indeed, the affirmation of an interior sense of calling—"I was made for this!"—can bear fruit not only for the person who is inspired to act on her sense of the Spirit's gifts, but also for those who are served by her deep sense of joy and "fit-ness" for the task to which she has been called.[67] "Vocating," then, becomes a creative act between what God has given and how we respond.[68]

Empathetic Response

Culturally, the dominant appeal to serve the neighbor is by way of compassion and empathy, the deep fellow-feeling that we can understand

and feel with the suffering and hardship of others. Once we feel with another, we are moved to do something about it. Several theologians point to feelings of compassion and empathy as intimations of a calling. Neafsey, influenced by the spirituality of St. Ignatius of Loyola (1491–1556), states, "in vocational discernment, it is important to pay close attention to our feelings, because authentic callings always begin with a stirring of the heart. Someone or something moves or touches us in some way, and our heart responds with a *feeling*."[69] Schuurman also turns to the religious affections as the experiential root of God's calling. A sense of dependence on the natural environment, on others, and ultimately on God gives rise to a sense of gratitude for "the gifted character of our lives" and the call to the stewardship of creation.[70]

A call to service through empathy and compassion considered across the span of our lives is not one thing. It takes on many forms. Children, for instance, may be called to learn the practices of stewardship for creation and hospitality to others, and teens awaken to compassion for others and learn to be advocates for those in need. Over time they see that the neighbor is both familiar and unknown, immediate and global, loved and labeled as an "enemy." Youth experience the joys and struggles of service, and when returning from mission and service trips will often say, "I got more than I gave." Compassion is in service to identity formation for the young.

Awakening to compassion and empathy happens throughout adulthood as well. New parents often have a sudden and strong realization of how much their own parents did for them and now see them with more compassionate eyes. Those in later adulthood who serve as mentors to younger adults in professional work reach out in empathy to those struggling as they make their way into a profession. They can also have more time and space for service after the busy years of middle adulthood. Experiences of illness and loss in later adulthood often give these adults renewed empathy for the struggles of older adults.

For the Common Good

Vocation is also connected to a larger communal good.[71] Advocacy and solidarity are forms of service that go beyond our immediate circle of kin and friends. As Jane Patterson notes in her biblical interlude on siblings, the calling to be a "brave keeper of one's brother" leads Miriam into a circle of women concerned for all children.[72] Neighbor love stretches us to embrace a broader social ethic: the call of the stranger, the suffering, and the poor. We may feel called to advocate in the name of others. "Advocacy means," according to Pope, "speaking up for victims of injustice or on behalf of the common good" in order to promote long-term systemic change.[73] As psychologist Matt Bloom notes in this volume, adults may feel called to advocate for others through the social and economic power they have in work, in civic duties, and in leading institutions.[74]

The call to solidarity moves beyond compassion to the work of building bonds of fellowship that draw people together in stronger unity and purpose. Hahnenberg builds his theology of vocation around solidarity with the poor: "The call to be *for* others is always a call to be *with* others, particularly with those who suffer unjustly."[75] Vocation is God's call not only to do something for the poor, but also to be in solidarity with all those who are killed by poverty. Their "suffering interrupts" me, he claims, and God's call "confronts who I am."[76] Solidarity, rooted in compassion, means awakening to the demands of economic and social injustice. Many Christians experience a call to advocacy, solidarity, and social justice as something they cannot *not* do.

For those who cannot do physical work (e.g., building homes for Habitat for Humanity) or give financially, advocating for others may take the form of witness. Being a witness is the calling to give voice to God's love for the world.[77] Despite their inability to serve as they once did, older persons can be called to give witness to what God is doing in the world. The prophets Anna and Simeon, for instance, continued to play a powerful part in salvation history by their boldness in speaking the truth about God's work in the world through the infant Jesus, as described in Jane Patterson's reflection on the vocational call of elders.[78]

A relational and communal view of vocation means that we are called to be agents of vocation in turn—identifying others' gifts, affirming and nurturing them, and supporting institutional structures that allow everyone's callings to flourish. But Christian service to the neighbor can easily become domination, paternalism, dependency, or self-righteousness. We may too quickly frame vocation as what I can do for others, rather than what I can do that builds up the whole community. What if we saw our first duty to the neighbor as calling forth their sense of being so called in community?

Duty Calls

There is a limit, however, to the call to service based on feeling, compassion, and empathy. Callings also entail responsibilities, duties, and obligations that may not feel so good; in fact, they may be in direct competition or tension with what we most desire in our lives. The parent who is raising a developmentally challenged child may have to give up a promotion at work; the husband who cares for his wife with memory loss becomes homebound himself and cannot travel or visit friends; the student who must meet requirements for the credentials she needs to practice accounting has to delay beginning a family.

Vocation does not escape the burdens, lost opportunities, and constraints that relationships entail. Our callings have their own dimensions of suffering. In fact, loving service for the other demands sacrifice at times, a giving of our whole selves for the good of another, even at a cost. Jane, a middle-aged woman and participant in our research, was helping the family care for her ill father-in-law and reported that she grew resentful as he declined and needed more care. She was not resentful of the other family members with less time, but of him. Initially, she felt he was "taking her away from her calling" at her work. But over time, she realized that her calling "was right here with him" but it meant letting go of what she wanted in order to give more time to him.

Obligation is at the heart of Luther's insight about vocation. As Schuurman notes, "the duties of one's stations fuse the general law of God with one's own life. God uses their demands to drive individuals to their knees at the foot of the cross, and to provide avenues for service born of the love and freedom that faith creates."[79] Callings, then, are not always of our own choosing. They may "choose" us, and we may have to wrestle our way through figuring out how best to respond.

Because we live in a culture dominated by choice and achievement, we cringe at the language of calling as duty and obligation. Of course, the cold hand of duty can strip callings of their joy, but, framed through the language of choice, callings appear as something we determine when in fact there are many situations not of our own choosing. Being so called often means responding in neighbor love because the situation demands it. But the language of calling can reframe such situations by engaging a sense of agency—the searching for God's purposes in that place despite what seems impossible.[80] Twentieth-century theologian Karl Barth recognized that vocation is the "place" where God's invitation meets us, a place that is particular and marked by "limitation and restriction."[81] Vocation also means that within the limitations of our lives, bodies, and ages, all persons have an identity, worth, and purpose in God's purposes through which they can find a sense of meaning and be called into service. As Townes writes about a beloved woman who seems to find a calling in a place of profound limitation,

> to be called beloved
> is to listen to the words of Baby Suggs
> holy
> who offered up to them (us) her great big heart[82]

In this chapter, by way of introducing calling across the lifespan, I have examined how relationality, embodiment, time, and communal dynamics provide new ways of understanding vocation. From this perspective, calling is less about figuring out a detailed plan and more about moving toward responsiveness in relationship. The questions of calling—identity, meaning, purpose, community, story—arise within the body's emergent capacities. Callings are neither single nor solitary, but communal and therefore deeply personal. Our callings are lived out in all the particularity of time and place where God, the One-Who-Calls, comes to meet us and we discern "the agenda between us," what in the end we can identify as our callings. Vocation, then, is a dynamic response to who we are, how we live, and what we give our lives to—questions that the following chapters explore across the full span of human life. And that perspective, we hope, casts new light on the meaning of being so called.

Suggested Readings

Cahalan, Kathleen A. *The Stories We Live: Finding God's Calling All around Us.* Grand Rapids, MI: Eerdmans, 2017.

Cahalan, Kathleen A. *Introducing the Practice of Ministry.* Collegeville, MN: Liturgical Press, 2010.

Cahalan, Kathleen A., and Douglas J. Schuurman, eds. *Calling in Today's World: Voices from Eight Faith Perspectives.* Grand Rapids, MI: Eerdmans, 2016.

Coombs, Marie Theresa, and Francis Kelly Nemeck. *Called by God: A Theology of Vocation and Lifelong Commitment.* Collegeville, MN: Liturgical Press, 1992.

Fortin, Jack. *The Centered Life: Awakened, Called, Set Free, and Nurtured*. Minneapolis, MN: Augsburg Fortress, 2006.

Hahnenberg, Edward. *Awakening Vocation: A Theology of Christian Call in a Postmodern World*. Collegeville, MN: Liturgical Press, 2010.

Neafsey, John. *A Sacred Voice Is Calling: Personal Vocation and Social Conscience*. Maryknoll, NY: Orbis, 2006.

Placher, William C., ed. *Callings: Twenty Centuries of Christian Wisdom on Vocation*. Grand Rapids, MI: Eerdmans, 2005.

Schuurman, Douglas. *Vocation: Discerning Our Callings in Life*. Grand Rapids, MI: Eerdmans, 2004.

Schwehn, Mark R., and Dorothy C. Bass, eds. *Leading Lives that Matter: What We Should Do and Who We Should Be*. Grand Rapids, MI: Eerdmans, 2006.

Volf, Miroslav. *Work in the Spirit: Toward a Theology of Work*. New York: Oxford University Press, 1991.

Wolfteich, Claire E. *Navigating New Terrain: Work and Women's Spiritual Lives*. New York: Paulist, 2002.

Introducing Biblical Interludes:
Vocation in the Family of God

JANE PATTERSON

The idea of the "family of God" is not unusual to many people, but the ways in which the familiar phrase functions in a specific way to structure biblical ideas about calling would probably seem new and even strange to many. The image of the people of God as somehow God's *family* is dependent for its understanding on ancient customs regarding family life, not all of which would be found appropriate or salutary today. For instance, the subordination of all family members to the will of the father would be seen as highly problematic in most of Western society. Like all metaphors, the image of the family of God has limits to its application and points at which the comparison breaks down entirely. And yet, there are also some ways in which increased attention to this ancient image may serve to energize a sense of vocation, even today.

> All who are led by the Spirit of God are sons of God. For you did not receive a spirit of slavery to fall back into fear, but you have received a spirit of adoption as sons. When we cry, "Abba! Father!" it is that very Spirit bearing witness with our spirit that we are children of God, and if children, then heirs, heirs of God and joint heirs with Christ. (Rom. 8:14–17a, author's translation)

In the passage above, from Paul's letter to the Romans, all people (male and female) who follow the promptings of the Spirit show forth that they are "sons of God" by virtue of their choice to live in a way that embodies God's care for all. They are people who undertake God's work in the world. The image depends on ancient notions of a family's work being carried forward, generation after generation, by sons who follow in their fathers' footsteps. In our own time, of course, sons and daughters are equal as heirs, and for the most part neither sons nor daughters have the absolute obligation to carry on the same work as their parents. But what was likely felt as liberating for women in Paul's communities was to be considered among the sons of God, those entrusted equally with God's work in their context.

Several things are novel in Paul's use of the metaphor. One is this inclusion of women among the "sons," by virtue of their baptism (Gal. 3:28). The other is the *adoptive* status of all the sons. In Greco-Roman society, a young man might be adopted into a family that had no male heir. The purpose of the adopted son was to manage the family business for the continued well-being of the rest of the extended family. Something like this situation is the context that makes sense of the metaphor in Romans 8. Christ is understood to be the natural son of the father (God). He fully carried out God's work in the world through his ministry, death, and resurrection. But he is no longer embodied in the same way, and so adopted sons are needed to continue the father's work, for the ongoing well-being of the creation. Today, men and women in Christian community together bear the dignity of adopted daughters and sons of God, with the shared responsibility of furthering God's work in the world around them.

Calling arises in this metaphor in two different ways. One is the calling to be adopted into God's family, to make the conscious choice to structure one's life by the shape of God's love and God's work. The second calling is to particular spheres of living out one's adoption: birth at a particular time into a particular family; the calling to learn from particular teachers and experiences; to serve a certain community and to enter a particular sphere of work; to know and love others in ever-widening but particular circles; to shape one's life over time by the gradual accrual of particular commitments and decisions over the course of the lifespan.

Among the chapters of this book are scattered brief biblical interludes that portray people from both the Old and New Testaments, living out their callings at different ages. One difference that characterizes the stories is the Jewish understanding that all "sons of the covenant" (Bar Mitzvoth) are *natural* sons and daughters of God. This understanding is actually the context in which the proclamation of Jesus as "son of God" makes sense: he was, to his followers, the epitome of what it means to be a son of God in Jewish terms, giving himself thoroughly to God's work in the world. The metaphor of adoption that comes to the fore in the New Testament, however, highlights the importance of *choice* in becoming a follower of Jesus, a choice especially significant to Gentiles. The fact that God would choose to "adopt" these non-natural daughters and sons into the family of God was a part of how the earliest followers of Jesus tried to make sense of their belief that in their time God was making a way for all people to answer the call to live a life that would be in right relationship to both God and neighbor. As a person responds to the callings that come to her, following the patterns of care for the most vulnerable that were put forward in the life of Christ, the whole creation is cared for and fostered, even when this care is costly to the one who gives it.

The biblical interludes between the book's chapters offer brief glimpses of people living into their callings at various stages of the lifespan, even if vocation is not the specific topic of the story. The interludes are not included here as sociological evidence for ways in which vocation was construed in the ancient world, but rather as lively narrative windows into the lives of people caught out unawares, living mostly unselfconsciously into age-specific vocations. Academic tools of biblical study (historical, rhetorical, literary) are used, but without being center stage. The tools do the behind-the-scenes work in imagining the biblical characters as clearly as possible so that they can take center stage, illuminated by the insights of the authors concerning vocation across the lifespan.

Childhood: One Such Child

JANE PATTERSON

–

That children are highly desired is obvious in the Bible from Genesis on. And yet, by the time Jesus pulls a child out of the crowd and says, "Whoever welcomes one such child in my name welcomes me" (Matt. 18:5), many children are living at the very bottom of the social scale, the most vulnerable in the generally fragile economy of Roman-occupied Judea. "One such child" is probably a child who is already at work for the benefit of his family. In a family of means, a child might be caring for animals, helping in food preparation, or running errands. In a family of no means, a child might be begging, or might even be sold to support the rest of the family: *one such child*.[1]

Jesus's own childhood has scant witness, but an interesting story is told of him in the Gospel of Luke (2:41–52), just as he is in his tweens, 12 years old. His family is obviously very devout, joining the group of pilgrims who undertake the journey on foot from Galilee to Jerusalem for the Passover. After the festival, the whole group of Galileans begins their journey home. We might imagine everyone talking, telling stories, laughing, enjoying the break from the daily routine. Jesus's parents don't notice that he is missing for a full day. When they finally do, they start a search among the families traveling together. Giving up, they return to Jerusalem, where they search for Jesus for three days (three days!), only to find him in the temple with the teachers. Because Jesus as an adult is often depicted as besting the rabbis in argument, many people overlay this story with those stories in their imaginations. But, in fact, Jesus is shown doing what would be appropriate for a bright 12-year-old, engaged in his favorite activity with adults who are mentoring him: he is listening and asking questions. The rabbis are amazed at his precocity, but there is no antagonism between them at this point. The story closes with

36

a pun that surely made its original hearers smile: "Did you not know that I must be in my Father's house?" (2:49). His parents are puzzled, but Jesus returns to Nazareth with them, and life as usual resumes, only with this hint of mystery still remaining, a shadow of his adult vocation falling across his entry into adolescence.

This story of Jesus in late childhood, being irresistibly drawn to the temple and the teaching of the Torah, is intended to point to his deeply embedded calling, one that adults, even parents, can fail to see, as Bonnie Miller-McLemore points out in the following chapter on children and vocation. But it might just as well serve as a way for others to recall their own late childhood; to remember the people who served as mentors and models; to recall childhood interests, hobbies, or fanaticism for some pursuit. In Jesus's case, he is actually pursuing an interest common both to his earthly parents and to his heavenly parent: the Torah—even though his earthly parents seem caught by surprise when their own dedication is manifested in their child with so much energy, curiosity, and giftedness.

3

Childhood

The (Often Hidden yet Lively) Vocational Life of Children

Bonnie J. Miller-McLemore

When I was 8 or 9, I promised myself I would never lie again. Whether in response to a lie gone awry or some other reason, I don't recall. But I do remember how solemnly I committed myself. No one in the immediate vicinity provoked my pledge—I think I was just biking around the neighborhood—although I no doubt heard about truth telling in my family, my school, and the Protestant church we attended.

One night I awoke to a full moon streaming its light through my bedroom window and felt inspired to rise and write. What I wrote is long gone, but not the memory. The impulse seemed to flow from a power greater than I to whom I felt I owed all. In the woods at church camp or looking at the stars from the backseat, sometimes I wondered, "Why is there anything at all rather than nothing?"—only to discover that this question unsettled camp counselor and parent alike. It bothered me too, and I didn't think about it for long because I got the creeps picturing nothing. Years later, I learned that a famous philosopher had called this *the* fundamental question of metaphysics.[1] This doesn't mean I had arrived; it means Martin Heidegger didn't get all that far or, better yet, young children are capable of asking big and sometimes disturbing questions.[2]

Some children have even more explicit call stories. "I was always going to be a writer," says popular novelist Ann Patchett. "I've known this for as long as I've known anything."[3] One Christmas Eve—a holiday she remembers as otherwise abysmal in a step-family with half siblings—her father read to her over the phone from his home in Los Angeles a short story clipped from the *LA Times*. The author grew up in a Catholic orphanage and recalls the year she gave away, on encouragement by the nuns, her only gift of colored pencils, made more dear because of her aspirations to become an artist, to gypsy children with even less than she. Like many parents, Patchett's dad could not anticipate the story's impact. But it triggered in Patchett "the kind of explosion of understanding that sometimes happens in childhood," and her 11-year-old aspirations stretched from writing to her place in life as a whole. "As much as I wanted to be a writer when I was a child, I also wanted to be a shining example of my faith."[4]

Children often know themselves as deeply faithful even if they do not convey this to those around them or articulate their memory of childhood knowledge until later in life. Their reserve partly comes from adults who actually discourage children from asking profound questions. School-age children quickly "learn that only 'useful' questioning is expected of them," as philosopher Gareth Matthews observes.[5] But adult discouragement does not end children's exploration. Practical theologian Kathleen Cahalan describes her hunger as a child to know scripture and learn to pray. When she decides in sixth grade that she will read the Bible "from beginning to end," she temporarily "borrows" a prayer book from her Catholic parish, believing that its daily readings will give her access to God even if she is not at daily Eucharist.[6] This pursuit is mostly hidden from adults. Although heavily involved in church, she "never let out what was an inner and private practice and neither did anyone inquire."[7]

I do not tell these stories to show how "kids say the darndest things," a twentieth-century phenomenon reflective of a society captivated by perceptions of children as cute and innocent, yet covertly convinced that they really do not know much, that they lead lives of emotional, philosophical, and spiritual simplicity.[8] Nor do I recount these stories to suggest that children's vocation is all about mountaintop highs, moral transformation, or what they want to be when they grow up. Children do, of course, have what Abraham Maslow famously called "peak experiences" that shape their future, even though researchers have seldom studied them.[9] But children also have vocational experiences that are entirely and appropriately mundane, discoveries and daily encounters that result merely from being children who encounter nature for the first time or learn how to do new tasks. My husband recalls an early memory of walking out the door as a toddler and finding himself captivated by the sparkle of dew atop the rubber front of his Red Ball Jet shoes. Aspiring a few years later to learn how to tie them, he had a dream in which he was shown the secret, and in the morning he woke up and knew how to do it.

I begin with these portraits of vocational inclinations in childhood to evoke your own memories and to confirm the place and power of this period in the vocational lifecycle. These stories remind us of our own experiences of encountering the divine in our early lives, and they offer an initial sampling of how children experience their common vocation to love God and neighbor and recognize their particular vocational gifts and talents.[10] In this chapter, I invite adults to imagine children's vocational lives afresh, exploring facets often overlooked. I argue that we need to include children more fully in our understanding of how vocation unfolds over the lifespan. I also want to show that as children engage their own vocation they contribute to the vocational development of those around them in ways that also go unnoticed. Ultimately, to paraphrase the words of scholars who have written about children and vocation, I hope to inspire us to "take notice" of how children are called and how they also "call us out."[11]

Children and Vocation

That children have vocations in matters sacred and mundane and that part of that vocation is to form adults may catch readers by surprise. People often associate "vocation," if we use the term at all, with entering a religious order, training for skilled labor, or finding the right career. It is something about which adults worry, not children. In addition, we assume children do not form adults; adults raise children. However, behind these reactions lie misperceptions about both vocation and children. Christian communities generally do not encourage either adults or children to interpret their lives through a vocational framework. We also tend to overlook children as full participants in familial and social households as well as in the greater household or family of God.

Although the idea of vocation has a distinct Christian history, vocational development ironically receives its most serious study today among secular lifespan psychologists and life-course sociologists instead of among theologians. While social scientists have generated considerable empirical data and even academic journals on children and vocation, there has been only one book in Christian theology that has broached the subject. This inattention to children and vocation among theologians is especially troubling because scientific treatments tend to reduce and secularize the term's richer theological meanings. "Vocation" merely refers to "career exploration, career awareness . . . career maturity/adaptability," and childhood becomes largely a "formative period" for paid work in adulthood.[12] These portrayals reflect the influence of a market economy that has little place for "unproductive" children, a view Christianity and other religions have good reason to question.

Christianity has its own challenges, however. According to the copy on the back of *The Vocation of the Child*, children's calling has been a "perennial puzzle for the Christian community."[13] How does one fit children, especially preverbal infants and unsteady toddlers, into classic Christian understandings that measure maturity in faith according to the acquisition of reason, the capacity for verbal confession, and the formation of moral conscience? For church fathers, such as Augustine and Thomas Aquinas, these notions relieve infants and toddlers of the moral and religious accountability placed on youths and adults.[14] But these adult-centered definitions of faith also raise questions about the purpose of childhood, fostering misperceptions of young children as insignificant and incomplete. Childhood receives greater attention among modern scholars influenced by the developmental sciences, such as James Fowler, who took young children's capacity for creative religiosity seriously. But the emphasis on "stages of faith" often falls on cognitive development and on adulthood, or "becoming adult, becoming Christian," to borrow one of Fowler's book titles, and less on understanding children's religious experiences.[15] This shift in focus to adults partly results from the nature of the theory itself. That is, stage theory tends to value where one is headed more than what one leaves behind.[16]

One result of this Christian inheritance today is a continued struggle to regard children as active participants in and contributors to the Christian life, a problem that resurfaces when we start talking about vocation. My own early research on mothering explored vocation as an adult dilemma of work and love, and then in later work I urged people to take children more seriously.[17] But I still did not connect children and vocation until other people began to invite such consideration. Yet if Christians see children as part of the community, then children have vocations too. Unfortunately, efforts thus far to study their vocation often define the term narrowly as moral and spiritual aspiration, thereby overlooking a holistic appreciation for how vocation touches every aspect of life. Vocation is often seen as a theoretical concept to be debated doctrinally or morally more than a concrete reality to be lived out in faith communities and families. Moreover, adult anxieties about preserving marriage, for example, or offsetting advocacy for children's rights with a Christian emphasis on responsibility overshadow deeper interest in children's own thoughts and experiences. When practical concerns do arise, the emphasis falls heavily on the role of adults tutoring children toward adulthood. The overriding question then becomes, "[How] can adults help or hinder a child's vocation to become and to be a moral, spiritual person?," turning "vocation" into a one-directional (adult-forms-child), forward-looking (child-becomes-adult), and spiritualized term.[18]

In this chapter, I hope to disrupt these patterns by exploring how children engage vocation *as children*, how they form adults, and how they do so in mundane contexts. Research in practical theology and childhood studies supports this reorientation and shapes the argument. In addition to an abiding interest in theology in particular contexts, practical theologians have paid close attention to children partly out of a focus on religious formation and an interest in what social scientists say about human growth. In the 1990s, European practical theologians such as German scholar Norbert Mette were already insisting on "children as subjects" rather than objects before the concept became academically fashionable. If children participate actively in the construction of reality from the beginning of life, as modern psychology suggests, then "there is more truth," as Mette argues, "in saying that children 'bring up' adults than is generally supposed."[19] Their upbringing is a more socially interactive process than previously imagined. A similar turn toward enhanced respect for children occurred in childhood studies, an interdisciplinary field that emerged initially out of sociology in the 1990s.[20] Its literature transforms common assumptions about children, including Christian ideas about their incompleteness, through a commitment to seeing them as active agents in the world around them. Instead of studying *the child*, childhood studies also underscores the complexity and multiplicity of *children's* experiences across history and society.

Entering: Birth, Recognition, and the Power to Shape a World

Acknowledging this diversity makes it difficult to accomplish one of my aims—to create a sense of what vocation means for children by itemizing central characteristics of this phase. I can generalize, but for every generalization there is an exception and another story to be told. It is also difficult to speak about infants and preteens in one chapter. In fact, one of the markers of childhood is the immense physical and social growth that occurs. Generalization also leads to romanticizing and essentializing childhood, especially in modernity where we have stereotyped children as innocent, pure, and cute, and then exploited these qualities. Variations also exist over when childhood ends. Some people identify puberty, others point to the time when the brain stops growing in the mid-twenties, and society makes up all sorts of artificial markers, such as readiness to drive, vote, or get into R-rated movies. Finally, all of us remain children of our parents for our entire lives, and the belief that people are children of God is central to Christian understandings of grace and adoption, as Jane Patterson also notes in introducing her biblical interludes for this book.[21]

Despite these qualifications, I still find the loose category of *childhood* useful, and I try to balance a sense of its cohesion with respect for differences and ambiguities. Birth is a wonderful example. It is an obvious commonality that marks the beginning of childhood regardless of time and place, but people understand its meaning and experience its reality quite differently. Even though it is questionable whether newborns undertake birth as a "vocational task," birth exemplifies vocation's irrevocably relational nature. One does not cause one's own conception or remember coming into the world. But if part of children's vocation is to form adults, they do so powerfully through birth. Although birth is not always joyous or celebrated and is often difficult, if not traumatic, giving birth can become a transformational and even miraculous religious experience for many adults, confirming "the grace of life itself" as one father and theologian says about the birth of his daughter.[22]

Although a few pre-modern theologians like Augustine closely observed and commented on early infant behavior as they considered questions of sin and baptism, most pre-modern and modern theologians have shown less interest in the awakening tasks of childhood. By contrast, modern psychologists have studied them closely. Prominent events include connecting in face-to-face encounters with caregivers, early language expression and acquisition, and the gradual development of a sense of self with the power to name and affect the world around oneself. While object-relations theorists and developmental psychologists, such as Margaret Mahler and Daniel Stern, have divided these tasks of connection and separation between birth and 3 years into finer and finer steps, earlier psychoanalysts such as Sigmund Freud and Erik Erikson had greater interest in broader awakenings from birth to puberty, what Erikson labeled "crises" and Freud called "stages of psychosexual development."[23] Beyond the initial task of connection (trust versus mistrust), Erikson's other three crises of childhood emphasize forms of assertion (autonomy, initiative, and industry)—an approach that feminist scholars criticize as one-sided in its focus on independence and neglect of relationship.

While recognizing the value of this critique, it is still helpful to notice that a major awakening vocational task for children involves gaining a sense of subjectivity and agency, moving into the world, and extending one's connections with it. Much adult care involves responding to and shaping constructively children's efforts to communicate and participate. Psychologists also describe nicely what children need for accomplishing these tasks—a safe, trustworthy "holding environment" (D. W. Winnicott) and "mirroring" or affirmation and role models worthy of imitation and idealization (Heinz Kohut).[24]

Characteristics: Small, New, Fresh, Vulnerable, and Open to the Divine

That children are *small* seems obvious. But this distinguishing mark of children's vocation is often overlooked. Adults forget what it is like to view the world from below and close to the ground except perhaps when a film (like *The Tree of Life*) adjusts the camera angle. Part of children's vocation is to remind us. Children are also *new* and *fresh*, like seedlings and hatchlings. In fact, there is something incredibly captivating about the young. Anyone who has sat behind an infant in worship or at the ballpark can confirm this. Only the most dedicated worshiper or avid sports fan can close eyes in prayer or watch for strikes while under the spell of a playful, curious child in the row ahead.

The appeal, particularly the capacity to smile and solicit another's gaze, actually represents an adaptive advantage for securing care and protection, according to evolutionary science. Although neurobiologists do not have a scientific explanation for social smiling, they detect early "appearance of brain activity" in newborns "specialized for face-to-face communication." Social smiling emerges in infant behavior across cultures around 6 to 8 weeks of age and "produces a marked change in parent-offspring relations."[25] Twentieth-century lifecycle theorist Erik Erikson said as much several decades earlier. The demeanor and needs of the newly born have a "power all their own," he observes, endowing the infant "with an appearance and with responses which appeal to the tending adults' tenderness and make them wish to attend."[26] Building on Erikson, developmental psychologist Robert Kegan says "recruitability"— children's capacity to "recruit" or "to hold the mother with a recognizing eye" and adult proclivity to be attracted—is as "fundamental to our development" as the physical ability to grasp an object. Nature endows the young with attributes that draw the welfare of others, and nothing is "more powerful" than the eyes and face.[27] In other words, part of children's vocation, embedded in their smiles and their smallness, newness, and freshness, is to provoke care from adults and to cultivate adult capacities for responsiveness.

Newness is also what makes the first scrape so injurious, the first lost tooth so poignant, and the healing of scrapes and bumps so rapid, eliciting adult appreciation for life's vitality. Freshness also surfaces in inexperience, näiveté, and boundless energy as well as the ever-changing bodies and growth spurts that make clothes suddenly seem small. Some scientists label the "long phase" of "slow growth" from age 5 until puberty "middle childhood," and point out that, unique to humans, it allows for "an enormous amount of vital and detailed cultural learning" alongside the biological changes.[28] Thus, biology itself suggests children have a vocational call to grow and learn, even though I doubt many biologists would say it this way.

For Christians, however, these attributes are not just biological and psychological survival mechanisms. They have spiritual and vocational relevance. In an essay frequently cited by scholars who write on children and religion, Karl Rahner, a prominent twentieth-century Jesuit theologian who had little immediate responsibility for children but significant influence on religious education, captures one of children's vocational gifts nicely when he describes childhood as "openness," even "infinite openness." By "openness" he partly means trust—"deep elemental and ultimate trust which seems inexhaustible in its endurance." But its qualities escape easy depiction—"harmony with the unpredictable forces" that confront us, "hope which is still not disillusioned," "a readiness to journey into the untried and the untested." Stated most starkly, openness is "total self-abandonment to the incomprehensible infinitude of the ineffable mystery."[29] The resemblance between this portrait and his understanding of God suggests how proximate Rahner sees childhood to knowledge essential for the Christian life.

Rahner is not just referring to children here, however. Nor is he talking metaphorically. He is talking literally about *mature childhood within adulthood*—"childhood as an inherent factor in our lives," not as a "secondary or incidental" reference but the "*reality* of childhood" that has "definitive and enduring validity in God's sight" as part of adult life.[30] In short, we might read Rahner as saying that if adults really want to know about God, they need to look at children and their own childhoods as vocationally and theologically relevant.

Here and with the other marks of childhood explored in this section, children's vocation differs from how adults usually understand the term as a subjective self-conscious claim about one's purpose that arises *internal* to the self and, in its modern aberration, a highly individualistic act of choice and agency aimed toward future productivity or, in evangelical terms, a personal response to God's command. For children, by contrast, vocation often arises in the here and now at the juncture of interpersonal interaction, in their *external* impact on and interchange with the world based on the very traits that comprise childhood itself. Children have their own personal vocational epiphanies, of course, whether in the moment, as with Patchett's early knowledge of her desire to write, or constructed in hindsight, as with my adult realization that even as a child I used writing to unravel puzzles. Still, children also experience and enact their vocation in small, mundane, incidental ways as a sheer result of being children and without conscious articulation, simply by evoking the sacred in the midst of everyday life and by having an impact on adults and the common good. In a way, they participate in their vocation *as children* without necessarily recognizing this except, possibly, through a kind of felt knowledge. That is, their vocation exists, and they have some sense of this even if not verbally proclaimed. Although children may not notice internally or assert overtly their childhood traits as vocational capacities, adults should welcome these traits as gifts bestowed indiscriminately on those who attend to children.

One of children's distinctive capacities—their openness to divinity as described by Rahner—seems almost incomprehensible because we cannot help but assume that, as adults, we surpass where we were in our faith as children and that, as Christians, mature faith and eternity lie out in front of us somewhere. But a Christian view of time, subjectivity, and vocation upsets our ordinary linear, individualistic, and progressive perception in which one stage follows another and selves exist as independent entities, leaving childhood behind as vocationally "subordinate and preparatory" in Rahner's words.[31] Instead, childhood goes forward with us not only in the decisions we make but also as invaluable *in itself* as a time when certain matters occur that can occur at no other time. Childhood touches the divinity of God "in a special way of its own." Humans are "allotted [a] task" and fully "endowed with grace . . . from the very outset," Rahner argues.[32] And vocation happens between us as much as within us, as an intersubjective matter. In a word, children have a vocation that is as essential to Christian life, if not more so, than our purpose as adults. Their task or "claim upon us all," which we must help children perform, is to help us become the children we began to be in our own childhood, again not metaphorically but in reality. For in childhood, our "first intimations of God are attained."[33]

Children have their own view of time that reorients adult assumptions about how vocation happens. Vocation for children is not, at least initially, forward looking or about becoming something else. Rather, it happens by living fully into the given or what we might call the is-ness of now. For infants and toddlers, time is negligible, not a matter to be considered. It only acquires meaning, as Freud implies, when young children have to wait and hence acquire what he calls "delayed gratification." Tempering the "pleasure principle," or the immediate indulgence of our desires, with the "reality principle" forces us to learn about time.[34] When children do begin to attend to time, it can seem excruciatingly slow. One moment for a child also seems longer because it represents a larger portion of the lifespan than it does for an adult.[35]

Children not only experience time differently, however. They are also more fully present to it and possess an especially sharp awareness of immediate experience. As I noticed as a mother of young children, they seem to have a capacity to absorb what is before them, seeing "what adults have long since failed to note," attending "religiously to the world's creations," and expressing concentrated awe in ants, fireflies, water, sand, and thunderstorms. Toddlers and preschoolers "do not hedge their bets with a thousand worries."[36] Christian mystic and activist Simone Weil famously likens this kind of receptivity to prayer—the "orientation of all the attention of which the soul is capable toward God."[37] By simply exuding such a stance, children live into their call and, potentially, reorient the adults around them to different and often more valuable, even ultimate, priorities, as the elderly sometimes do also.[38]

Pastoral theologians Herbert Anderson and Susan Johnson use the term "immediacy" to describe this quality. But by this they mean candor and spontaneity, as when children "say things that adults have learned to mute." They also list "imagination, play, and celebration" as "variations."[39] I would say there are so many sub-qualities of this characteristic of immediacy that it is hard to name them all. Children unabashedly express amazement, astonished when they first balance a bike or receive candy just by saying "trick-or-treat." Their contagious awe reminds adults to prize what they have come to take for granted. They cry often and easily, especially in the first three months—what scientists recognize as a "vital built-in survival mechanism" and Swiss theologian and therapist Dieter Seiler describes as not just a "signal of need" but also "an expression of power over adults who have to hear it and act."[40] They are eager to learn and inventive in their acquisition and use of language. They create surprising, even humorous metaphors. One of our sons who loved anything round—from balls to balloons—continued to call out "balloon, balloon!" whenever he saw a looming Chicago water tank despite our efforts to teach the "correct" word (odd structures, which we had, by the way, ceased to notice). Because children's imaginations are big, their terrors are also vivid. Dreams are never as real as in childhood, calling forth adult help in reinterpreting reality and offering protection. Finally, one facet of immediacy seldom lifted up is how fully children inhabit their bodies until they learn to fret about appearance, dampen their exploration, or, most tragically, fear adult intrusion.

Until now, I have assumed the best of circumstances—an environment in which children are provided opportunity to flourish. Sadly, this well-being is not always the case. Illness, disability, parental absence, abandonment, and death dramatically reshape children's vocational experience. Moreover, in a world in which the powerful and the hardened easily take advantage of the trusting and the weak, qualities of smallness, freshness, openness, and immediacy put children at greater risk than most people in other age groups. These traits also render childhood one of the messiest, noisiest, most restless, unpredictable, chaotic, and disruptive times of life. As a result, many children struggle in situations of neglect, abandonment, domestic violence, and sexual abuse where adults refuse or violate children's efforts to "recruit" adult care. Some find unique, resilient ways to follow their calling and secure vocational meaning in the midst of adversity. Others pay a high price for poverty, war, famine, and disease. The immediate and long-term consequences for children of human calamities are often overlooked or discounted by adults. Human potential is wasted, callings are missed or unanswered, and dreams are deferred. When adults cause or contribute to such loss, and miss the chance to welcome "one such child" as Jane Patterson suggests,[41] the warning words of Jesus in Luke's Gospel come to mind: "It would be better for you if a millstone were hung around your neck and you were thrown into the sea than for you to cause one of these little ones to stumble" (17:2, NRSV).

Not surprisingly, therefore, *vulnerability* is a final vocationally relevant trait. Children's acute vulnerability makes the anomalies and harsher re-

48

alities that can disrupt any life phase all the more painful and accentuates their need for protection and advocacy. "Small, weak, and needful," as Anderson and Johnson observe, children are dependent on others for care and survival and thus are even more "susceptible to being wounded."[42] This precariousness is true in a purely biological sense, according to scientists who observe that, in a trade-off with the female pelvic anatomy that accompanied upright posture, infants actually "should be born about twelve months later" simply in terms of the brain's growth, which doubles in volume during the first year. Early birth creates a period of dependency more acute and prolonged than that of any other mammal.[43]

As with other traits, however, the place of vulnerability also has vocational meaning as a "locus of God's grace" (David Jensen) or a part of God's "risking love" (Anderson and Johnson).[44] For Jensen, our creation in God's image is distinguished not by openness, as Rahner suggested, or other qualities earlier Christians identified, such as reason, dominion, or morality, but by vulnerability, exemplified in childhood.[45] As Jensen argues, God's vulnerability runs through the Old Testament where "the God who becomes vulnerable in relationship to Israel calls the covenant people to become vulnerable to those on the margins"—the widow, the orphan, and the stranger. It continues in the New Testament when Jesus reaches out to the most vulnerable, including children, and makes himself vulnerable unto the cross.[46] Returning to its Latin root, *vulnerare* ("to wound"), Jensen offers a helpful definition: "To be vulnerable is to expose oneself to possible harm and injury—to live on the edge, open to the world's profound beauty and its threatening violence."[47] The very asymmetry and imbalance in power between children and adults then serves a vocational purpose as an important destabilizing effect that, like children's openness, can disorient and reorient adults to deeper meanings in life and faith. In a sense, children and aging adults both "live on the edge," more exposed than others to life's precariousness and perils. Therefore, their vocation, in many ways, is to remind those in the middle years about the value and limits of life, to live well at life's extremes, and to call forth the gifts of others to ensure they are able to do so.

Reckoning with children's vulnerability also alters how adults have understood human sin or fallibility. For Christians, children never occupy what Rahner describes as "a sort of innocent arcadia." They are always already located in and conditioned by a human history that is, as he says, "also a history of guilt, of gracelessness, of a refusal to respond to the call of the living God." So childhood does not escape the "forces of bitterness"

and complexity that belong to human life.[48] Recognizing children's fallibility allows us to take them and their vocational needs and choices more
seriously.[49] However, given their limited power and dependence, they
"are more often sinned against than sinners themselves," a distinction that
arises from liberation theologians attuned to the experience of those without power.[50] An "inherited vulnerability" captures the reality of our shared
fallen nature better than the classic Christian idea of inherited depravity,
especially for the small, weak, and dependent whose power to act is often
at the mercy of others.

Vocational Experiences: Working, Playing, Learning, and Loving

As these characteristics suggest, vocational experiences in childhood are
more nebulous and fleeting than in adulthood even though the decisions
and dilemmas center on similar domains of work, play, learning, and love.
There is simply less pressure than at any other stage to make the right
choice. Ideally, children can experiment with roles and choices without
ultimate consequence, with room for error and less grief over mistakes.
So the turmoil of discerning vocational call that marks most other stages
is lessened in childhood.

In fact, Anglican bishop Rowan Williams makes a profound plea for
social recommitment to this phase of life as rightfully one of "indetermi-
nancies." One cannot learn how to use language—so central to human
life—without allowance for "utterances that I *don't* have to answer for."
We need a protected sphere for "legitimately irresponsible talking" and,
by extension, irresponsible working, playing, learning, and loving. If we
commit to this, adults must allow for speech and action that are not "uni-
formly nice, docile or harmonious."[51] Adults also must be ready to dispel
children's fantasies when they become overly vivid and out of control.
To say it simply, "children need to be free of the pressure to make adult
choices if they are ever to *learn* how to make adult choices."[52] This quality
itself—practicing choosing—is definitive of childhood.

Among the four areas of work, play, learning, and love, Western
middle-class adults have the most difficulty imagining children's vocation
as workers. When Marcia Bunge, a Lutheran theologian and major contributor to childhood studies, lists six "primary duties," or "offices," that
comprise children's specific vocation, work is not among them.[53] This
oversight of work is partly because children have been progressively ex-

cluded in modernity not just from paid labor but also from contributing substantively to domestic life. As one historian of childhood observes, in place of pre-modern ideals of a "useful childhood" where children helped sustain families, people now picture a "sheltered childhood, free from labor and devoted to play and education."[54] Modern misperceptions of childhood as devoted solely to play have deprived children of other valuable vocational experience. For Christians, children have a vocation to serve families and communities through meaningful domestic and social labor that explicitly affects family and communal welfare. That is, they are called to contribute in ways that go beyond token activities assigned because they build character or provide an excuse for an allowance, even if opportunities for children to work have become harder to envision. Children who assume domestic responsibility learn that "no one in the home exists just to serve them," as moral theologian Julie Rubio states, and they "come to understand that they are connected to others" and "have an obligation to engage in loving service."[55]

Play still has a significant place even if it is neither unique to childhood nor its sole focus. Even if the dichotomy between children who play and adults who work is a modern Western misrepresentation of childhood as innocent and carefree, children still have distinctive gifts and needs for play. They usually enter into it more easily, earnestly, and imaginatively than adults. Like their altered sense of time, they often lose themselves more fully, manifesting what psychologist Mihaly Csikszentmihalyi has famously labeled "flow."[56] Different from the "flow" that Katherine Turpin describes in the following chapter as a disciplined pursuit of a singular gift in adolescence, children delve into play to learn an amazing cross-section of human activities—playing house, playing church, playing games, and so forth.[57] Play and work are not opposites here. As lifespan psychologists observe, children "playfully construct possible future selves" and use play to "explore the world-of-work much earlier than theorists and researchers have typically assumed."[58] Play allows for vocational experimentation and a suspension of consequences for the roles one assumes—casting a vocational "shadow" across children's entry into adolescence without forcing anyone to own up to anything yet, as Jane Patterson suggests happens with a preadolescent Jesus in the temple.[59] Winnicott describes a child's need for a "holding environment," his creative and popular term for a nurturing, safe, low-pressure space in which children can engage in imaginative play, an essential activity in the process of self-discovery and understanding of others.[60]

Like smiling, play is another "biological puzzle" that evolutionary biologists cannot wholly explain because of its "apparent pointlessness" and "multiple functions." But the "smartest mammals . . . are the most playful."[61] It is interesting to note, as we did with Rahner, Jensen, and others, what qualities theologians choose as essential in childhood and crucial for religion. For nineteenth-century Congregational minister Horace Bushnell—the "quintessential American theologian of childhood," according to historian Margaret Bendroth—play is pivotal.[62] He describes play as both instinctual in children and a "forerunner of religion." In his words, "God has purposely set the beginning of natural life in a mood that foreshadows the last and highest chapter" of the human pursuit of the good.[63] Mature adult faith without a playful spirit is deeply problematic. In his classic book *Christian Nurture*—"one of the first extended reflections on the religious lives of infants and young children," according to Bendroth—his advice to parents, in Jensen's words, "is simple: play with your children."[64] In scripture, playing children are integral to wisdom at creation's beginning, "growing up" and "playing before" God (Prov. 8:31), and at the end of the world in Zion's restoration with "boys and girls playing in the streets" (Zech. 8:5).[65]

In industrial and postindustrial societies, the value of education and the amount of time children devote to it has grown. But it may be as rare for adults to recognize children as having a vocation as learners as it is for us to see them as workers. Some scholars argue that doing well in school assumes today the importance that domestic and paid labor served in preindustrial days since it is "every bit as tied to the economy" and children's future well-being.[66] Even child advocates who argue for fewer restrictions on children's paid employment recognize the necessity of balancing paid work with educational opportunity. Lack of education perpetuates poverty and makes children more vulnerable to exploitation. Children have an aptitude for learning that adults lose, evident in the ease with which they acquire languages, for example, or adapt to new technology. For Christians, studying diligently also has a religious purpose, serving as a means for children "to cultivate their unique skills, gifts and talents so that they can love and serve others and contribute to the common good," as Bunge says.[67] Over the centuries, both Christian and Jewish traditions have upheld the importance of providing children with a good formal education (mostly restricted to boys until modernity) as well as informal training in domestic skills as a fundamental parental and adult responsibility.

Finally, of the four areas, children's vocation in relational matters has received the most attention from Christian theologians. Both Jewish and

Christian traditions have stressed children's calling to honor and obey parents and to love God and neighbor. The first four "offices," or duties, that Bunge names fall in this arena—honor parents, obey parents, disobey parents, and fear and love God. Only then does she turn to schoolwork and play as additional responsibilities. Her articulation of children's duties reflects a heavy reliance on what she finds in scripture and tradition. She begins with the fourth commandment to honor parents and then turns to another command that appears almost as frequently, obeying them. She interprets both honor and obedience in terms of respect and appreciation for parental nurture and the acquired wisdom of one's elders. She does not point out that key passages asking children to "obey your parents in everything" (Col. 3:20) appear in the Household Codes in the deutero-Pauline letters of Ephesians, Colossians, Timothy, and Titus that also counsel wives and slaves to submit to husbands and masters. These codes have received plenty of critique, including the recognition that they reflect a desire among Paul's followers to reassert patriarchal order within an early and turbulent period of Christianity's history.[68] However, by also including disobedience as an explicit task, Bunge underscores an often-neglected vocation—that "children are not ultimately subject to their parents" but made in God's image and, foremost, dedicated to God and neighbor.[69] Precedents for disobeying parents abound in the tradition, from Martin Luther to Francis of Assisi to Jesus himself.

Of all these relational duties, I would say children's foremost calling in this sphere is the one Bunge puts toward the end—to love God with their whole heart, soul, mind, and might (Mark 12:30). Embedded in the Jewish Shema, or affirmation of faith in one God, is the parental imperative to "recite [these words] to your children and talk about them when you are at home and when you are away, when you lie down and when you rise" (Deut. 6:7). This command echoes an earlier passage in Deuteronomy: "make [God's commandments] known to your children and your children's children" (4:9).

Unfortunately, the emphasis on honoring parents and elders often overlooks children's calling to treat their peers, including siblings, with respect. "Do not put down the other person," your brother included, as we used to say to our sons, "in order to make yourself feel better." Christian ethicist William Werpehowski expresses well the importance of extending honor beyond parents to peers when he says, "the fourth commandment may attain its fullness of purpose as a central moment in a history of learning to honor *every* human being."[70]

Communal Dynamics: Adults Form Children, Children Form Adults

Under optimal circumstances in each of these four realms, children as well as the adults who care for them seek to recognize and actualize their distinctive talents. As with any stage, gifts rise naturally to the fore, and they also depend heavily on environmental reinforcement and opportunity. Children surprise parents who are called to welcome and "handle with care" the unexpected capacities and challenges that come with vocational gifts. It took my husband and me years to honor drumming and climbing as among one of our son's desires and gifts. Seeing percussion as a rich musical endeavor and the rock wall as a good place for honing discipline and attention was not part of our repertoire. But as it turned out, our son's early predilection to climb whatever tree limb or wall was at hand cast a wonderful "shadow" over his longer vocational trajectory, which has included a love of the outdoors and outdoor education with children.

As our parental experience suggests, there are at least two reasons why it is important for adults to know more about children and vocation. Adults have an impact on children's vocation and should claim their influence as a valuable Christian responsibility. Inversely, children form adults more than adults realize, a distinctive vocational role to which adults should be alert and receptive. Vocational call is personal and individual, *and* discovered, confirmed, and affirmed in the give-and-take of relationships with others, including family, peers, mentors, and communities.[71]

"There was no gift that could have made me feel my father really knew me," Patchett claims, "the way that [Christmas newspaper] story did."[72] Patchett and Cahalan both talk about crucial acts by adults that guided them, often unbeknownst to the adults. A nun asks Cahalan and a few others to return to church after school and help set up the sanctuary for Mass. Cahalan remembers the experience, whether a purposeful or simply pragmatic invitation, as pivotal to her receiving the church as her own to care for.[73] Patchett still has a valued friendship with a Catholic sister who essentially took it upon herself to tutor Patchett through serious learning deficiencies in second grade. Only as an adult was she able to transmute a lingering 7-year-old's sense of persecution into appreciation.[74]

Most adults looking back on childhood recognize similar formative persons and moments. Do adults notice the steps children are taking as they live out their vocation? Do children honor these moments as graced, a sign of God's presence? Often, we do not notice unless encouraged to do so by reflecting on and sharing the experience, as Patchett does through her writing or as I did by participating in a group that discussed vocational epiphanies in childhood. As researchers observe in their analysis of childhood peak experiences, "a number of participants told us that they have never related the stories before and how significant it was for them to have their stories heard and accepted." There seems to be "a silencing of peak experiences" among children similar to the discouragement of philosophical musings, even though these musings have significant influence. Adults who notice and affirm children's experiences "can have a positive impact."[75]

On a practical level, from the perspective of social science research, adult attention to children's aspirations has job implications. "What children learn about work and occupations," according to one survey, "has a profound effect on the choices they make as adolescents and young adults, and ultimately, on their occupational careers"—again, casting a vocational "shadow" on what is yet to come. The survey also shows that children explore the "world-of-work" sooner than researchers and parents recognize. Rather than seeing childhood as a "passive, quiescent period," adults should see it as a "period of active precursory engagement."[76]

From the perspective of Christian theology and faith, however, more is at stake than a future livelihood. Arriving early and staying late at the convent because of her mother's long work hours, Patchett now sees that more "rubbed off over the years" than she realized.[77] Never pressuring students to enter religious life, what the nuns told them "repeatedly was to *listen*: God had a vocation for all of us and if we paid close attention and were true to ourselves we would know" God's intent.[78] Many people, such as the contributors to *The Vocation of the Child* and church leaders, underscore the parental vocation of passing on the faith and nurturing love of God, neighbor, and self. Bunge lists "best practices" for adults who want to guide children vocationally; these practices range from inviting them into worship and service to cultivating knowledge about the world, their bodies, and vocations.[79] Others, such as Rubio and myself, underscore the family's "public vocation" or "social mission" to inculcate in children a sense of the common good and their role in contributing to it.[80]

Adults assume they must educate children. But all the while, children are significantly making over the adults in their midst in both subtle and dramatic ways. Adults should become more aware of how children form them, seeking it out and welcoming it.[81] Some parents have powerful experiences of children's formational impact. Religious ethicist Christine Gudorf says her two adopted children controlled their relationship at least as much as she and her husband did, determining "where we went . . . what we ate, all home activities, who we saw, even how much sleep we got." More profoundly, her children expanded her racial boundaries and moral commitments.[82] Sometimes children lead in more subtle ways. When Dorothy Bass read through a Taize Picture Bible with her step-daughter, she helped form in the child a love for living within the Christian narrative, but the activity also allowed scripture to take hold anew within her as the caring adult. Later, this same step-daughter insists that her two families (each parent having remarried with children of their own) spend time together in the same remote retreat village to which they had previously traveled separately, essentially helping the families move past conflict and discomfort toward greater reconciliation. In a word, children lead adults vocationally, with the full force of the eschatological words heard in Advent from the book of Isaiah, "And a little child shall lead them" (11:6).[83]

Neither church education nor psychology considers seriously enough how adults are formed and transformed when they attend to children. Church schools focus on teaching children, seldom on the impact of care of children on adult spirituality, and psychology often focuses on how absent mothers or overbearing fathers wreak developmental havoc in children's lives. Erikson, however, is an exception. He calls the interconnection or "interplay" between generations "cogwheeling"—an intertwining or "interliving" in which the "stages of others" move people along as they in turn foster the movement of others through life's stages.[84] Although he does not use the term "vocation," his analysis of the ego strengths or virtues that result from the resolution of conflicts at each stage (hope, will, purpose, competence, fidelity, love, care, and wisdom) is relevant to vocational formation. "Each virtue and its place in the schedule of all virtues is vitally interrelated to other segments of human development."[85] The connections between people at either end of the lifecycle are especially pivotal and paradigmatic. The adult, searching for meaning in crises of generativity and stagnation, integrity and despair, needs the claims a young child places on her just as much as the child, facing early crises of trust and mistrust, needs welcoming arms, encouraging words, and a place in the world. In Erikson's words, the "adult cannot help smiling back" in response to the infant's smile, "filled with expectations of a 'recognition' which [the adult] needs to secure from the new being as surely as [the infant] needs [the adult]."[86]

Children form adults in countless ways. They compel us to move at a different pace—"according to the pace of the cattle [and] children," as Jacob says to his brother Esau (Gen. 33:14).[87] Children remind adults about life's limits and mortality, and how to live well enough within the fixed parameters of our choices. In their struggles and judgments, they reflect our own foibles, giving us opportunity to revisit and reconcile with our past. In nearly overwhelming us with physical contact, they remind us of the significance of bodily care. In the chaos of care, they invite and even yearn for structure and ritual at mealtime, bedtime, and worship time, highlighting the value of binding our hearts in good daily habits. "If I forget [to cross myself]," an associate pastor remarks, "my five-year-old reminds me." In fact, the youngest congregants are sometimes the "most ritually alive," even though adults "tend to segregate" them "until they are past the age when it is likeliest to fascinate them."[88] Caring deeply for children also requires reserves of trust and relinquishment, letting children disappear around corners where we can only call out from a distance. A range of theologians, such as Gudorf, Elizabeth Dreyer, Janet Soskice, Wendy Wright, and myself, describe care of children as having ascetic dimensions that hone the capacity for attention and love, including the capacity to let go.[89] What one gives up and how one comes to regard life differently can incline one's heart to God. Pope John Paul II used a common and important Christian term for this honing of the spirit, saying that children even contribute to the "sanctification of parents."[90] Not always and not easily, but one can sometimes see in children's faces the face of God, as the Gospel accounts of Jesus's welcome to the children suggest.[91]

Children also form people in larger communities. When a small urban congregation in Buenos Aires grew increasingly unsettled by the social problems and poverty surrounding them, it was children, according to professor of applied theology Nancy Bedford, who played a major role in pushing people to deliberate and take action. She testifies on how "God's Spirit [used] the voices of children":

I would hold that the questions of young children—when taken seriously—are often among the most important catalysts in the process of discernment, especially in societies where small children and their conversation are valued highly, as in Argentina. Their questions are insistent, often incisive, and display an unconscious hermeneutic of suspicion. Some questions posed by my oldest daughter, three years old at the time, that were significant to me in clarifying my priorities were: "Does that woman sleep outside at night? Why? Shouldn't we find her a place to stay?" (observations made on the street). "Does God give all people food or just some?" (asked after giving thanks for the food).[92]

This profound account of children's transformative influence is tucked away in a long footnote in an essay otherwise devoted to moving liberation theology from global pronouncements on social justice to concrete steps or what Bedford calls "little moves against destructiveness." As her testimony about her daughter's impact reveals, children see what adults, even the best liberation theologians, have missed, and they also do theology. Such revelatory capacity can make pastoral work with them "tricky," as another scholar says. "One cannot take children seriously in worship and at the same time want—for example—foreign workers to be deported without further ado."[93] Bedford concludes with a condensed verbatim of a conversation with her daughter that took place over a couple of days about whether God is active if invisible, and her daughter's own discernment of the Spirit telling her, as the girl says, that "we need to find a place to live for those people that sleep outside . . . and teach the bad people to be good and share with the poor people."[94]

In sheer scientific terms, it is no surprise that community matters when it comes to vocation. Communal interconnections have fostered human survival and evolution. Extended social help in the nurture of infants, toddlers, and young children, also described as "cooperative breeding" or "allocare," "probably made a difference between us and our last common ancestor" in terms of our evolutionary success.[95] Although mothers have a primary connection in early years of care, an extended network has always surrounded the mother-child dyad until the modern deviation of isolating mothers in nuclear households. Children need and benefit from many caring adults beyond the immediate family. Christianity underscores this and provides additional religious rationale and institutional support, such as godparents, adoption, "other mothering," and "fictive kin," terms black feminist Patricia Hill Collins uses to describe care by non-biological relations within African American communities.[96] Although theologians have emphasized parental responsibility to rear children in the Christian faith, they have never assigned this duty to parents alone; it is a shared task of church and state, including the provision of social and political infrastructures of support. The more formal ritual act of baptism or baby dedication is one way Christian communities mark the invitation into God's family and the initiation of Christian vocation and God's calling, both general and particular to each child. Such rituals underscore the welcome of infants and children into the congregation and assign responsibility for their nurture and welfare to the entire community. Pastoral theologian Jeanne Stevenson-Moessner reminds us that God's position as essentially an adoptive parent sanctifies such care as a central God-act.[97]

One final crucial and perhaps unnoticed place where children encounter vocation in community is through friends and siblings. Today I watch with deep appreciation as my three young adult sons set examples for each other on how to live a full and centered life, developing one's talents and giving to the wider world. Although they have their differences, they have been their "brother's keeper," to use Jane Patterson's words from the next biblical interlude, standing by each other like Miriam by her brother as they have made early adult decisions about next steps with their lives.[98] Deliberations on vocation often underestimate the influence not only of sibling support, but also the place of friends. Growing up, I spent hours with a neighborhood buddy climbing trees and rafters of homes under construction, book in hand, so we could each find a perch and read. Few friends welcomed the joy of a good read or the out-of-doors as she did, and she paved the way for these loves to grow in my own life then and now. We moved into entirely different circles in high school and adulthood as peer and social pressures impinged (she ended up on Wall Street). But childhood friendships in general retain an element of freedom and unadulterated affirmation often lost in the teen years.

Ending: Shifting Perspectives of the World and One's Place

The onset of puberty has served as an easily identifiable marker for the end of childhood. However, as the age at which children enter puberty drops, this has fluctuated, and children have had to deal earlier with bodily changes for which they are less than emotionally and socially prepared. The tasks that define the termination of childhood vary across culture and time. I have focused on birth to 12 years, but young people in their early twenties still have lingering traits from childhood (e.g., dependence or even brain immaturity). Conversely, in past centuries children entered into adult tasks much sooner than many children do today, and this is often still true for many children in poor and low-income communities in the United States and worldwide.

A better marker or task that falls at the end of childhood, regardless of age and context, is acquiring a changed perspective of the world and one's place in it. Even the word "unadulterated," which I used above in describing children's friendships, suggests that childhood is a period of life not yet "contaminated" by adult knowledge, responsibility, and striving. Although children definitely recognize otherness and are bold to call it out, they generally disregard social ranking—what Rahner calls a "lack of false ambition," "not seeking for dignities or honours," and "lack of artificiality."[99] Of course, early signs of such concerns do arise in preschool and grade school when children pick teammates, buy clothes, or compare grades or grade levels. Brand name marketing and school tracking can push the age of such competitive comparison lower and lower. And adversity of all sorts can also push children out of childhood early. But the ranking and the striving are still more ephemeral and fluctuating with less dire and extended consequences for children than for adolescents and adults. Children are literally and figuratively closer to the earth (humus), humble without striving to be so. They simply do not (yet) see status as meaningful or have sufficient power to affect it. They do not (yet) censor themselves in compliance with convention. Although we should avoid falling back on modern views of childhood as wholly pure or innocent, one ending task is giving up a certain view of self and world. We slowly begin to leave childhood when positioning ourselves in terms of rank, expectation, and responsibility assumes greater and greater import and consumes more time.

In this ending task, there are other awakenings. Children recognize that a parent does not know everything, that adults are both bad and good at the same time, that Santa might not exist, or that recognized religious and scientific beliefs can be questioned. They become more conscious and even critical of their bodies. In a word, they encounter complexity and disillusionment. Gaining a wider, more complicated, and disenchanted view of one's world coincides with acknowledgment of external standards and greater interpersonal responsibility and accountability. As self-psychoanalytic theory suggests, when children internalize functions previously fulfilled by caregivers and assume activities performed by adults, they begin to leave childhood behind. This expansion of one's world also comes with the first experience of loss, which is often felt quite deeply even if it is only relatively minor, as when a first best friend moves or a treasured toy is lost. In naming these endings, we can see why sadness and grief come with growth, and why we moderns have chased futilely after a romanticized childhood, the daring and self-centered Peter Pan who never grows up.

The author of Luke's Gospel likely had many reasons for including the story of Jesus at age 12 staying behind in the temple after Passover, leaving his parents to search for him, the only New Testament post-infancy story (2:41–52). But perhaps the account should be read as an ending task in his own childhood. Jesus's parents seem to recognize this, and so does Jesus. Even before they miss him, they assume he is among the company with whom they are traveling and no longer in need of immediate supervision. Meanwhile, he has the confidence and interest to sit in the temple listening and asking questions and offering his own thoughts. "Did you not know," he says to his parents, "that I would be here?" (2:49). That Jesus, God incarnate, grew as we grow reveals the vocational potential within the early years of our own evolving lifespans. May children follow him, increasing "in wisdom and in years, and in divine and human favor" (2:52).

Suggested Readings

Anderson, Herbert, and Susan B. W. Johnson. *Regarding Children: A New Respect for Childhood and Families.* Louisville, KY: Westminster John Knox, 1994.

Brennan, Patrick McKinley, ed. *The Vocation of the Child.* Grand Rapids, MI: Eerdmans, 2008.

Bunge, Marcia J. "'Best Practices' for Nurturing the Best Love of and by Children: A Protestant Theological Perspective on Vocations of Children and Parents." In *The Best Love of the Child: Being Loved and Being Taught to Love as the First Human Right,* edited by Timothy P. Jackson, 226–50. Grand Rapids, MI: Eerdmans, 2011.

Bunge, Marcia J., ed. *The Child in Christian Thought.* Grand Rapids, MI: Eerdmans, 2000.

Coles, Robert. *The Spiritual Life of Children.* Boston: Houghton Mifflin, 1990.

Jensen, David H. *Graced Vulnerability: A Theology of Childhood.* Cleveland, OH: Pilgrim, 2005.

Mercer, Joyce Ann. *Welcoming Children: A Practical Theology of Childhood.* St. Louis, MO: Chalice, 2005.

Miller-McLemore, Bonnie J. *In the Midst of Chaos: Care of Children as Spiritual Practice.* San Francisco: Jossey-Bass, 2006.

Miller-McLemore, Bonnie J. *Let the Children Come: Reimagining Childhood from a Christian Perspective.* San Francisco: Jossey-Bass, 2003.

Miller-McLemore, Bonnie J. "Work, Labor, and Chores: Christian Ethical Reflection on Children and Vocation." In *Children, Adults, and Shared*

Responsibilities: Jewish, Christian, and Muslim Perspectives, edited by Marcia J. Bunge, 171–86. Cambridge: Cambridge University Press, 2012.

Rahner, Karl. "Ideas for a Theology of Childhood." In *Theological Investigations,* vol. 8, translated by David Bourke, 33–50. London: Darton, Longman & Todd, 1971.

Siblings: Am I My Brother's Keeper?

JANE PATTERSON

The biblical stories of sibling animosity seem especially vivid, perhaps precisely because parents usually hope so much that their children will not only get along, but carry the family's values forward together into subsequent generations. The call to be a brother or a sister is not the result of discernment, but is a given, like the call to be a son or a daughter. But once given, the calling presents many chances to grow in the vocation or to deny it. Sibling strife shows up in the Bible almost from the very beginning, though it could be argued that the stories in which it occurs are not strictly about sibling rivalry. Rather, the familiar tensions between siblings are used to explain other kinds of fractures in a society that should, like siblings, be more cohesive.

Cain and Abel, the first siblings in creation, enact the most dramatic conflict of all (Gen. 4:1–16), over the relative value of their offerings to God. It is here that the word "sin" makes its first appearance in the Bible, when God chastises Cain for his anger at his brother: "If you do well, will you not be accepted? And if you do not do well, sin is lurking at the door; its desire is for you, but you must master it" (v. 7). The question that most sticks in the hearer's mind long after the story is over is that of Cain, when confronted by God after the murder of Abel: "Am I my brother's keeper?" (v. 9b). Younger children often are, in fact, entrusted to the care and keeping of their older siblings. Outside of parents, siblings are each other's most important safeguards.

One sibling who rises to the challenge to be her brother's keeper is Moses's sister Miriam. Their family, descendants of the tribe of Levi, was among the Hebrew slaves consigned to forced, hard labor in the building of cities and work in the fields of Egypt. The reigning Pharaoh is described as both ruthless and paranoid. Seeing the strength of the Hebrew people, he "made their lives bitter with hard service" (Exod. 1:14). The tension between Pharaoh and the Hebrews escalates as Pharaoh sentences all infant boys born to Hebrew mothers to be drowned in the Nile. In the face of Pharaoh's decree, the Hebrew midwives know clearly what their vocation requires of them, and they do not kill the infant boys. Moses's mother hides her newborn son as long as she can. When he is three months old, she places him in a waterproofed basket and nestles the basket among the reeds on the riverbank. His older sister Miriam hides and waits to see what will become of her brother.

The child is discovered by Pharaoh's daughter, who knows immediately that he is "one of the Hebrews' children" (2:6), and she takes pity on him. Like the courageous Hebrew midwives, who refused to kill the Hebrew baby boys outright, Pharaoh's daughter ignores her father's policy as she reaches out to the squalling Moses. Out pops his sister Miriam from her nearby hiding place, and she offers to find a Hebrew woman to nurse the baby. Pharaoh's daughter and the slave-girl meet eye to eye over the basket with the infant Moses. The simplicity of the storytelling invites the reader to imagine the expressions on the girls' faces: complicity? amusement? daring? Of course, the nurse Miriam "finds" is her own mother, who returns Moses to Pharaoh's house after he is weaned. Miriam embodies what it means to live into the calling to be the brave keeper of one's brother. At the same time she is initiated into a conspiracy of women, united across boundaries of ethnicity and social class by compassion and concern for the well-being of *everyone's* children. The depth of her commitment to her calling as a sister pulls her, together with Pharaoh's daughter, into the tow of God's care for all children.

Adolescence: God Looks on the Heart

JANE PATTERSON

In yet another sibling story, the future King David is introduced in 1 Samuel 16 with a brief, but vivid, account that hides none of the complexity of his entry into Saul's court. Chapter 15 ends with the ominous line, "And the LORD was sorry that he had made Saul king over Israel" (v. 35). While Saul is still king, God sends Samuel, the priest and prophet, to search among the sons of Jesse for the future king, and to anoint this young man as king, even while Saul continues to reign. In a folktale kind of narrative, the sons of Jesse are brought before Samuel, from the eldest on down. But the one whom the Lord has chosen is nowhere among them. "Are *all* your sons here?" Samuel asks Jesse. Jesse replies, "There remains yet the youngest, but he is keeping the sheep" (1 Sam. 16:11). For anyone familiar with the Hebrew scriptures this is an inside joke. Biblically, a skilled shepherd is the very model of good leadership. The prophet Ezekiel proclaims God's frustration with the self-serving leaders of Israel, who have not been good shepherds: "You eat the fat, you clothe yourselves with the wool, you slaughter the fatlings; but you do not feed the sheep. You have not strengthened the weak, you have not healed the sick, you have not bound up the injured, you have not brought back the strayed, you have not sought the lost, but with force and harshness you have ruled them" (Ezek. 34:3-4). Jesse's youngest son is keeping the sheep.

As a late adolescent, David has been shepherding his family's flock, training (unbeknownst to him or to anyone else) for his future calling as king. For a family like David's, their wealth was in their flock. While the work was frequently entrusted to younger family members, it required extraordinary diligence, the ability to endure boredom and then to be suddenly on high alert if there was a threat to the flock, to be aware of the condition of the sheep at all times, and to put the sheep's needs first.

No one familiar with David has seen anything unusual in him, but Samuel is God's means for seeing into the heart of this young man. Samuel anoints him, an act by which the spirit of God comes "mightily upon him from that day forward" (1 Sam. 16:13). At the same time, "the spirit of the LORD departed from Saul" (16:14), and he becomes tormented by destructive thoughts. David is invited into Saul's court due to another skill he has developed while tending his father's sheep: playing the lyre. Anyone who has shared space with a teenager who is obsessed with playing the guitar may be able to imagine the young David practicing his lyre hour after hour in the field, completely absorbed in a "flow experience," losing all track of time. Again, skills honed in childhood and adolescence become transformed into tools for the young adult to use in God's service. David is invited to court to play his lyre for Saul, soothing the man's ravaged soul. One of the interesting aspects of the story is the list of qualities David possesses, as they are enumerated by the courtier who is recommending him: "I have seen a son of Jesse the Bethlehemite who is skillful in playing [the lyre], a man of valor, a warrior, prudent in speech, and a man of good presence; and the Lord is with him" (16:18). David becomes not only lyre-player to the king, but also Saul's armor-bearer. The qualities Samuel saw in the young man begin to be evident to all who meet him.

But the story also introduces the complexity and irony of the challenge that the younger generation presents to their elders as they begin to exercise leadership. David becomes a king according to a different model from Saul, and Saul's era is waning. Across all of 1 Samuel, the two are locked together in love, suspicion, admiration, tragedy. Even though David is exercising a calling that he has been preparing for since childhood, this preparation and clarity of calling do not prevent him from confusion, bad decisions, reversals of fortune, traumas of love and loss. His story prevents us from idealizing vocation. When David is mentioned in the genealogy of Jesus in Matthew 1:6, his entry into the lineage is both confirmation of Jesus's messianic legitimacy and a poignant reminder of David's frailties as a man in ordering Uriah's death so that he could have Bathsheba as his wife: "And David was the father of Solomon by the wife of Uriah."

4

Adolescence

Vocation in Performance, Passion, and Possibility

KATHERINE TURPIN

I come home one afternoon from walking the dog to find my 13-year-old daughter sobbing on the floor. Her younger brother is in his room slamming things around. "What happened?" I ask. She is heaving and hiccupping from heavy tears. "He never does what I tell him to do, even if what he is doing is dangerous or embarrassing and I ask him to stop. Then, I try to tell him why this is so frustrating, and I sound like I'm being overdramatic. I'm not, but I sound like I am." Upon further conversation, she says she wants to be helpful around the ranch where we live in the summer, but she doesn't always know what to do. When she is asked to babysit the young children of the caretakers, she is worried because they always want to do things that she is afraid will be dangerous. She'll feel responsible if they get hurt. She wants to help make cookies in the kitchen, but she doesn't quite know where things are, and she feels like she should know, because she's done it before, but never without adult help. She knows she has "happy rushes" and "down days," and wonders if they are related to hormones. She gets frustrated with the girls her age, who seem ready for teenage stuff, but she's not interested. Not yet, she says, wondering if it may be coming soon. In short, Elizabeth is becoming an adolescent.

Entering Adolescence

Awakening to adolescence can be a rude shock. Childhood comes to an end with the achievement of independence in many self-care tasks. As the body begins to take on adult shape in adolescence, the mind opens to new understandings of what is going on in the world. Adolescents shift from a matter-of-fact curiosity about the world to the more charged task of staking a self-aware identity within the political and relational dynamics of ever-increasing social circles. As Elizabeth's story demonstrates, and as biblical stories such as Jane Patterson's accounts of Cain, Miriam, and David in this volume illustrate, the taking on of adult roles and responsibilities while recognizing one's own inexperience and lack of skill in navigating them can be difficult. Adolescents feel the drama of interactions differently, and they know that they are playing a role that may or may not be done correctly. From navigating the relationships of school hallways to understanding the impact of social roles and cultural expectations, adolescents begin to understand that they have to respond to the expectations of both interpersonal interactions and impersonal institutions. Suddenly, their lives are not an unexamined given within the intimate circle of home and classroom, but an exploratory quest to be a self in the midst of expectations and possibilities that can seem confusing and exhilarating. With these transformations, the explicit quest for vocation, an emerging search for who one is called to be before God and in the world, rises to the fore in powerful ways.

I am echoing the work of practical theologians Dori Baker and Joyce Ann Mercer in their use of the word "quest" as it relates to vocation in this stage of life, a helpful metaphor that points to the self-conscious embodied search for identity and life purpose that emerges in adolescence.[1] But the quest for vocation is not a linear process from adolescence to adulthood. Many persons writing about vocation in adolescence discount the understanding of adolescence as a time of discernment and preparation for a future vocation, arguing instead that adolescents hear *and respond* to the call of God *as adolescents* in significant ways. These colleagues are right to emphasize the trivialization and domestication of adolescent energies to primarily entertainment and economic-oriented notions of the purpose of human life.[2] They illuminate the need for an increasing sense of contribution, agency to make a difference, and opportunities to discern the call of God on their lives and to respond to it as adolescents.

Megan was trained at 15 to be a Planned Parenthood peer sexuality educator. She confidently produced a kit of birth control items to teach both her friends and strangers in organized settings, feeling that teenagers deserved to have good information about STDs and contraception.

68

She felt called to participate in this mission, and she took her role as a peer educator very seriously.[3]

We often underestimate the sense of calling to do something worthwhile vocationally in adolescence and teens' willingness to work hard, as Megan did in her role as a peer educator, to be able to make a contribution. Teenagers' responsiveness to opportunities for service, to care for younger children, and to collaborate on artistic ventures all point to their desire to respond to callings as adolescents. As Jane Patterson explores, Miriam's willingness to answer the call to protect and care for her infant brother embodies the often heroic willingness of young people to rise to the occasion of calling's invitation.[4]

Adolescence is also a time of experimentation and risk-taking, of exploration and engagement in callings that may not be lifelong, but may contribute to the narrative arc of a life story in unexpected ways. Adolescents can experience a heightened sensitivity to inspiration and suffering, an openness to the influence of beloved adults and powerful cultural stories, and serendipitous and unexpected life encounters that can have lasting effect on the timbre of vocation. Adult fears can inhibit this needful exploratory vocational work in the period of adolescence, such as worries about future economic prospects or sexual involvement. Vocational quests in adolescence are not usually a linear progression to an imagined future, but rather a gathering and strengthening of the experiences of God's calling and faithful response that contribute to a longer narrative of faithfulness throughout a lifetime.

By adolescence, I am referring to the period of life that begins with puberty, the rapid transition to an adult body and emergent forms of complex thought associated with brain development. This dramatic transformation usually begins in children between the ages of 10 and 15, with girls entering earlier and boys later within that time frame. Although there is disagreement among researchers on the end of adolescence due to discovery of extended brain developments as well as delayed economic independence beyond the teen years (which I will discuss in the following chapter), for the purposes of this chapter the transition out of adolescence occurs when a person becomes at least partially responsible for providing his food, clothing, and shelter. Another key marker of the end of adolescence is living in a way in which others are not fully structuring the decisions and environments in which a person navigates. This can occur while a young person is living at home as early as 16 or 17, if his paid work is necessary to provide food and utilities and he has little parental oversight in the shape of his daily activity. For those who remain under the economic and directional over-sight of parents or highly structured institutions, adolescence may extend into their early twenties. Class, cultural, and economic differences make a definitive ending to adolescence difficult to associate with a particular age.

Characteristics of Adolescence

Vocational experiences in adolescence are influenced by extensive bodily, mental, and emotional transitions. Like the rapid decline of the body for some older adults, the major bodily changes at this phase raise insistent vocational questions and challenges. The new power associated with developing adult physical and mental abilities allows for different contributions and increasing agency essential to developing a sense of having something to offer to the world in faithful response to God's calling. New awareness of the social landscape and its expectations invites adolescents to understand the self as a performance in front of an audience, which changes the way they perceive calling.

Becoming a New Creation, Literally

With the onset of puberty, adolescents' transforming body signals a new self to the social worlds in which they live. Bodily changes raise questions and concerns about who they are becoming and what it means for who and what they are called to be and do in the world. For example, girls' bodies mature in a period of two to three years from child to woman. With the emergence of breasts and hips comes an avalanche of cultural expectations, norms, and practices about the significance of gender, sexual desire, and attraction (both wanted and unwanted), and the legacy of sexism and het-eronormativity. For young tweens, this confusing mix of cultural messages gets navigated through day-to-day experiences such as arguments with parents over clothing choices, being sexually harassed in public places, and noticing some awkwardness around trusted male adults who begin to withdraw and seem less comfortable expressing the physical affection they offered a girl when she was a child.[5] Youth become aware that a new body entails new powers and new risks, which impacts who they understand themselves to be in the world.

Likewise, adolescent males experience their bodies as an insistent presence, whether because of the power of a larger, stronger body or its absence as other boys begin to shoot up and fill out. Youth who experience an extraordinary appetite, spontaneous erections, or rapid growth spurts are concerned about staving off their hunger, being sexually normal, and being physically coordinated. Male adolescents experience cultural expectations, fears, and monitoring. They are expected to be independent and strong, feared for being threatening or disruptive, and monitored for "compulsory heterosexuality." Proper masculinity is negotiated through mundane experiences such as working part-time jobs, participating in gym class, and being followed in stores.[6] Like their female counterparts, and those youth who perform gender along a broad spectrum, the new body triggers vocational questions about who they are supposed to be, what they are supposed to do, and whether people value them in the world.

One of adolescents' key spiritual issues is whether the self they are becoming is worthy. Their physical transformations lead to acute body consciousness, and sometimes physical and emotional awkwardness. Spiritually, many struggle to believe that this new body and mind is "fearfully and wonderfully made" rather than a freak of nature.[7] The love and support (or lack thereof) that surrounds adolescents can witness to an ultimate sense of their value and significance grounded in God's love for them, which makes the vocational quest possible. Baker and Mercer note the importance of parents and other adults in communicating trust and confidence in who the young person is becoming: "When parents communicate their belief in their daughters' gifts and abilities, they support those aspects of their daughters' religious lives tied to vocational seeking and decision-making."[8] Without the assurance that who they are, as they are, is worthy of love and respect and capable of contributing to the community, a vocational search is unlikely to occur during adolescence.

Performance of Self

The emerging self-awareness of adolescents fuels their sense of being people with a unique and particular life to live out, another key moment in the development of vocation. Faith development theorist James Fowler describes this self-awareness as "I see you seeing me: I see the you I think you see." He captures vividly the relationship between the cognitive achievement of mutual perspective taking and the impact it has on an adolescent sense of self as performed for the audience of trusted persons around them.[9] Adolescents are particularly attuned to social relationships and ideologies where they have gained the painful awareness that their own perception of themselves is not the same as other people's perceptions of them. Their life becomes more of an intentional social performance, and questions of the acceptability, viability, and valuing of that performance surge into emerging self-awareness. For those with the vocabulary of Christianity in their bones, a sense of whether their life is the one God would choose for them comes alive in new ways in this period.

On a more mundane level, adolescents begin to get the sense that they might need to amount to something. School records start to matter in new ways for future educational and economic prospects. Social pressures to acquire a skill or develop a talent through consistent practice become more evident. The burden to have a presence in a social circle arises, to be somebody special and worthy of respect by others. Young people begin to realize that they can move in circles where their parents have no presence, sensing dimly that in the future they will have a story beyond the one linked to parents and home. The provisional taking on of the powers of adulthood, whether sexual maturity or freedom from parental supervision, combined with new cognitive and emotional abilities, brings a greater sense of responsibility for self-creation. Young people gain the capacity for autobiographical reasoning: a sense that they are creating a life story with thematic and temporal coherence that other people experience.[10]

Openness and Malleability

Beyond these obvious changes and social ramifications, adolescents are also undergoing a less visible brain transformation over a ten-year period. Neural networks that are regularly used become myelinated and interconnected in ways that speed mental processing and enable complex thinking. Simultaneously, the brain prunes neural branches that are unused, eventually increasing the brain's efficiency for adult functioning. During brain restructuring, emotional processing shifts to the amygdala and consequently the full martialing of the brain's frontal cortex that coordinates cognition and emotional response suffers during adolescence. Because frontal-lobe functioning is transitioning, primal fight-or-flight emotional responses are more dominant in everyday interactions, creating what we commonly call "drama" in adolescent social life.[11]

But depending on the amygdala to process affect also creates a capacity for awe, wonder, and emotional sensitivity. Youth are more emotionally capable of deep encounters with love, beauty, and suffering that are central to spiritual experience. This receptivity to the divine means that many people's narratives of awakening to vocation begin during adolescence. Encounters with something awe-inspiring, whether deeply beautiful or terrible, changes the way they see the world and their role in it. Mercer and Baker call adolescence a *"kairos* time" in the lifelong vocational process. "That is, it can be a period of life ripe with the sense of God's presence and calling, a time of deep sensitivity and openness to the purposes and activity of God."[12]

> *Rose took several international trips during her adolescence with her mother and father, whose conservation work took them to places such as Mongolia, Kenya, and India. Travel helped her to encounter the need for sustainable economic development for the poor and to recognize the damage caused by aid workers living the "white savior" complex. She is majoring in international relations with a focus on economic development because she wants to work on sustainable models of culturally appropriate development across the globe.*

Emotional receptivity also opens adolescents like Rose to the call of others who suffer, one of the ways that vocational clarity emerges.[13] Such opportunities to form and articulate passions in relationship to the world's needs rather than focusing on triviality that keeps them busy or out of trouble can be rare for adolescents. The spaces that help fan those initial sparks into full ignition are deeply consequential for the development of vocation.[14]

The miraculous and complex process of cognitive and affective transformation can feel alienating for the people experiencing it. A new emotional palette and increased self-awareness leaves adolescents feeling as though they are constantly on display for others to view. The increased depth of interiority and self-reflection feels both powerful and terrifying. Simultaneously they gain an increased capacity for abstract thinking that enables deep exploration of the world. Awakening to self and world opens up new territories in peer interaction and friendship, as well as new opportunities for social stigma and shame. New capacities for emotional and sexual intimacy also increase possibilities for loneliness and becoming an existential stranger even to one's self. Exploring the worldviews and perspectives of others can throw comfortable understandings of one's home environment into new and sometimes harshly critical light.

Developing Adult Capabilities

Adolescents' emerging cognitive and physical abilities mean that they can engage certain tasks with the same skill as the adults around them, particularly those activities that interest or engage them. Because they gain stronger powers for concentration, adolescents can experience intense immersion into hobbies and relationships, as is the case for the young David playing his lyre. Psychologist Mihaly Csikszentmihalyi first documented the experience of "flow" in his research with adolescents, an unself-conscious experience of engaging so deeply in an activity with joyful concentration that time seems to stop.[15] Whereas in young children, immersive experiences of play can be experienced as flow experiences (as Bonnie Miller-McLemore describes in the previous chapter), in adolescence flow begins to take the shape of more disciplined practice, such as in music or athletics. Experiences of deep absorption and loss of self-consciousness in the pursuit of excellence are a form of practicing disciplined response to something larger than oneself. Such experiences also help point to vocational self-knowledge such as: What do I love? What am I good at? What can I uniquely contribute? Where do I feel most fully alive?

Religious rituals of accountability, such as confirmation or believer's baptism in Christianity, require these adult levels of cognitive ability and self-awareness. Many traditions expect adolescents to demonstrate their competence in performance of adult ritual practices. Whether it is reading from the Torah, public profession of faith, or reciting a catechism from memory, communities expect that teenagers become responsible for themselves and their faith life during this stage. In times of evangelistic fervor such as Christian revival meetings, youth have been targeted for conversion experiences that witness to their adult faith. These religious rituals acknowledge the emerging adult capacity in young people, honoring their ability to respond maturely to God's call to faithful living.

One of the trials adolescents face is the mismatch between maturation into adult capabilities and cultural, primarily Western expectations about what is appropriate to their development. Educational theorist Nancy Lesko argues that contemporary understandings of proper adolescent development were shaped at the beginning of the nineteenth century.

She notes that in this period "youth were defined as always 'becoming,' a situation that provoked endless watching, monitoring, and evaluation."[16] The emergence of adolescence as a distinct phase of life coincided with the outlawing of child labor, extended schooling, and new forms of juvenile justice and leisure activities such as scouting and youth groups. These environments were meant to protect and control adolescents so that their emerging energies were not misspent but rather channeled into the proper activities designed to create citizens to build a great nation. This now century-old ideal continues to influence public understandings of the proper timeline and activities of adolescence.

Vocational Experiences during Adolescence

Adolescence provides a time of consequential possibility, where young people experience many "firsts." Young people begin to practice social roles in order to discover their capacities to contribute to the social world. Whether in love or work, these first impressions of what it means to be an employee, a romantic partner, or a responsible leader begin to form the scaffolding of vocational life narratives of young people. Through these experiences, young people develop interpersonal relationship skills, empathy, organizational skills, and the ability to motivate others. They practice responding to the call of neighbor, noticing the needs of the world that evoke their gifts, and begin to understand their place in the patterns of interaction of the larger whole. Through experimentation with possible selves, development of friendships and romantic relationships, experiences of suffering, and navigating cultural stories and school, adolescents begin to author their stories of vocation.

Experimentation with Possible Selves

Many adolescents explore different selves, believing they can reinvent themselves through a change in hair color or a new way of dressing. They explore new hobbies, pursue interests and passions with specialized social media groups, and participate in fandoms. They join new social groups with different norms than those of their childhood friends. Educational theorists Michael Nakkula and Eric Toshalis identify experimentation and testing as one key mode of adolescent identity formation. Adolescent humans, like other mammals, have evolved to have a desire for creativity and risk that allows them to venture forth from their parents and establish independent lives. This need to take risks can be expressed in any number of environments, from physical challenges to social ones.[17] As Baker and Mercer indicate, one of the gifts of youth is their "probing questions, openness to new possibilities, energy, and fearlessness."[18] Because they have not yet made lifelong commitments and because the social space allows for experimentation, the grooves of their selfhood are not as deeply worn. This openness to experimentation is particularly attractive to teachers who enjoy their willingness to approach different ideas and ways of understanding the world. This identity flexibility can raise concerns as well when young people seem easily swayed by authoritative speakers, peer trends, or cultural trends. The experimentation is an embodied form of discernment, as teens risk new ways of being and figure out whether they are called to live into these new selves long term.

Creating Friendships and Significant Relationships

With puberty, friendships shift from enjoying time together with people who like to do the things I like, or chums who mirror me unselfconsciously, to social entities that must be navigated and negotiated because they reflect who I am and what I want in the world. Friendships can be a source of extreme joy and an experience of deep wounding during this period. Peer relationships can feel exaggerated to the adults who witness them; there are great highs and lows of connection and rejection dotting the landscape, but these interactions are not trivial. They are a place where testing the social self and its audience is a critical aspect of developing vocation.

Because of the sexual maturing that happens during adolescence, young people's experiences of love often shift to include attraction, flirtation, desire, and coupling. Explorations into romantic relationship serve as searches for possible selves even as they also experience sexual attraction and embodied connection with other people. Through relationships, adolescents try on various commitments, lifestyles, and ways of being in the world. By fitting themselves into both friendship and romantic relationships, they are deciding and shaping who they like to be and how they want to be that person. This form of embodied vocational discernment teaches teenagers to read and respond to the feedback, both external and internal, that they are receiving and hones their sense of calling as relational beings.

To trivialize these relationships because they do not endure beyond this life stage is to denigrate important vocational discernment about identity and partnering that occurs even in short-lived relationships. For example, there has been some movement in Christian circles to end dating as a teen practice, with the rationale that it is a waste of time (and a risk of premature sexual involvement) to build relationships that are not leading to marriage. It seems there is an element of fear about adolescent sexual expression in this movement, but there is also a fallacy about the linear and instrumental view of friendship and romantic relationships. Dating and friendship building are not just about finding a mate, but are a current expression of the vocation to be in relationship and connected to other humans, to love one's neighbor as one's self. Creating support and convivial ties to get through hard times, learning to be peacemakers in the midst of interpersonal conflict, as well as gaining self-knowledge and awareness are all part of the vocational expression of relationship.

Experiences of Suffering and Loss

As this project's authors and collaborators gathered and talked about our experiences of calling in our adolescent years, we recognized the ways in which experiences of suffering and grief shaped our callings over a lifetime. Often we think of calling as a positive response to inspirational moments, but it can also be a compassionate or determined response to darkness and sorrow. Two of us had siblings who were terminally ill during our adolescence, and two had parents who struggled with mental illness or addiction during our teenage years. These experiences of grief, loss, and trauma no doubt had an impact on our becoming adults who studied the intersections of psychology and religion and who attended to the deep questions of meaning-making in our adult work. For other teens, experiences of personal illness or disability during adolescence, experiences of war or cultural conflict, or experiences of hunger and poverty inform their commitments to participation in healing and justice work. Learning difficulties or cultural dismissal in school may lead to commitments to be better teachers to the next generation. Suffering during adolescence may forge a sense of the needs of the world; a passion to end the conditions that led to such suffering may be the cornerstone of a calling across the lifespan.

Other teenagers become parents, commit major crimes, or otherwise perform life out of sequence according to social expectations for this age.

These experiences can cause grief and suffering because they violate what Lesko calls "the dominant life script of adolescence," which requires a "slow, over-a-long-time development from young person to adult" in a protective environment.[19] Those young people who experience an "all-at-once" growing up, either because they have done something or had something done to them, violate this script. Teens who experience pregnancy, parental illness or death, or situations that cause them to take on responsibility may lose space for vocational experimentation in their adolescence. Lesko investigates the way this cultural norm of a leisurely adolescence is gendered, raced, and classed in ways that are often ignored: "It assumes and maintains a youth sheltered by affluence, white privilege, and a male body who can grow up slowly, planning and reflecting on his future adulthood."[20] Young people who enter the workforce to support their family, who become sexually active and reproductive, or who commit crimes violate this narrative and become "problems." Such anomalies to the dominant life script of adolescence often raise additional vocational questions because adults surrounding these young persons do not know how to respond to such experiences except with grief and a sense of loss.

Negotiating Cultural Narratives

Adolescents' rising awareness that they will be the authors of their own life stories sets them on a journey to build the narratives that will integrate their experiences across time and serve as "internal guideposts for ongoing decision-making, everyday behavior, and self-understanding."[21] However, such stories never have solo authors. The stories are written in relationship to the larger stories of the culture. Individual expressions of vocation are written in concert "with the people with whom we are in closest connection and within those contexts that hold the most meaning for our day-to-day existence."[22] They may be written in harmony with those voices, in contrast to those voices, or as an extension of those voices, but the cultural stories and values of the context cannot be ignored in their story construction.

Because adolescents have particularly keen antennae for social ideologies, peer approval and sanctions, and the opinions of adults close to them, these influences play an important role in the formation of vocation at this stage. In his faith development work, Fowler named the kind of faith lived into by most adolescents "synthetic-conventional." He describes the connection between the stories offered to young persons and their constructive work in this way:

> In this stage a person struggles with composing a "story of my stories"—a sense of the meaning of life generally and of the meaning and purpose of one's own life in particular. My research suggests that this involves a process of drawing together into an original unity a selection of the values, beliefs, and orienting convictions that are made available to the adolescent through her or his significant relationships and face-to-face interactions with others.[23]

Following Erikson's linking of ideology to identity development, Fowler emphasizes the importance of the bigger stories offered to adolescents by their culture as they pull together a unique vision of their life's purpose. Adolescent vocation is both shaped and distorted by cultural scripts that offer visions for the good life and communicate social expectations for their outcome (e.g., gender, consumerism, privilege, success). Whether these are embraced or rejected, they are the raw materials from which a personal narrative is shaped, and during adolescence they have particular sway. Adolescents' heightened attunement to cultural norms may make them voracious consumers of popular culture, but their position as targeted consumers makes them particularly vulnerable to the "you are not enough as you are" messages of advertising.

Adolescents may begin to understand how broader social categories such as race, gender, class, immigration status, and sexual orientation affect the way their bodies are welcomed and rejected in various social spaces, and what this means for their sense of self and their social contribution. When cultural messages are toxic, adolescents, for their own health, must find ways to counter them. In her work on racial identity development, Beverly Daniel Tatum explores the protective aspects of oppositional identity development in adolescents of color that can occur in the midst of racial oppression, naming a dynamic that can affect those from other minority groups as well. Religious educator Evelyn Parker calls the resistance to these devaluing narratives a "place of holy rage."[24] Tatum also speaks to the importance of "identity-affirming experiences and information about their own cultural groups" as well as the power of affiliative groups with other young people as a way to navigate identity challenges raised by oppression.[25] When the social environment denies or pathologizes the social group to which they belong, adolescents need intentional positive intervention to counter the devaluing dominant narratives in order to develop positive vocational sensibility.

Schooling

School has a particular importance for the development of vocation in adolescence because by early adolescence "students clearly associate their school performance with possibilities for the future."[26] Focus on academic success can be particularly difficult if young people have learning disabilities or other emotional or behavioral struggles that hinder their ability to function well at school, such as Allison experienced:

> *Allison struggles academically because of learning disabilities that made reading difficult in elementary school. Her favorite times at school come on internship day, when she serves as a teacher's aide in a second-grade classroom. She likes having the opportunity to contribute as a respected leader with the younger children, and the setting matches her own vocational desire to teach elementary school, to make a difference with kids like her who struggle early on to learn to read.*

Students like Allison can experience enormous self-doubt and feelings of unworthiness because of school difficulty. School struggles can cause young people to wonder if they can succeed in life more broadly, and given the extended time that teenagers spend either in school or in school-related activities, that environment can have a strong impact on vocational self-perception. Schools tend to promote a narrative involving college acceptance and graduation as its vision of success. Given that less than one-third of adults in the United States complete a college degree, this narrative does not adequately fund the vocational quests of two-thirds of adolescents. When churches concelebrate school success with the broader culture, they fail to provide their unique voice to what matters most in human life. By abandoning their particular visions of the good life, they can be co-opted into imagining young people primarily as citizens and economic resources without offering their particular religious wisdom for the broader purposes of human existence.

Because the school success narrative is dominant, it is helpful if church and other communities can offer alternative categories of what is meaningful and valuable in life, such as love of God and neighbor, glorifying God and enjoying God forever, or doing justice and loving kindness. Here, the religious tradition as gift to the faithful imagination provides a layered and time-tested vision for what makes a human life beautiful, just, and good. This counter-narrative to school (and by extension economic success) is essential to broadening the categories by which adolescents can value their own emerging life experiences.

Providing such alternatives should not be the work of churches alone. Religious educator Bert Roebben stresses the need for education that is hopeful and that attends to the concrete quests and inspirational needs of young people. "Their little stories are given space in order to be seen and told in relation to the big movements of our culture that are happening in depth (historical), in breadth (socially) and in the distance (with respect to the wellbeing of future generations)."[27] Teachers who pay attention to students' abilities, desires, and cultural values can help adolescents navigate a sense of what they can bring to the world. But vocational discernment is made difficult in public schooling given increasingly standardized curriculum and teacher pay structures linked to success on statewide tests. These institutional structures can hinder the vocational development of young people by eliminating the relational space for mentoring and discernment of young people's unique gifts in schools.

Communal Practices for the Nurture of Vocation in Adolescence

Vocational experiences in adolescence are deeply impacted by the adults and the culture that surround teenagers. Putting together a life that honors one's deepest inner desires, the complexity of the world's needs and structures, and a sense of God's calling is not an easy task. Often young people jump into the fray of curating a resume for college applications before they have a chance to ask what is really valuable in the world and what they have to contribute to it. They need trusted adults to recognize, validate, and encourage them in the form of "interactive mirrors" rather than "didactic evaluators," sharing their own experiences not as exemplars but as "empathic possibilities designed to connect with them."[28] Mentoring young people in their vocational quests requires presence and availability rather than intentional shaping of their vocational paths. Adults who resist offering quick interpretation or answers but instead listen carefully over time, as an informal practice of spiritual direction, offer critical space for conversation, reflection, and connection. Given such space, adolescents' vocational paths may deepen to the strong currents of God's desires for them and the world.

Living Commitments Heroically

In addition to individual adult mentors, adolescents often experience God as Caller through the narratives their communities embody. Given their sensitivity to the heroic, teenagers particularly respond to communities that live into their commitments with clarity and flair. The availability of heroic role models is critical to invoking vocation in young people. Many adults recount vocational narratives deeply influenced by the environments they grew up in and resonant of the possibilities that were made available by the adults around them.

> *Kristen, now a Baptist minister and adjunct professor at a divinity school, remembers hearing and taking to heart the passage "Here I am, send me" in Isaiah as a teenager. She knew she was called to the mission field. That moment of heightened awareness and calling was supported by attending a church throughout her childhood that counted many women Baptist missionaries who lived in a nearby retirement home among its members. (She remembers as a child checking her birthmarks as a potential sign from God about where she should serve, then discounting this method when her only birthmark was shaped like India, where she didn't want to go.) Women who had served in China, Vietnam, and Indonesia taught her Sunday school classes, told their life stories from the pulpit, and invited dedication to a life of full-time Christian service. Their unusual and exotic forms of faithfulness profoundly shaped Kristen's sense of call to be of service to God, even in a Southern Baptist environment where girls were not supposed to hear a call to ministry.*

The layers of faithfulness that contributed to Kristen's calling point to a congregation that lived into its commitments to foreign missions in vivid color. From ritual life to storytelling to personal care and connection, the communal value of mission-orientation and service to God played out in Kristen's church on a weekly basis. Even though her adult vocation did not replicate this path of foreign mission service, the commitments and passion embodied by the elders around her influenced her in profound ways.

The development of awareness about the perceptions of others dramatically increases the importance of relationships with both peers and trusted adults during adolescence. The audience for this new social self has an authority that is distinctive when compared to other periods of the lifespan because of the particular sensitivity to cultural and personal relationships at this stage. As the critical involvement of adolescents in the Children's Marches during the civil rights era as well as current protests by high school students related to policing in communities of color attest, the energies of young people can be roused by communal witness.

Their increasing capacity for an interior life and new recognition of others' corresponding interiority makes young people especially interested in hearing about the vocational experiences of other people, particularly those whose lives are distinctive from and yet similar to their own. By encountering these narratives (both in person and through the media), young people test the validity of their own perceptions, either by contrast or by confirmation. Educational theorist Kieran Egan describes the way that adolescents seem particularly primed to respond to the heroic stories of transcendence and resistance in everyday persons.[29] Adolescents tend to be inspired by stories of vocational heroes, persons who respond to callings in ways that are extraordinary, courageous, and ideologically consistent. Later, in young adulthood, people turn to vocational exemplars, who tend to be more realistic, everyday persons in a young adult's social circle who model vocational possibilities for them.[30] By contrast, adolescents are drawn to larger-than-life examples. Historically, religious communities used the lives of the saints and martyrs to encourage passionate response in young people to the highest ideals of the community.

Much of that energetic response to the heroic today seems to be channeled into attachment to entertainment and sports figures, although sometimes heroes' commitment to philanthropic and political causes is a part of the inspiration. Exposure to stories of people who put their lives on the line for the common good, whether contemporary martyrs such as peace activist Rachel Corrie and photojournalist Jim Foley or teenage women's rights and peace activist Malala Yousafzai, can help young people develop visions of the way that their gifts and passions can be expressed faithfully. It is important work for educators, both religious and secular, to consider where in our culture young people hear the inspiring stories of meaning and commitment that spark faithful response in a way that calls into question their immersion into consumer and economic narratives of success and opens other possibilities.

Opportunities for Real Work

A vocational issue for many adolescents is the sense of spiritual restlessness or malaise caused by the construction of adolescence as preparation for a far-off future. Nearly a century ago, early feminist and founder of the social work movement Jane Addams lamented the "snare of preparation" that can cause disengagement in young people: "Somewhere in the process of 'being educated' they had lost that simple and almost automatic response to the human appeal, that healthful reaction resulting in activity from the mere presence of suffering or of helplessness."[31] Remember the stories of Megan, the peer sexuality educator who felt a calling to help her friends be safe, and Allison, the second-grade teaching intern who had struggled to learn to read as a child? Both delighted in the "real work" they participated in that resonated with their sense of calling. Adolescents experience a desire to be taken seriously as contributing members of the human community in some area of their life, and they experience a deep spiritual satisfaction when they are met in this way by the adults around them.

The local community of faith may support these emerging capacities by beginning to call forth gifts in young people, validating them publicly as more than child's play. Communities and congregations can provide social space for youth to express their charisms and to practice offering themselves to causes and concerns greater than themselves.

Paul grew up in a congregation that fought publicly for marriage equality in both the public and denominational realms. In his own high school, he has become the president of the Gay-Straight Student Alliance, a struggling organization in a working-class environment with conservative political and traditional family values. Despite the difficulties, he has learned from the adults in his congregation (and his cultural heroine Lady Gaga) that silence in the face of injustice will not lead to change.

As religious educator Evelyn Parker notes, "education that nurtures hope with young people recognizes them as equal participants in the vocation of their congregations. . . . Together youth and adults prayerfully discern their call to ministry, determining those institutions that help and hinder justice for their neighbors."[32] Congregations have long invited youth into worship leadership and preaching, mission trips and service opportunities, and care and teaching of young children as a way of validating their extant gifts and callings. In a liability-conscious and litigious environment, often the smaller, local stage of school, congregation, and extended family is one of the few places that will trust adolescents with real labor that makes a difference in shared life. When communities participate in expressions of faithful response to disaster, tragedy, or institutional poverty, young people's energy and compassion are honored. Opportunities to participate in responding to the world's needs with others out of love for God and neighbor contribute to the development of vocational capacity in adolescents.

Resistance to the "One True Thing" Narrative

When I was a youth minister, I worked with a young woman named Claire who was a serious poet and fiction writer. Her parents began to worry as she moved through high school that she was not participating in organized sports or school activities, which could be listed on college applications. Eventually, they pressured her to join the newspaper staff so she would have a legitimized outlet for her writing. As the values informing college acceptance have changed in the past twenty years, Claire would fare better today because she had found her "one true thing." In a time when unique passions and clarity of focus are valued on college resumes (as opposed to the well-rounded student of the 1990s), Claire's status as a poet would perhaps make her stand out. However, both "resume-building" and "the one true thing" unhelpfully focus young people on making their life a marketable product desirable for college admissions or future employment. Similarly, consistent adult questioning about "What are you going to be when you grow up?" or "What are you going to major in when you attend college?" sends a message about vocation that frames calling as singular and outcome-oriented.

In contrast to this single-path understanding of vocation, young people benefit from adults who understand that the experiences of life often add up to a sense of calling in unexpected and nonlinear ways. As an example, when I have asked seminary students in my youth ministry classes to write autobiographies of their adolescent years, I have been surprised by how many of them were involved in band. In hindsight, it makes perfect sense that people called to ministry were groomed for that vocation in marching band. They practiced affiliation with an institution considered uncool by many of their peers. They learned to work together as a community, often to lead sections or the entire band as drum majors, to produce something beautiful together. They learned to build group identity and camaraderie in the midst of difficult, hot, tedious work. Adults around those young people might view band as primarily a precursor to a life in music performance. In reality, the experience of being in marching band lends itself to preparation for a variety of callings as well as expressions of beauty and camaraderie that are vocationally worthy in their own right.

One gift that adults can give young people is the opportunity for taking creative risks and turning down the "pressure cooker" of success linked to the single-path narrative. Science journalist Barbara Strauch issues this challenge:

> In response to our new knowledge about how the adolescent brain grows and develops, it may also be time to give teenagers a wider definition of what success at this age means, give them more wiggle room to make their own mistakes and come up with their own answers. Why not lighten up on the oversupervised, overstructured activities and get-into-a-good-college-or-else-you're-dead culture we've created and, instead, figure out ways to let teenagers have some space to find their own path? Maybe we should stop robbing them of the time they need to take risks and roam intellectually, physically, and emotionally.[33]

Very few young people decide what they are called to as adolescents and move doggedly toward that goal, and few will work at the same paid employment as a fitting expression of vocation until retirement. By recognizing that young people will be called to be parents, lovers, workers, leaders, followers, and friends within a variety of callings over their lifetime, the adults around them might begin to ask other questions of vocation that honor the need for experimentation and risk-taking.

Adolescents need help broadening a sense of what their gifts are in light of the needs of the world and recognizing abilities or capacities that are emergent—while being careful not to expect that a particular mentor's voice is the only interpretation available. Engaging in practices and conversations that enable their ability to be self-reflective, to contemplate, and to see what their "best self" responds to may be helpful. Beyond the tiresome question "What do you want to be when you grow up?" young people need opportunities to answer: "What breaks your heart about the world? What are you doing when you feel most fully alive? What are you doing when you feel most connected to other people? What moments have made you feel proud of what you are able to contribute to a group or project?"[34] Adolescents need help discerning how these moments of clarity about what gives them life connect with further opportunities to contribute to the broader world.

Taking Them Seriously

Adolescents need adults to offer vivid visions of wholeness and transcendence and to express clear expectations that young people have something worthy to contribute to them. Adults sometimes inadvertently send the message that it does not matter what they do or are interested in as long as they are "happy." In a valuing of happiness deemed neutral by the culture, the only feedback young people may get from school and parents has to do with the economic ramifications of vocational decision-making or a desire for their personal happiness. Adolescents also need adults to communicate an expectation that their lives will make a contribution to the world in significant ways, and that they have something to give. Vocation is not always about fulfillment; callings can also include sacrifice and obligation to respond to what is needful. A young woman, "Julie," is quoted by Baker and Mercer as saying: "But I think the people with the biggest influence on what I do with my life are my parents. They want me to do some kind of good work, different than they could do, but they also show me all the time that there are lots of ways to matter in the world."[35] By communicating that what adolescents do does matter, even in an ultimate sense, adults show interest and care in hearing their perspective about the world and what they find exciting and horrifying about it. This can help adolescents begin to sense a place that they can uniquely contribute to the healing and nurturing of the world.

Vocational Gifts from Adolescents to Other Generations

Adults can trivialize and stigmatize adolescent transitions. Stereotypes of adolescence include beliefs that they are impulsive risk-takers, lazy, clumsy, hormonal and moody, obsessed with sexuality, cliquey and mean, disrespectful, and overdramatic. While most of these have some basis in the physical and cognitive changes that are taking place, they highlight only the negative aspects. Adolescents are also courageous, passionate, growing at an unbelievable rate, vibrant, socially attentive, empathetic, open-minded, and lively because of these very same changes. These particular energies can re-invoke and enliven the energies of other generations when they are allowed to be expressed in intergenerational communities.

The close attunement to ideology and cultural narrative causes adolescents to raise wise elders as they force their parents and other caring adults around them to come to terms with their own failures, call out their hypocrisies, and loudly notice their dulled cynicism about the world's possibilities. They often demand integrity from adults who have moved into a stage of appreciating paradox and the gray zones of what once seemed black-and-white. While some of this demand for ideological purity can be maddening, it also reawakens important questions of integrity and renewed commitment from adults who want to be good mentors to young people. After this intense relational period of negotiation and reawakening about what really matters, adolescents create new space for vocational work in members of their family as they break away from parents and home to pursue their own adulthood. They remind their parents that they had a life before children that they now have more time to pursue, thus launching their parents into their vocational search.

> *Jacob's youth group got involved with the Appalachian Service Project, one of many nonprofits designed to have youth groups assist in home repair for impoverished communities. Jacob's passions developed through this work and led not only to his adult calling to be involved in affordable housing ministry, but his father's ongoing volunteer work for three decades with the local Habitat affiliate, including managing the warehouse on a part-time basis during retirement.*

Jacob and his father developed a new sense of vocation in tandem, with Jacob's enthusiasm enlivening his father's post-retirement gifting of his time and capacities.

Like artists, adolescents' keen ability to read the social dynamics and hypocrisies of adult society are a gift to the broader community. Their hopeful visions of the future possibilities of their own lives, their biting critiques of adults who don't live up to their own stated commitments, and their appreciation for the absurd make them vibrant and lively members of the human community. "If we are skilled enough to witness it, adolescents' theoretical imaginations offer some of the richest, most critical, and deeply hopeful worldviews we might find."[36] Living in close community with adolescents often allows adults to experience the social world, its suffering and its beauty, with a renewed sense of possibility and a refreshed appreciation for deep connection to it.

I spend my summers at an intergenerational retreat center, and I have been surprised by the depth of emotion that guests express at seeing adolescents connect with the natural world and the profound spiritual conversations that happen with them. Many of the older guests say, "It gives me hope for the next generation," even as they see those same gifts with reawakened appreciation. A similar dynamic occurs with young people's presence and involvement in churches. Their interest can reawaken adult commitments and faithfulness because their passion is so infectious. As Baker and Mercer remind us, "the vocation of youth in the church and in the world places young people in a distinctively prophetic role that is necessary to the life and transformation of both the church and the world."[37]

Ending Adolescence

The period of adolescence starts with two fundamental disruptive changes: a new physical body and a new mental capacity for self-reflection and awareness of others. These two changes throw a young person into a vocational quest to discover the features and limitations of her life's purposes in God's purposes. Contemplative mystic Thomas Merton points to the quest for individual identity before God: "No two created beings are exactly alike. And their individuality is no imperfection. On the contrary, the perfection of each created thing is not merely in its conformity to an abstract type but in its own individual identity with itself."[38] Young people begin adolescence believing that they can mold the self into an infinite range of possibilities. By the end of adolescence, a better sense of the givenness of the raw materials of the self emerges: this particular body and disposition, this particular experiential history, this particular cultural locatedness, this unique instance of incarnated life. A best-case scenario allows for a dawning recognition that the self is not infinitely malleable, but rather expresses a particular instance of God's creation that is beloved and capable of responding to God's calling.

Merton asserts that the problem of salvation lies in the problem "of finding out who I am and of discovering my true self."[39] With adolescents, this language of true and false self may not be particularly helpful. The rawness and sensitivity of newly acquired self- and other-awareness may set up the quest for a true self in a way that can be striving to conform to external standards rather than what Merton means by the true self. The true self is not the "better self" or the "more faithful" self that rises above mere everyday existence. Rather, the true self is the one that lives fully into the particularity of individual identity in connection to God's love, which allows for detachment from the self's importance and an infusion of that love in one's engagement with creation. The vocational work of adolescence includes the process of becoming painfully aware of that self and coming to understand that this particular self, in all of its awkwardness and beauty, is the one that is called to love God and neighbor and be loved in return. Young people may also seek places to deploy that true self in faithfulness: "Our vocation is not simply to *be*, but to work together with God in the creation of our own life, our own identity, our own destiny."[40]

Obviously, this task of "finding out who I am and of discovering my true self" is not limited to adolescence, nor is the self that is discovered in adolescence likely to remain stable throughout a lifetime. However, there is a quality of settling into the self that occurs throughout adolescence, a movement from the younger adolescent who follows a school clique's standards to an older adolescent who begins to understand that he does not have to conform completely to be acceptable. Hopefully, with experiences of affirmation and companioning, older adolescents begin to understand their unique giftedness and capacities for love and response to the needs of the world. They are poised to begin to take on with more seriousness the commitments and responsibilities of adulthood.

Suggested Readings

Baker, Dori Grinenko, and Joyce Ann Mercer. *Lives to Offer: Accompany Youth on Their Vocational Quests.* Cleveland, OH: Pilgrim, 2007.

Dean, Kenda Creasy, and Ron Foster. *The Godbearing Life: The Art of Soul Tending for Youth Ministry.* Nashville, TN: Upper Room, 1998.

Mahan, Brian J., Michael Warren, and David F. White. *Awakening Youth Discipleship: Christian Resistance in a Consumer Culture.* Eugene, OR: Cascade, 2008.

Parker, Evelyn L. *Trouble Don't Last Always: Emancipatory Hope among African-American Adolescents.* Cleveland, OH: Pilgrim, 2003.

Turpin, Katherine. *Branded: Adolescents Converting from Consumer Faith.* Cleveland, OH: Pilgrim, 2006.

Turpin, Katherine, and Anne Carter Walker. *Nurturing Different Dreams: Youth Ministry Across Lines of Difference.* Eugene, OR: Pickwick, 2014.

White, David F. *Practicing Discernment with Youth.* Cleveland, OH: Pilgrim, 2005.

Yaconelli, Mark. *Contemplative Youth Ministry: Practicing the Presence of Jesus.* Grand Rapids, MI: Zondervan, 2006.

Younger Adulthood: A Voice from Within

JANE PATTERSON

The angel of the LORD appeared to Moses in a flame of fire out of a bush; he looked, and the bush was blazing, yet it was not consumed. Then Moses said, "I must turn aside and look at this great sight, and see why the bush is not burned up." When the LORD saw that he had turned aside to see, God called to him out of the bush, "Moses, Moses!" And he said, "Here I am."

(Exod. 3:2–4)

"I wish God's voice would be as clear to me as it was in the Bible," people often say, as they approach the significant decisions of adulthood. The classic model for vocation seems to be that of a voice that comes clearly and surprisingly to a person caught in the midst of some other activity: to Abraham standing in his father's tent; to Hagar in the wilderness; to Moses while shepherding his father-in-law's flock; to Miriam as she raises her tambourine; to Elijah at the entrance to his cave; to the young Jeremiah at the time of Josiah's reforms; to Mary of Nazareth in her home. Traditional paintings of the angel's annunciation to Mary show her surprised as she looks up from her book, or her knitting, or her prayers. In none of these stories is there any doubt that God, or an angel of God, has appeared and made a direct request to the person. Yet, as our exploration in this book makes evident, rarely is vocation so clear for most people.

An example of the dominance of this kind of story is in the disjuncture between the way in which Luke describes Paul's life-changing revelation in the book of Acts and Paul's story as he tells it in his own words in Galatians. Luke tells of Paul's encounter in this dramatic and memorable way:

> Now as Paul was going along and approaching Damascus, suddenly a light from heaven flashed around him. He fell to the ground and heard a voice saying to him, "Saul, Saul, why do you persecute me?" He asked, "Who are you, Lord?" The reply came, "I am Jesus, whom you are persecuting. But get up and enter the city, and you will be told what you are to do." The men who were traveling with him stood speechless because they heard the voice but saw no one. (Acts 9:3–7)

Luke's narrative has become the way in which most people think of Paul's radical change of life. In fact, the phrase "a Damascus road experience" has come to mean a dramatic, life-altering encounter with God. Not only Paul, but also his companions, hear Christ speaking. Note, too, that the directions are clear, and more specific details are said to be coming.

But when Paul recounts his story to the Galatians, it sounds like this:

> You have heard, no doubt, of my earlier life in Judaism. I was violently persecuting the church of God and was trying to destroy it. I advanced in Judaism beyond many among my people of the same age, for I was far more zealous for the traditions of my ancestors. But when God, who had set me apart before I was born and called me through his grace, was pleased to reveal his Son *in* me, so that I might proclaim him among the Gentiles, I did not confer with any human being, nor did I go up to Jerusalem to those who were already apostles before me, but I went away at once into Arabia, and afterward I returned to Damascus. (Gal. 1:13–17; emphasis added, author's translation)

The most critical difference between the two accounts is so small that you might miss it: the preposition "in" in Paul's own account ("was pleased to reveal his Son *in* me," 1:16). His sense of the revelation of Christ was apparently an interior one, a feeling in his gut rather than a vision for the eyes. The feeling rocks his world so much that he goes off alone for several years to ponder and process what has happened and how to respond. Another interesting aspect of Paul's self-understanding is the way in which he uses Jeremiah's call story to shape his understanding of his own calling, including both his early zeal for all things Jewish and his insight that the God of the Jews (the God of Christ) was calling him now to a special role, to proclaim God's sovereignty to the nations ("I appointed you a prophet to the nations," Jer. 1:5). Paul's understanding of his call includes both phases: his preparation as a devout young man and his sending forth by Christ to the nations. As Katherine Turpin notes in the following chapter, sorting out vocation in young adulthood is not automatic. It can take some time.

Paul's story of the revelation of Christ within him contains many of the elements that make a calling difficult to perceive for many people, especially in their younger adult lives: the ripening of an interior sense; the need to process and ponder what God seems to be doing in one's life; changes of course and abrupt turnarounds; and sometimes the need to grieve and repent of earlier decisions and actions. Yet among all of these changes, Paul expresses the sense that his calling by God has been deep within him from his birth, like a single river flowing through varied terrain. The way I hear people express this feeling sometimes is, "I was made for this!" They might be at work on a project in their cubicle or hiking up a mountain trail, holding a child or a book, chopping vegetables or digging into black soil, singing or painting, comforting a friend who has moved to long-term care, bandaging a wound, giving wise counsel in a meeting, or hosting friends around their table, when the feeling comes over them: "I was made for this." These are the manifold ways in which the adopted family of God senses a vocation, ponders it, and lives it out, loving and tending the world as God loves it.

5

Younger Adulthood

Exploring Callings in the Midst of Uncertainty

KATHERINE TURPIN

As adolescents transition into the early years of adulthood, social expectations that they perform a meaningful adult life that contributes to the shaping of families and communities increase dramatically. The questions central to vocation are perhaps at their most visible in the lifespan as the decisions and commitments begin to have lasting and irreversible consequences on the shape of one's life. Social and economic conditions can make the discernment and affirmation of callings quite difficult within the novice navigation of the complex waters of employment, household establishment, and relationships. For older adults looking back across the lifespan in retrospect, younger adulthood is the period of time most closely associated with vocational decision-making. However, from within the lived experience of this phase of life, vocational discernment can feel elusive, experimental, and even chaotic to the emerging adults who wrestle with it.

> *Madison, a college graduate with a business major, lives at home with her dad and stepmom and waits tables to pay off student loans while she tries to make something interesting happen in her chosen field. She feels different from the servers who understand waiting tables as their "real" job, but worries that it might become her career permanently as well, given the economy. Her parents are understanding, but keep making comments about her growing up and moving on with her life. They argue over her social life and how much she is contributing to household labor and funds. She hopes to at least get her own place, but can't imagine how to sustain that given her debt load and lack of*

job prospects. The guy she's been dating suggests they move in together in order to save on finances and keep her parents out of her sex life, but she worries that he is no more stable than she is at the moment. Trying to maintain an apartment, pay the bills, work at the restaurant, and network or intern for jobs seems completely overwhelming, but she hates the fact that she hasn't been able to move out and start her life already. She thought the promise was if she got a college degree in a practical field, she could have a good job that would help her have a nice life.

Perhaps this story sounds like those of the emerging adults you know.[1] Maybe other stories come to mind: stories of young adult felons serving time because of youthful mistakes, of young moms attending to the multiple needs of babies and young children, of law students clerking for judges, of medical residents struggling to become surgeons, or of young adults on the autism spectrum losing their state educational benefits when they turn 21. Younger adults are a diverse group of persons in U.S. culture, much less across the global stage, and any attempt to describe how vocation is experienced at this time of life requires the humility to admit that the range of experiences exceeds what can be captured here. As choices and experiences accumulate, life stages become more difficult to track as the various life paths and configurations diverge.

With the phase of younger adulthood, we begin to see that the length of time spent in each period of life can vary greatly based on the life experiences, bodily limitations, and social and economic opportunities available to each person. For some, younger adulthood can extend for more than a decade, filled with vocational experimentation and an extended process of growing into various roles and callings. For others, a series of early commitments to long-term relationships, forced economic independence, childrearing, or pre-scripted professional tracks can shorten what we are calling younger adulthood and thrust people into the vocational experiences of middle adulthood much sooner.

Entering Younger Adulthood

The distinctions between adolescence and emerging or young adulthood resemble the subtle transitions of ombre dye rather than the bold delineation of color blocking. One way to talk about the transition between these two phases of life would be biological, paying attention to the end of puberty and the achievement of a mature adult body. Tracing this border between life periods is more difficult than previously considered, as research on the brain demonstrates that the timelines of maturation are more complex and hidden than once thought. Long after bones have lengthened and hair has appeared in new places, full neuronal pruning and myelination that allow for complex long-term decision-making and appropriate risk-assessment in the fully adult brain do not occur until as much as a decade later.

This discovery of ongoing biological development has caused some social scientists to push the end of adolescence to ages 20 to 25, a period that clearly would have been understood as full adulthood half a century ago in developmental literature in the United States. Economic independence and establishment of families and households are delayed compared to earlier generations. Even as biological and economic markers make a case to extend adolescence well into the early twenties, parents complain that adult thinking about sexuality, violence, and other complex issues is pushed onto adolescents at younger and younger ages through media exposure. Because this age group has different life struggles and living situations than either older adolescents or middle adults, psychologist Jeffrey Arnett has argued for establishing a new life stage called "emerging adults."[2]

Although we recognize the realities of brain development and delayed economic independence, the expectations of a 17-year-old and a 24-year-old in U.S. culture are quite different, and so for the purposes of this book we have not linked the transition into adulthood with biological development but rather to cultural expectations and vocational markers related to them. During the period after high school there is an awakening to commitments and responsibilities normally assigned to adults. Developmental psychologist Sharon Parks speaks of the "post-adolescent quality of emerging strength" in this life period that requires appropriate mentoring persons and environments in the realms of higher education, economy and workplace, politics, religion, and family.[3] Indicators of emerging strength include being responsible for some of the economic burden of providing for shelter, food, utilities, and clothing for the household in which one lives. Additionally, being considered an adult involves movement out of highly structured and protective environments led by another (sometimes a parent's home, high school/college dorm, or early military service) and into situations where adult responsibilities are tried on and other people become dependent on one's contribution. Participation in providing income, being a caregiver, or pursuing specialized education for job or career comes to be expected as a full-time endeavor.

Social science research on young adults often over-represents those with college or graduate degrees, given that less than one-third of younger adults in the United States complete college. Sociologist Robert Wuthnow notes that "because research about young adults is often based on studies of college students—and produced by faculty in academic settings for readers with advanced education—it is easy to forget that the experiences and opportunities open to college graduates are not part of the typical young adult's life world."[4] Many younger adults spend their time in one or more service-sector jobs, in learning trades, in military service, or in parenting children rather than in college. In this chapter, I am trying to keep young adults in all of these contexts in mind as I explore the vocational characteristics, tasks, practices of nurture, and gifts to other generations in this phase of life.

Characteristics of Younger Adulthood

The transition into younger adulthood pushes vocational questions and decisions to the center of daily life. As adolescence winds to a close, the people who matter to emerging adults begin to expect them to make decisions and take steps that firm up the shape of their adult identity and livelihood. Things become serious in terms of performing adult identity, and young people step directly into life's deepest vocational questions. As Parks puts it: "In young adulthood, as we step beyond the home that has sheltered us and look into the night sky, we can begin in a more conscious way to ask the ancient questions: Who am I under these stars? Does my life have place and purpose? Are we—am I—alone?"[5] Finally, young people have the adult body, the social approval, and hopefully the economic possibility of authoring their own lives. Big questions press in on them: What story will I write? Will it be a story that people care about and listen to? Will it be a story that feels true and right to me, or one that is beholden to outside forces? What bigger realities does my life serve, and to whom am I accountable? Will I find companions to join me in the life I have composed? The demands of vocation can be experienced as both gift and curse, as young adults struggle to launch their own life story of significance and purpose into the demands of social scripts that privilege economic success and romantic triumph. Some of the characteristics of this period in the lifespan include the exploration of identity in relation to larger social narratives, navigating dual callings to economic and relational life, seeking full adult status in difficult economic times, radical impermanence and transitions, and forward orientation in time.

Exploration of Identity in Relation to Larger Social Narratives

Young adult vocational experience is marked by a new internal awareness that all persons have the authority and responsibility to decide what feels right and makes sense to them out of all of the ways that people understand how the world works—more of a gut feeling, as Jane Patterson notes in Paul's experience.[6] This new sense of internal authority is companioned by the emerging social and material capacity to participate in the world according to personal beliefs and values. Parks also focuses on the internal sense of authority that arises in the years from ages 17 to 30: "This mode of making meaning includes (1) becoming critically aware of one's own composing of reality, (2) self-consciously participating in an ongoing dialogue toward truth, and (3) cultivating a capacity to respond—to act—in ways that are satisfying and just."[7] This self-awareness heightens the conscious sense of responding to the demands of creating a good life as a responsible person even if the person is also scrambling to get through school, make ends meet, or build relationships while working multiple part-time jobs.

A central part of vocation in younger adulthood is the exploration of identity outside the structures provided by the family and context of origin. Because an initial step in vocational discernment is acquiring "true self-knowledge," an accurate internal sense of who we are and what capabilities, personal characteristics, and core commitments we have to offer, this identity work is a cornerstone of vocational exploration.[8] When developmental psychologists speak of young or emerging adulthood, they often point to the drive for self-dependence and identity exploration in the midst of relating to social structures that marks this phase of life, an idea first proposed as a task of adolescence in a different social and economic era by developmental psychologist Erik Erikson.[9] Contemporary developmental psychologist Robert Kegan labels this stage the "institutional self," where the focus is on identity and self-authorship in relationship to the ideologies and institutions that one must participate in as part of being a social creature.[10] This work of self-discovery often occurs in contrast as young adults move out of the settings in which they grew up and navigate workplaces, roommates, neighborhoods, and educational settings with quite different values and rhythms of life from the ones assumed normative in their contexts of origin.

Navigating Dual Callings to Relational and Economic Life

Angelo, a young U.S. Marine about to be deployed overseas, struggles to decide whether to marry his high school girlfriend and endure the strain of a long-term, long-distance relationship or cut ties and see what the world brings him. A commitment would mean that she has access to survivor benefits if something happens to him, but his family feels that he should grow up and live a little before he marries. He finds boot camp exhausting and disorienting. Maybe getting married would create one point of stability in his life, but would people expect them to start having kids? He wants to see the world and grow up a little, and the structure of the military seems a good way to do that. Now he's trying to figure out how that goal meshes with his relationship with his beloved.

The multiple aspects of identity related to vocation and the potential conflict of multiple callings becomes evident to young adults like Angelo who are trying to sort out the balance between their work and relational life. Military deployments and other jobs that require a great deal of travel can highlight the struggles between relational and economic demands that are also common among young adults with less extreme conflicts. While the competing demands of multiple vocational commitments and obligations are more strongly marked with the increasing responsibilities and establishment of middle adulthood as explored in Matt Bloom's chapter, young adults also begin to feel pressure from the ways that being called to love and to work can be at odds with each other.

Many young adults watch middle adults closely, seeking exemplars of vocational integration, people who have been able to live into multiple callings in their lives. Matt Bloom and Amy Colbert discuss the importance of exemplars in the early discernment stages of those called into the professions, but exemplars are also needed for navigating multiple callings to love and to work. "Exemplars were important because they were real, salient models of individuals who appear to be living their own calling in and through their work. Informants used exemplars to gauge whether their own true self elements might fit a particular professional role—an identity work task we called mapping."[11] For example, as a young adult woman beginning a doctoral program in religion, I weighed the possibility of living into a felt calling to be married and start a family with my professional calling. At the time, I lacked exemplars, women who seemed to be able to have both a satisfactory family life and a strong career in the professorate. As I was making steps toward responding to these various callings in my life, I struggled to see how they could be integrated and lived out simultaneously, and I actively searched for women who were living into these particular simultaneous callings.

Seeking Full Adult Status in Difficult Economic Times

As a culture we are still negotiating the boundaries and expectations for this phase of life, and that uncertainty can cause existential angst for the people attempting to live through this time, about whether or not they are "real" adults capable of living into a vocation. These transformations in the cultural patterns of adulthood and economic limitations on meeting social expectations for adults can hinder young adults' sense of their own capacity to live into the callings that they discern.

Cultural expectations of the tasks necessary to becoming an adult have outstripped the economic realities that allow these tasks to be completed. Wuthnow summarizes public opinion about the necessary tasks for being considered an adult and when they should be accomplished: "When the public was asked about these expectations in the 2002 General Social Survey, nearly everyone agreed that becoming an adult involves being financially independent, not living with one's parents, being employed full-time, being able to support a family, getting married, and having children."[12] According to this survey, the U.S. public believes that these tasks should be accomplished between the ages of 21 (stop living with parents and begin working full-time) and 27 (begin having children). How are young adults doing at fulfilling these expectations? According to Pew Research analysis of U.S. Census data, 36 percent of 18- to 31-year-olds were residing with their parents in 2012, a number that has stayed fairly constant since 1968, the first year comparable data were tracked. However, between 1968 and 2012 the number of adults in this age range who were married and living with a spouse in independent households dropped from 56 percent to 27 percent, while those living with roommates, unmarried romantic partners, or children increased fivefold.[13] A new category of household has emerged where nearly one-quarter of young adults are cohabitating with friends or romantic partners, while also, at times, parenting children alone.

Pew Social Trends data demonstrate a more complex story of young adults living in intergenerational households than is visible in the Census data. An increasing number of young adults are returning home to live with parents because of economic limitations, even after completing a college education. They are driving an increase in intergenerational households (those with two adult generations residing together) since the 2007–9 recession. By 2012, about 24 percent of young adults lived in intergenerational households, up from 18 percent before the recession and a dramatic increase from 11 percent in 1980, when intergenerational households hit an all-time low in U.S. culture.[14] Whereas in 1968 many of the young adults living in their parents' household were unmarried young women or men who never left home after high school, often working to contribute to household income, more young adults are now moving back home after college, military, or work experiences that took them away for some amount of time. Some of these young adults bring spouses and children back into their parents' or grandparents' homes, consolidating living situations to reduce living expenses. Because moving back into their parents' home violates one of the dominant cultural markers of successful adulthood, it raises existential questions about whether or not a person has achieved full adult status and agency.

Several socioeconomic factors lead to delayed achievement of once-standard markers of adulthood and may cause some young adults to struggle spiritually with the significance of a perceived "failure to launch." Households headed by those under the age of 40 are often impacted by student loan debt, as 37 percent of young adults carry some debt, which impacts their economic viability; on average they owe $13,000.[15] Due to such economic pressures, reduced social stigma about cohabitation, the rise of part-time employment, and the lack of a living wage for those without college degrees in full-time jobs, the average age of first marriage has climbed into the middle twenties for women and closer to 30 for men.

Thus, adulthood can seem like an elusive identity marker that may or may not be viably achieved and maintained for many young people. The inability to demonstrate competency and full social recognition as an adult can cause spiritual anxiety about one's fundamental worth, a significant vocational problem in this time of life. Many hear derogatory terms and phrases as disciplinary mechanisms to enforce maturation. Emerging adults may fear being labeled "incompetent," "unable to contribute," a "slacker," or a "man-child," all terms used to sanction failure to get established. Likewise, they try to avoid the stigma of "living in their parents' basement," or of being "such an adolescent" (when used to refer to someone beyond their teen years), and other cultural sayings that question their fundamental worth as human beings because of the structural inability to meet the expectations of "real" adulthood. Being caught in between the material realities and social norms can be vocationally traumatic for young and emerging adults who may experience these delays as vocational failure.

Economic instability raises the vocational question of whether young adults will be allowed to express their unique capacities and perspectives in the world or whether they will be forced to shape themselves into existing structures and institutions (whether romantic partner roles or work roles). Rather than finding themselves cogs in the great machinery of consumptive capitalism or faceless participants in impersonal bureaucracies or corporations, many young adults want to find ways to work and forge relationships that are significant and engage their particular gifts and commitments. The theological language of vocation provides a possibility for reframing their life narratives after times of crisis or closure in the experimentation phase. Rather than succumbing to the sense of themselves as losers in the marketplace or underdeveloped characters who have failed to grow up, a theological understanding of vocation may encourage other possibilities, such as naming younger adulthood an appropriate period of actively seeking connection to God's purposes in the world. By working to connect to the ways that significant and loving contributions can happen within situations that feel less than ideal, younger adults can experience a sense of vocation in the midst of not fulfilling cultural expectations about adulthood. Unfortunately, this kind of vocational reframing may be difficult given the strength of cultural markers of real adulthood and the barriers to achieving them.

Even for those young adults who successfully graduate college and enter the workforce, living into a felt sense of vocation can be deeply challenged by economic realities. In her study of twenty-seven college graduates who participated in intensive vocational exploration communities at Loyola University Chicago, Jennifer Haworth discovered five themes that participants wished the program "would have done differently to equip them 'better for the vocational challenges' they had 'actually experienced since graduating from college.'" Four of these themes directly related to difficult economic conditions and resulting limitations on living into a calling: a need to give more attention to "the 'hard realities' of following a calling in the 'real world' (e.g., a weak job market, heavy student loan debt, dual career couple tensions, how to 'pay the bills' in low-paying social justice fields)"; to place more focus on "'vocation beyond 9-5 (i.e., sometimes our jobs are not necessarily where we feel our deepest sense of vocation)"; to address "the challenge of vocational burnout in high-stress, low-paying service fields"; and to help with "how to live a life of purpose and meaning when 'a job is just a job and not a calling.'"[16] These young adults who "made it" out of college and into full-time paid employment felt economic pressure on their ability to respond to felt callings in the workplace and believed that those jobs would not be where their sense of calling was lived out.

Impermanence and Multiple Transitions

As young adults begin to compose a life through choices about where to live, with whom to relate, and where to give their energies, one vocational characteristic common to many younger adults is the temporary nature or impermanence of their life choices. An extended period of impermanence can have an impact on younger adults' sense that they are in the process of responding to God's callings upon their life, leaving them with the feeling of multiple, chaotic, and transitory experiences that are not building to anything in particular.

Young adults begin to try on provisional identities through what Parks calls "probing commitments," such as work roles and relationships that represent possible forms of truth about the world, self, God, and others.[17] Many of the work experiences young adults have are considered "entry-level" internships or jobs that one does to pay the rent and gain experience for a "real job." Those who have entered professions such as law or medicine face extended graduate education and residencies into their twenties and beyond. Many of the young adults I teach in seminary struggle with the reality that they are in their late twenties or early thirties and have never had this elusive "real job." Of course, they have often worked for ten or fifteen years, but never at a job that felt like it would be the job to which they would give their full adult energies. They have only had jobs that were a means to another end, such as paying tuition, covering the rent, or buying groceries. Most of this work is part-time, often in service or retail industries, where worker scheduling increasingly is driven by management software that understands workers as manageable assets to the company rather than human beings with complicated lives and commitments. Nearly 10 percent of the labor force works in the four most-common occupations in the United States: retail salesperson, cashier, food and beverage server, and office clerk.[18] Such contexts do not generally encourage introspective practices that might lead to deeper currents of self and a felt sense of vocation related to paid work.[19] Indeed, many working-class adults experience job impermanence throughout the lifespan because of the tenuous nature of employment in a service-oriented economy.

Impermanence is also demonstrated through mobility in living situations and geographic location more than any other generation in our culture. Young adults are more likely than other generations to experience high turnover in employment, occasionally seen as a benefit of moving up with increasing experience and increased pay. But Wuthnow notes a downside to this experience: "From a different perspective, high turnover also means greater difficulty for young adults seeking to make plans about marriage, children, healthcare, housing, and other major financial decisions. If a person is unlikely to be employed at his job for more than three years, it becomes very difficult to make long-range commitments."[20] In addition to the mobility through cities and towns, young adults tend to change residences more often, shifting living spaces as roommates follow jobs and romantic partners from place to place, as they pursue further education, or as job loss or gain causes changes in availability of rent money. These temporary communities and alliances can be a source of camaraderie and learning about human nature, but they can also be a frustrating source of conflict, drama, and disappointment.

Gathering of varied life experiences and experimentation can feel adventurous and exciting, on the one hand, and lead to an increase in self-knowledge and understanding central to vocational discernment. On the other hand, adjusting to multiple situations, tending new relationships, and learning new contexts can feel exhausting and overwhelming. What can be romanticized by other generations—"It must be nice not to be so tied down, and to be able to pick up and move across the country with your girlfriend"— can also feel like a situation in which nothing is stable, settled, or secure. Sometimes what is characterized as flakiness or lack of commitment by parents or grandparents, or a failure to successfully discern and live into a calling, can be a rational response to economic challenges that delay establishing a household and securing permanent employment.

Either way, the sense of improvisation and impermanence through this period may cause young adults to feel like their search for a felt sense of integrated vocation is stymied, unclear, or forever under negotiation based on forces beyond their control.

One popular source of life wisdom that resonates deeply with many young adults seeking vocational clarity in the midst of impermanence has been the poet Rainer Maria Rilke's advice from *Letters to a Young Poet*:

> You are so young, so before all beginning, and I want to beg you, as much as you can, dear sir, to be patient toward all that is unsolved in your heart and to try to love the questions themselves, like locked rooms and like books that are written in a very foreign tongue. Do not now seek the answers, which cannot be given to you because you would not be able to live them. And the point is, to live everything. Live the questions now. Perhaps you will then gradually, without noticing it, live along some distant day into the answer.[21]

Because of the extended period of trying to get established, "living into the questions" becomes a central marker of vocation in emerging adulthood. Indeed, dealing with the unsettled nature of things becomes "a task unto itself" and "a primary characteristic of the young adult era."[22] Rather than reveling in an unmistakable calling experience like the story of Moses and the burning bush, young adults often feel that the questions—and not the certainty—become their vocational companions in this stage of life. Although the young person may be working hard to discern vocation and to take steps toward responding to callings, the internal experience of vocation may remain uncertain until experiences of validation and affirmation occur. For many professionals and working adults, such affirmation doesn't occur until commitments have been made to move into adult roles, where efficacious performances are recognized and appreciated by clients, beneficiaries of services, or co-workers.[23]

In the midst of all of these transitions, some vocational discernment may occur through intentional introspective practice or through conversation with trusted family members, friends, or mentors in professional settings, but much of it occurs through trial and error. With exposure to exemplars and the introspective space to imagine oneself into a variety of roles, vocational discernment can occur through a reflective process in which young adults compare realistic self-knowledge against vocational possibilities with wise guidance from elders.[24] In the absence of these guided reflective opportunities, many younger adults engage vocational discernment through an embodied process of trial and error.

Employers, long-term volunteer opportunities, and faith communities can meet young adults and help them with exploratory modes of vocational discernment when they offer worthy work in this experimental phase. Work that gives younger adults a chance for taking risks, for being in charge of decisions that matter, and for making a contribution to something bigger than themselves is essential to the process of discernment of vocation—allowing young adults to affirm, in Jane Patterson's words, that "I was made for this."[25] However, offering a place to test the emerging strengths of younger adults is complicated for workplaces and other institutions, which long for the energy and passion of young adulthood, but also desire loyalty and stability of presence that can be unrealistic given the sociological and economic factors. Finding places of employment that aren't mere exploitation of their energies, but rather communities that provide opportunities to take on significant roles and responsibilities can be a difficult quest for younger adults.

Forward Orientation in Time

Emerging adulthood, like adolescence before it, assumes a lengthy life-span ahead that stretches out with openness and possibility. While that forward orientation in time can be ripe with possible alternatives, one of the vocational losses experienced at this stage requires coming to terms with the reality that every choice made, every decision rendered closes some doors and opportunities. For some emerging adults, the decision of where to attend college is one of the first decisions where there is full recognition that this choice closes off other good choices. As one young adult pursuing an internship lamented: "It's like all the fruit is on the tree, and you can't eat it all." The realization that the decisions made about where to live, what to study, what job to pursue, and who to live with will permanently shape who you become and your future possibilities may be experienced as a frightening ending of openness as much as a joyful opportunity.

Sometimes young adults, because of their sense of an extended future, are willing to invest in learning new things because they have the time and the energy it takes to take on a new career, a new hobby, or even a new way of being in the world.

Andrea, now a professor of social work, remembers the moment when her sense of vocation solidified as a young adult. She was a novice social worker in the field, trying to gain health services for people living with HIV/AIDS prior to the wide availability of antiretroviral drugs. One of her clients was also undocumented and was handcuffed to the bed in the hospital with two guards for the last three days of his life. She went to court to try to get him into hospice care without the imprisonment so he could die with dignity. The judge hurried the case because he had a tee time he was trying to meet and turned her down flat because "she didn't understand the dangers he posed." Frustrated because no one would listen to her, she decided that if she had a doctorate people would pay more attention when she advocated for her clients. She began a degree program that fall with her emaciated client on her mind and in her heart, calling her to change the system that had abused him so viscerally.

Looking back as a middle adult, Andrea understands that her belief that a doctorate would make the system listen to her was perhaps naïve. However, the determination and willingness to throw herself into an extended degree program on behalf of her client and others like him has continued to fuel her work in the field for more than two decades. It was a clear moment of vocational call from those who suffer, as theologian and psychotherapist John Neafsey names one of the sources of a sense of calling.[26] That forward-looking young adult who knew the system was broken and had to be fixed threw herself into the future in a way that put the middle adult in a place to make some changes that matter.

A sense of a long future of openness puts young adults in a different position in relation to the institutions they inhabit and the relationships they nurture. Presbyterian pastor Carol Merritt puts it this way: "The problem is that young people usually do not have power, time, or money. But they have other things: potential, creativity, imagination, vision, and ideas. . . . Younger people have a natural orientation toward planning while older people have an inclination to reminisce."[27] While Merritt's point can be oversimplified, this basic sense of forward-orientation is necessary to businesses, communities, and religious organizations. When complemented by the wisdom of experience offered by older generations, this revitalizing forward-looking energy is essential for renewal. For example, young adults may offer facility with technological and social advances that their generation grew up with but that older generations learned with more difficulty as established adults. Whether this involves an ease with social media or comfort with interacting with diverse racial groups or persons of different sexual orientations, sometimes younger generations bring as their home culture what was hard to achieve or considered aberrant in earlier generations.

Key Vocational Experiences of Young Adulthood and How to Nurture Them

Leaving Home:[28] *Reworking Relationship to Context of Origin*

Many young adults are negotiating and renegotiating their relationships, identity, and sense of vocation with regard to their environments of origin. Moving away from these environments provides the opportunity to see other ways of organizing life, to bump into values that are important to people in other communities, and to fashion new ways of being in the world. While exposure to alternatives is available through media and relationships with friends in adolescence, the ability to immerse oneself in a different environment or to have the power to shape one's own environment according to choices becomes more available with at least provisional entry into economic structures of income at young adulthood. All sorts of possibilities for vocational expression emerge, at times dizzying and at times exhilarating. While the economic limits of this period of life can be very real, the social and communal restraints on behavior are less stringent than at many other stages of life.

Authoring a life in new and powerful ways draws on the strengths and images developed in one's context of origin. Young adulthood is not a totally new start, so some of the energy of composing a life requires working through both the gifts and the wounds that come from the family of origin. As Parks note, "To become a young adult in faith is to discover in a critically aware, self-conscious manner the limits of inherited or otherwise socially received assumptions about how life works—what is ultimately true and trustworthy, and what counts—and to recompose meaning and faith on the other side of that discovery."[29] The shift from navigating the values and location provided by the home of one's childhood to creating a unique composite of one's own authoritative sense of the world and the capacity to live into it requires spiritual courage and fortitude. Asking big questions, particularly of the narratives, traditions, and life patterns that once made you who you are, can be a risky business. Will the interrogation of given narratives of meaning and purpose lead to a stronger sense of grounded and owned commitment, or will it lead to a time of nihilism, cynicism, or despair? There are no guarantees. From the outside, parents and other caring adults fret about whether young adults will get it all together and make something of themselves. From the inside, young adults often find the work of composing a life a lonely and sometimes discouraging place.

Because of the risk involved in maturing a sense of vocation through deep questions and independent construction of meaning, young adults need examples of the complexity of adult lives informed by a strong sense of vocation. They need diverse narratives and experiences of how middle and older adults have navigated their own vocational decisions in the midst of the various cultural scripts. In addition to the presence of exemplars in their social circles who model vocational integrity, access to such lives through relationship, film, and memoir may help inspire visions for why moving into full adulthood, committing to forms of work, institutional life, long-term relationships, and the raising of the next generation is worthy and good. Haworth discovered that seeking out and listening to "call stories" was an important practice to the young adults of Loyola Chicago's program, and one that they continued on their own after leaving school.[30] A good friend in my young adulthood found reading Madeleine L'Engle's account of marriage in her memoir *Two-Part Invention* helpful to his decision to marry a long-term girlfriend.[31] L'Engle's account of the meaningfulness of her marriage helped him make a choice to commit to marriage despite his own disillusion following his parents' divorce in his young adulthood. These mediations may help young adults gain a broader sense of ministry, new language, and images of God's work in the world that serve as a resource for constructing their own responses to callings.

Negotiating Competing Narratives of the Good Life

Young home construction leaders working as Americorps volunteers for Habitat for Humanity struggle to pay rent and live off their meager stipend. They hoped to make a difference in the world while they figured out what to do with their lives, but find themselves unable to sustain that idealism in the midst of the complex structures of poverty and immigration in which the people they serve are caught up. Now life seems just hard, and the struggle to eat, keep their clothes functional and clean, and pay rent is overwhelming. Being the responsible leader on the worksite with adults much older is intimidating and exhausting, even as it feels good to have people listen to them and benefit from their instruction. Moving back to an entry-level job, without a sense of helping others and after being in charge of the work site, seems like a step down. But having a better paycheck and benefits seems like a good deal. Or should they use the Americorps vouchers to continue their education, but stay poor longer?

One of the vocational tasks of young adulthood is sorting through the multiple narratives of significance from religious traditions, cultural values, workplaces, and familial traditions to discern which ones they will stake their lives on. Because these scripts are increasingly complex, young adults must sift through varied and often contradictory frameworks to fund their own life narratives. Should I strive to be as wealthy as the people in shared media and entertainment outlets? Should I live a balanced life of work and family, sacrificing material wealth for time for myself and loved ones? Should I serve my country like my grandfathers? Should I be committed to social justice and work for good living conditions for all? Should I live my life as a pure and holy sacrifice for God, and how would I do that?

Families and communities can provide intergenerational connections to traditions and the broader sources of wisdom. Merritt describes the experience of finding connection to these traditions: "These moments—when we feel as if we are a part of something larger than ourselves and we sense our connection to God and neighbor—these moments feed us. In our hunger, when we cannot grasp on to anything else at the end of our fingertips, we long for these rare Spirit-filled times. They are the reason that younger generations go to church."[32] Merritt warns against treating young adults as consumers in faith communities because of their deep suspicions that they are being sold something, particularly in an economy in which they have been the chief losers.[33] Instead of entertainment or distraction, young adults are seeking "connection, a place where they can be grounded in a spiritual community."[34]

Connections with other generations, with the wisdom of a tradition that is older than their parents, and with a spiritual source are all important contributions of faith communities to young adults. It takes a special community to serve the particular vocational quests of young adults:

Questing for meaning, searching for answers, willing to live with a higher degree of ambiguity, sorting their way through the stunning variety of beliefs, values, cultures, faiths, and social norms that compete for their interest and allegiance, this generation deserves a church that is at least as willing to engage them and their questions as they are to engage the future.[35]

Younger adults need the gift of larger stories to fuel the energy of the worthy dream. Whether the stories of contemporary saints who have responded to calls faithfully, communities whose practices of advocacy and witness to the gospel are inspiring, or workplaces that are particularly good at articulating the "good" that they serve and inviting others into their mission, younger adults respond to larger shared stories of significance into which their lives can be incorporated.

Trying on Adult Roles

One of the joys of young adulthood arises from the increased freedom, agency, power, and choice to form the environments in which you live, the work that you do, and the companions that you enjoy. Increased opportunity for participation in the structures and institutions of society can allow young adults to pursue passions, relationships, and collaboration in ways unimaginable to the average adolescent. Many young adults have the experience of looking around for experienced help in a particular situation and realizing for the first time that they are the responsible adults. That moment of recognition that no other adult is there to back you up or to fix things if you fail can be both exhilarating and terrifying. While some emerging adults experience dismissal and devaluing because of their youth and lack of experience, the capacity to be recognized as a contributing, responsible member of society is a heady thing, an integrational moment affirming one's sense of being capable of responding adequately to a calling.

The potent mix of finding relationships, communities, and work to give oneself to requires special environments that nurture and evoke the gifts of young adults. For some younger adults, a sense of calling is never internally validated until the opportunity to try on a role has been explored. Bloom and Colbert found that this process of trying on the role was one of the forms of vocational discernment that was common among the professionals that they interviewed:

Rather than a powerful feeling of knowing that preceded actually pursuing the profession, explorers experienced their sense of call only after engaging in the professional role itself. They moved forward into the early parts of the final period of identity formation, what we call integration, continuing to explore and search for that professional role for which their true self-elements were an ideal match. By enacting the professional role, explorers eventually came to a similar, deep feeling that they had found their call.[36]

For those without exemplars, without opportunities to know that certain sectors of work were even possible, trying on of roles becomes essential. It should not be cast as a mere learning experience (starter marriage, internship, job-for-now), but crucial for discerning the way.

Finding a Tribe

Probing commitments make belonging a key spiritual and vocational issue for some young adults. Finding a tribe, a multigenerational group with which to identify, may be the spiritual counterpoint to the drive to establish independence and personal authority at this stage.[37] The spiritual need for belonging also counters the mobility and impermanence of young adult relationships to institutions and communities. This task may be why relationships to grandparents, where they are still possible, often become particularly precious in young adulthood. Grandparents often do not have the anxiety about their grandchildren "making it" that the parental generation carries, and as bearers of stories of generations of family before, often provide context and perspective on the source of family norms and experiences. For others, the tribe is a group of chosen family, of other young adults trying to make it and facing some of the same struggles.

Many emerging adults who lack caregiving responsibilities for older and younger generations have time to invest in maintaining close friendships as a form of spiritual tribe. These connections allow for extended conversations about the shared struggles to navigate, sometimes mediated in person and sometimes in social media spaces. These friendships can become a primary place of wrestling through the questions of meaning and purpose that are central to the life of vocation. When these tribes are single generational, the lack of experience may often feel like the "blind leading the blind," but they can also provide a sense of shared challenges and hopes for the future. These spiritual tribes are markedly different from the youth groups and other sponsored organizations of adolescence. Many churches go wrong in trying to create a "young adult ministry" similar to a youth group with structured activities created by a sponsor. Such a structure ignores the significant difference in needs and strengths of the two groups, and the organic, intergenerational tribe-building that funds young adult vocational development. Spiritual tribes are more ephemeral, more porous, but no less important to the sense of belonging necessary for identity work related to vocational development.

Faith communities and other intergenerational tribes can allow younger adults to watch older adults navigate their own vocational paths, as both exemplars and cautionary tales. Emerging adults crave mentors who model complex lives of integrity, but who also validate efforts that are different from their own particular trajectory. These communities may also helpfully witness to a God who companions younger adults in the midst of vocational struggle and unknowing, as opposed to the more common image of how God participates in calling, as a distant person with a distinct plan for you that you must get right.

Young adults need conversation partners and listening ears as they make decisions. Lingering places where conversation and warmth allow for exploration and reflection are what Parks call the practice of "hearth." She notes the importance of offering places for extended and intense re-flection: "The dialogue of which we speak—for example, between power and powerlessness, success and failure, alienation and belonging, right and wrong, despair and hope—cannot usually be accomplished in fleeting sound bites. It requires something more like a hearthside conversation."[38] Hearth space can occur with friends, with mentors at work and school, and with family members both given and chosen.

Dealing with Vocational Failures and Obstacles

When young adults find themselves unable to take care of basic needs and contribute to caring for others, vocational crises may arise. Whether this limitation is imposed by inability to access educational and economic live-lihood, by irresponsible decisions, by experiences of illness or disability, by failing at a job, or by other obstacles, additional questions of mean-ing, purpose, and worth impose themselves. As Jane Patterson notes in her earlier biblical interlude on youth, King David's story exemplifies that vocation cannot be idealized. His path looks fairly clear and good at the outset but his calling is beset with "confusion, bad decisions, reversals of fortune, traumas of love and loss."[39] How younger adults deal with these moments of vocational disruption, whether from external obstacles or situations they create themselves, is crucial to their vocational development.

For the daughter of an African-American colleague, a crisis arose the first time a less-qualified white-male candidate received a position they were both applying for internally in an organization. For another well-qualified young adult with cerebral palsy and autism, getting past in-person interviews for technology jobs that would not require tremendous interpersonal skills was extremely difficult. Both emerging adults who face the loss of established roles to which they feel called and the parents and community members that so want them to "make it" experience grief and lament.

Many young adults experience the closing of vocational possibilities not of their own choosing. A childhood dream to become a pediatrician is ended by a low grade in organic chemistry, a good job ends in a round of mass layoffs, aversive racism leads to a lack of employment opportunities, or a partner breaks off a perceived long-term relationship. Such losses are experienced as disappointment, failure, or suffering and are more difficult to navigate the first time they happen. Without the experience to know that life can continue, and that even failures and barriers provide opportunities for growth and development, these losses feel devastating.

These experiences challenge the primary ways that vocation has been framed in theological literature by raising questions about what happens to calling when there is no longer a choice to respond. Many young adults understand these experiences of closing off as God's will for their lives, but there may be other ways to interpret these experiences as part of the discernment of vocation, even when they are caused by evil, tragic, or unjust situations. Experiences of vocational mistakes or barriers require finding a deep sense of trust in both the calling and the caller, even in the midst of evidence that contradicts the experience.[40]

Vocational Gifts of Emerging Adulthood to Other Generations

One of the gifts young adults offer the human community is the energy and strength of the no-longer-growing and not-yet-declining adult body. Young adults are often in the prime of their physical lives, able to work hard and play long. Sometimes this energy is used for physical or mental labor in the workplace, pushing institutions into creative adaptations for challenging new situations. Sometimes the energy is used for caregiving for a younger or older generation. Many young adults perform everyday caregiving tasks for their younger siblings or aging grandparents, such as driving them on errands, doing home maintenance and repair, or taking them to doctor's appointments and negotiating online systems. Because they have adult intelligence and strength, plus the time to invest, they can also be a group that has the energy to engage in volunteer work, political campaigns, and social activity.

Young adults also offer other generations the excitement of launching and a sense of possibility and future hope. Because they have fewer commitments and are mobile, young adults can move away and have adventures that the other generations enjoy vicariously, whether entering graduate school, accepting overseas military deployments, moving to a new city for work or relationships, or enjoying extended travel. Young adults also provide the possibilities of a new generation through the anticipation and birth of grandchildren. Younger children and adolescents look forward to the freedoms that young adulthood affords through its freedom from protective environments. Through observing the vocational choices of young adults, older adults remember and reminisce about the choices they made and are invited to reckon with the life they lived.

Young adults combine their physical and intellectual strength with inexperience and naïveté, which allows for courage, fearlessness, and lack of cynicism. They are sometimes less cowed by the knowledge of what barriers will arise, and they do not always recognize the full weight of the consequences of their choices. This can allow for dramatic expressions of vocational faithfulness. Young adults are the generation who historically have been willing to risk their lives for the ideals they hold, which is why many revolutionaries, martyrs, soldiers, and participants in social movements are young adults. For example, the Freedom Riders during the civil rights era were primarily young adults who responded to the call for an end to the oppressive segregation between the races and a vision of freedom greater than their personal experience. Risking everything for a cause can also be exploited, as recruits to cults, terrorist groups, and wars are often young adults. The hopefulness, idealism, and passion of young adulthood can provide reinvigorating energy and encourage communities that have experienced stagnation, defeat, or despair.

Young adults sometimes reclaim traditions that earlier generations have abandoned, giving them new meaning when embedded in the context of the values and purposes of a younger generation. Sometimes what they pick up is surprising to their elders, such as a recent renewed emphasis on home canning and preservation and raising chickens by urban young adults, practices left behind by their parents' generation. When coupled with new commitments to ecological awareness and connection with the earth, these ancient practices are renewed by their adoption by young adults.

Young or emerging adults need mentors, but mentors and elders also need to see the younger generation taking up their work and taking it to new and exciting places. A friend who is an Episcopalian priest has a son who also entered the priesthood. She said, "I can retire now, because he's got the church in good hands." This renewal of commitment to things that older generations have worked hard for complements the need for generativity in other generations.[41]

Inexperience can also sometimes give emerging adults a more critical eye than persons in other generations. When faced with the inevitable absurdities that move into systems and structures over time from the weight of repetition, young adults are sometimes the ones who naïvely ask, "Why not do it another way?" The answer to their inexperience may lead to an avalanche of "we tried that," but at other times the fresh eye of a young adult opens new possibilities that renew communities, policies, and practices. When this critical eye is met by the hospitality of mentors in other generations, cultural revitalization and strengthening occur.

Ending Tasks of Young Adulthood

The transition from younger adulthood to middle adulthood may extend over a period of time. The markers of middle adulthood, such as increased responsibility for the care of other generations and for the institutions and communities of society, may accrue slowly. Taking on one major not easily reversed life commitment can happen within younger adulthood, such as becoming a parent, pursuing graduate education to enter a profession, having a full-time job with major responsibility, or getting married. When several of these identity-stabilizing commitments converge in one life, the transition to middle adulthood has occurred.

Successfully navigating into a situation where one can not only take responsibility for one's own needs but also contribute to the building of community through one's work and care for others marks the transition into the vocation of adulthood and full recognition of adult status by a larger community. Sometimes young adults may have one of these but not others, for example, successfully raising a child while working jobs that feel limited and unfulfilling in terms of responsibility or status. Or a person may feel deep satisfaction with work, but struggle with personal relationships and finding communities of trust and mutual support. Young adults often watch these experiences and wonder whether they will be able to navigate the multiple vocations of adult love and work given the gifts and background that have been given.

Middle adults settle into communities, institutions, and relationships in such a way that ending these commitments would not be understood as a normal part of the stage but would cause significant change to one's sense of self and calling. Younger adults are more likely to be able to shift these commitments without major reworking of their sense of identity and vocation, as marked culturally by terms such as "starter home" and "starter marriage." When probing commitments and trial relationships become enduring commitments and are affirmed by others, middle adulthood has begun.

Suggested Readings

Arnett, Jeffrey Jensen. *Emerging Adulthood: The Winding Road from the Late Teens through the Twenties.* 2nd ed. New York: Oxford University Press, 2015.

Kegan, Robert. *The Evolving Self: Problem and Process in Human Development.* Cambridge, MA: Harvard University Press, 1982.

Merritt, Carol Howard. *Tribal Church: Ministering to the Missing Generation.* Herndon, VA: Alban Institute, 2007.

Parks, Sharon Daloz. *Big Questions, Worthy Dreams: Mentoring Young Adults in Their Quest for Meaning, Purpose, and Faith.* San Francisco: Jossey-Bass, 2001.

Wuthnow, Robert. *After the Baby Boomers: How Twenty- and Thirty-Something Adults Are Shaping the Future of American Religion.* Princeton, NJ: Princeton University Press, 2007.

Points of Decision in Adulthood

JANE PATTERSON

Multiple vocations, changes in vocation, beginnings and endings of vocations: these issues call for repeated discernment in adulthood, even after some of the larger commitments in life seem to have been made, as the following three chapters demonstrate. Sometimes the impetus toward change happens because of a tragedy, failure, or loss, as in the story of Naomi and her two daughters-in-law Orpah and Ruth (recounted in the book of Ruth). During a time of famine, Naomi and her husband Elimelech moved from Bethlehem to the other side of the Dead Sea, in Moab. Their two sons, Mahlon and Chilion, moved with them. Soon after their arrival in Moab, Elimelech died, and because Naomi and her sons remained in Moab, the two young men married Moabite women, Orpah and Ruth. But again, the family was struck with tragedy when the two young men died, leaving the three widows in Moab. Hearing that the famine was over in Judah, Naomi begins to make plans to return to the place of her people, but she makes it clear to her daughters-in-law that they are free to return to their own original homes, to start their lives over again.

This turning point is the spring from which the rest of the story flows. Orpah decides to return to her people, while Ruth decides to journey with her mother-in-law to a land she has never seen. We know nothing of the families the two women came from, but there is a sense that Orpah is choosing to return to what has been for her a greater love, while Ruth is deeply attached to Naomi. Both are good decisions, but each will change the person forever. Early and middle adulthood presents options like this, in which one can see two ways to go, each valuable, but each of which will shape the person in a very different way. A powerful and significant calling can arise from tragedy, as this story shows. As a consequence of her decision to remain with Naomi, Ruth becomes one of the foremothers of David and of Jesus, her decision a part of the working out of salvation on a scale she could not have seen.

We encounter Mary and Martha of Bethany (Luke 10:38–42) also at a point of decision, though perhaps not as dramatic a turn as that of Ruth and Orpah. Their story follows Jesus's encounter with a lawyer (an expert on the Torah) who wants to know what he must do to "inherit eternal life." Jesus asks him what the Torah has to say about that, and the man responds with the double commandment to love God and neighbor. This teaching could have been the end of the encounter, but the lawyer presses for more: "And who is my neighbor?" (10:29). Jesus responds with the provocative parable of the Good Samaritan, redefining the lawyer's question and elevating care of the neighbor to the level of a sacrificial offering in the temple. The vivid gestures of the Samaritan pouring oil and wine over the broken body of the wounded man call to mind the libations poured over offerings in the Jerusalem temple. The Levite and the priest who had passed by the injured man missed the significance of care for the neighbor, in God's sight. In the parable, neighbor-love and love of God are portrayed as deeply embedded in one another.

With the parable still ringing in our ears, we journey on to the home of Mary and Martha. Their household in Bethany is within an easy walk of Jerusalem, and makes a good stopping place for Jesus and his group of followers. Together, these two women are shown sharing the responsibility of the head of household, even while their brother Lazarus is alive. Mary's anointing of Jesus in the Gospel of John is a passionate portrayal of a host's duty to a guest (12:3–8), and when we encounter the household in Luke 10, Martha is engaged in all the tasks of food preparation, finding places for people to sleep, and the various duties that go with hosting a large crowd of probably unannounced overnight guests. Despite centuries of Martha's denigration by interpreters who belittle her anxiety over how to carry out all the tasks involved in the family's vocation to hospitality, the text itself does not denigrate her. Rather, Jesus calls her by name, twice: "Martha, Martha." And then he simply names her predicament, without judgment: "You are worried and distracted by many things." Finally, he invites her to a finer level of discernment: What is it time for *now?* "There is need of only one thing." He points to Mary as one who is doing what this moment calls for: focused listening. Mary's choice is not the right one in all times and places, but she is attending to what is most important at this moment. Martha's practical wisdom and service are still essential to the community that depends on her. But for now, stillness and listening are called for.

This story forms an important second form of discernment, following on the story of the Good Samaritan. Where the parable unfolded the difficulty of discerning neighbor-love, the story of Mary and Martha exposes a moment of decision to focus on the sheer love of God, even when the needs of the neighbor appear pressing. Their story is a very important one for all who feel the press of obligations, so typical of middle adulthood, as we see in the chapter by Matt Bloom that follows. Love of God and love of neighbor are completely intertwined, and yet they become manifest through different practices at different times. On the day we encounter Mary and Martha, they are being invited to discern a shift in vocation, perhaps awkwardly and without confidence at first. Martha hears her name called, she sees clearly that her habitual way of living into her vocation is not what is needed at the moment, she begins to discern a new direction for her attention, and she is pointed toward Mary, who models the moment's calling. This is not meant to suggest that Martha and Mary will never again shoulder the responsibilities of hospitality, but that they have been challenged to live into that vocation with more flexibility. From this day forward, they will live by closer attention to the alternating rhythm of listening and service.

A third poignant story of discernment in adulthood is that of Jesus in the garden of Gethsemane (Mark 14:32–42). Although he has been continually confronting opposition from authorities of various kinds up to that point, the power of God has also been clearly manifest through him. For those who believed that Jesus was God's Messiah, it must have seemed that, amid Roman oppression, God had finally remembered Israel, and that through Jesus they would be liberated from the sinful structures of life under Roman rule, and restored to right relationship with God and justice with their neighbor. At last, the hungry would be fed, those in debtors' prison released, children respected. The Passover, the commemoration of Jewish liberation, was frequently a time for unrest, and Roman authorities were nervous about anyone who appeared to be marshaling opposition. In the garden at night, Jesus wrestles with how far to push the situation. His movement is still gathering strength, there is much to do, and he knows all too well from the execution of John the Baptist just how quickly and without justification a prisoner may lose his life. Should he back down or continue to push God's cause in some dramatic way during the Passover celebrations? That long night of prayer is agonizing, as Jesus attempts to discern the path of God's will: he "began to be distressed and agitated . . . he threw himself on the ground and prayed that, if it were possible, the hour might pass from him." He entrusted himself to God: "Abba, Father, for you all things are possible; remove this cup from me; yet,

yet not what I want, but what you want." Jesus's ministry, hardly begun, hangs in the balance. The well-being of the people of God hangs in the balance.

From this point on, it appears that the forces opposed to God begin to win. Jesus is quickly arrested and summarily made to stand trial. Even the Roman authorities are not convinced of Jesus's guilt, but the unfolding events toward his crucifixion seem as inevitable as water rolling downhill. Jesus's discernment in the garden has caused him to plunge unreservedly into this river, allowing it to move him where it will. Even on the cross, Jesus expresses the bewilderment of the faithful person caught in incomprehensible events: "My God, my God, why have you forsaken me?" (Mark 15:34). Is his work over? Was he a failure? Did he not play his role in God's vision for Israel? The original, unadorned ending of the Gospel of Mark finishes with the empty tomb, a young man's message, and the women followers fleeing in confusion (16:1–8). As the other three Gospels were written, other endings to Mark were crafted in a more upbeat tone. But the original ending of Mark is stark, ironic, and provocative. The events that make sense of Jesus's discernment in the garden are all outside the frame, in the lives of Jesus's followers who composed this Gospel and who continue to live from it and to encounter the risen Christ. According to the community that preserved this particular way of telling the story of Jesus's last days, his alignment with the will of God in the garden was the turning point in salvation history, even though the earthly Jesus never got to see his vindication. The silence of the empty tomb spoke the first cryptic Alleluia.

The story of Jesus's discernment in the garden of Gethsemane under-scores the mystery of vocation that arises with a particular poignancy in middle adulthood. At some point, Jesus knew what he had to do, even though he didn't understand the ultimate point of it. He honored that calling with his whole self, speaking the truth to the authorities and to God all the way to the end, all the way to a new beginning.

6

Middle Adulthood

The Joys and Paradoxes of Vocation

Matt Bloom

Find work you love, and you will never work a day in your life.

—Attributed to Confucius

This book, being about work, is by its very nature about violence—to the spirit as well as the body. . . . It is above all about daily humilia-tions. To survive the day is triumph enough for the walking wounded among the great many of us. The scars, psychic as well as physical, brought home to the supper table and the TV set, may have touched, malignantly, the soul of our society. . . . It is about a search, too, for daily meaning as well as daily bread, recognition as well as cash, for astonishment rather than torpor; in short, for a sort of life rather than a Monday through Friday sort of dying.

—Studs Terkel[1]

When I was 32, I was unhappy in my work. I was an advisor for a financial services company, making good money, earning regular promotions, and receiving coveted accolades, but my work was unfulfilling. It was clearly important to others, some of whom I respected greatly. But for me, some-thing was missing, something I had difficulty identifying, yet I was spend-ing hours and hours at work. At the same time, I was the primary income earner for my family—my wife Kim was the primary care provider for our children—and maintaining a solid financial foundation for my family was important. I loved being a father; raising my two young sons was deeply meaningful to me; and I oriented much of my life toward this vocation. I was also a life partner to Kim—we were ten years into our marriage—and continuing to build our life together was an essential part of my life. My identity included all of these vocations: professional, income-earner, father, life partner. Even as I yearned for a professional role that fit me, one in which I could find meaning and even fulfillment, I knew that changing my work would have serious repercussions for these other vocations. My choices about work could not be simply about *my* needs and wants; my vocations were deeply intertwined with the lives of my family. I was struggling to find a truer center for my interdependent, complex life, one that would lead me forward with greater confidence that I was making good choices and living my life well. I was searching hard to find work that I would find meaningful—what I wanted, I thought, was a true vocation. And I was also searching to integrate that professional vocation with the other aspects of my life. I was in the deep throes of middle adulthood. My complex, many-faceted life and my struggles to not just balance but integrate the several callings of my life were hallmarks of this long and important life stage.

Entering Middle Adulthood

Middle adulthood is one of the longest stages of life extending roughly from age 35 to retirement. It usually begins with several important transitions: starting a career, being financially independent, and, for many people, finding a life partner and beginning a family. When people think about "being an adult," they often think about the potential downsides of middle adulthood: lots of responsibilities and hard work, constrained freedom, the burdens of providing for dependents, and (seemingly) not much time for fun. But many middle adults in fact find their lives rich, rewarding, successful, and sometimes even fun. They also find themselves pulled in different directions, responsible for things they never imagined would be theirs to manage, and they often reflect that they did not feel adequately prepared for the demands they face.

For many people, one of the awakening tasks of middle adulthood is understanding the multiple vocations that define who they are and that give shape to their lives. In addition to work, other vocations become important: life partnerships, parenthood, civic pursuits, religious and spiritual commitments, and caring for children or parents. Integrating and balancing this plurality of callings—and finally achieving that elusive goal of attaining work-life balance—is a dominant concern for middle adults. Many middle adults worry about overinvesting in work and underinvesting in their other vocations, even as they long for a rewarding career. A successful attorney, spouse, and mother of three adolescent boys describes middle adulthood this way:

> *Sometimes I wonder if I have made the right choices. Maybe I should have given more to my career—I should be a partner by now. But I also love my boys, I want to be their mom now before they leave home for good. Some days, work is amazing, some days it is hell. I can't quite seem to find the right balance between giving enough to work and giving enough to home. And, you'll notice I haven't even mentioned my husband, whom I adore. What about him? What about us?*[2]

At times, being an adult is wonderful because of the possibilities adulthood offers. At other times, middle adults want to give up the responsibilities and let someone else make the decisions and bear the burdens. This is the time of "real" adulthood: what you think, feel, and do really matters for your own self and for others. And, this is the life stage where, as one of my colleagues put it, "the rubber of vocation meets the hard road." For better or for worse, middle adults have to make important life choices, and then live out those choices, knowing that what they choose and how they live will have a profound impact on their own well-being and the well-being of others. When they do find vocation, many middle adults experience these as the best years of their life (at least the best they have experienced so far).

I did find a vocation, both in and outside my work. I quit that unfulfilling job, pursued an advanced degree, and became a researcher and professor. Now as a social psychologist, I study well-being at work to learn more about what makes work a positive, life-enriching experience. Throughout this chapter I will draw on a large research study that my team and I conducted (see note 2) on how people discern and live into work they experience as a life's calling. While I cannot offer evidence about whether our research can inform how people experience a calling as a parent, life partner, or civic volunteer, I believe the insights we gleaned provide a useful conceptual framework for thinking about a wide range of callings in the middle adult years. As I have studied how people came to encounter their own work as a calling, I have come to understand my own experiences better. I do experience my work as a calling: this research is deeply important to me, and I think my capabilities, personal characteristics, and core commitments "fit" this work very well. That research, and my own life's journey, inform what I share in this chapter.

Defining Characteristics of Middle Adulthood

Middle adulthood is a period of making important decisions. Just at the time in life when individuals' freedom and capacity to make their own choices peak, they face the need to make choices that cannot be easily reversed: a career path, entering into marriage, and having children, to name just a few.[3] In addition to opportunities for enriching life, these commitments and responsibilities also carry a loss of independence; middle adulthood entails awakening to the reality that one's life is deeply intertwined with the lives of others.

Middle adults experience the rush of months and years passing by all too quickly and, suddenly, time *really* matters. "I am *so* busy" is a common refrain in middle adulthood because there simply are not enough hours in the day to give proper attention to all of one's vocations. In earlier stages, most of life was focused on one's own needs and wants, but like the press of obligations felt by Martha and Mary in Jane Patterson's reflection, in this stage significant portions of life involve the needs and wants of several, perhaps many, other people.[4] Middle adults talk about "juggling priorities"—an apt metaphor for their experience that everything is up in the air, precariously whirling around, and that life seems only one small slip-up away from everything crashing down. Understanding the difference between the eternal now (*kairos*—sacred time, God's time, everything in its proper season, the right thing at the right time or the "moment's calling" as Patterson calls it) and one-dang-thing-after-another (*chronos*—measurable time, the sequence of time we experience in terms of hours, days, weeks, and years) is difficult, and much of life, too much, seems to be focused on simply getting through each busy day.

Middle adulthood raises challenging ethical, religious, and philosophical questions about life's purpose and meaning. Underlying choices, commitments, and responsibilities are the struggles middle adults encounter about the values and beliefs that are, or should be, guiding their life. During this life stage, individuals are concerned about living well—living a good, worthy, noble life.[5] They feel that their life choices and commitments should not only be effective, but they should also be the "right" ones. They feel that there are standards they should live up to, and they struggle to discern and understand what principles and ideals they should use as standards to determine what is best for themselves and the other people and groups with whom they are interdependent. Psychologist Crystal Park proposes that, to figure out the important problems and decisions in life, people try to fit them into a "global meaning system," an overarching worldview they can use to explain what their experiences mean and how they should respond.[6] Philosopher Charles Taylor agrees, positing that to answer the big questions of life, we must have a "horizon of significance," a framework we can use to determine what is valuable, what is worthwhile, what we ought to do, and what we can stand for or against. Taylor goes further, proposing that this horizon is part of our identity:

> In other words, it is the horizon within which I am capable of taking a stand . . . the frame within which [I] can determine where [I] stand on questions of what is good, or worthwhile, or admirable, or of value. . . . We are selves only in that certain issues matter for us. What I am as a self, my identity, is essentially defined by the way things have significance for me . . . we are only selves insofar as we move in a certain space of questions, as we seek and find an orientation to the good.[7]

The values and beliefs we hold most dear define how we understand ourselves and how we imagine our place in the world. But as I will discuss below, this overarching worldview, this horizon of significance, can elude middle adults, leaving them more or less adrift when making decisions that are central to their lives and also to the lives of other people.

Part of figuring out what is a worthy life centers around the challenging questions of stewardship related to protecting and caring for children (and often elder parents), tending a home, safeguarding family resources, cultivating a career, contributing to the larger society, and fostering personal and family spiritual life. Many adults at this stage know that some things they do now have sacred significance and they struggle to honor those things through principled commitments and hard work. They also feel a deep yearning to integrate and experience *kairos* in the midst of the *chronos* of their lives. They know things matter not just for their immediate outcomes, but also for their eternal, spiritual outcomes. But middle adults can lose touch with the idealistic dimensions of vocation they held in young adulthood even as they continue to feel the yearning toward significance. Theologian Edward Hahenberg describes how idealism inspires vocational yearnings: "vocation has to do with the wide-open space above.

Love has no ceiling, and so my vocation is, quite simply, the way that I will rise. Yet, like picking a point on the dome of the sky, there are an infinite number of ways up. So what will be my unique way of responding to God's living call? What will be the transcendent trajectory of my life?"[8] Like Park and Taylor, Hahnenberg thinks that middle adults need a larger worldview, one rooted in understandings about what really matters, what is really true and good and right, as a framework for discerning and living out their callings.

Middle adulthood also brings many paradoxes related to dependence and independence. At the very time in life when people have the economic resources to live independently, they find that others are economically dependent on them, as Jane Patterson's reflections on Ruth illustrate.[9] Dreams of freedom from the constraining power of one's parents and other authority figures give way to assuming responsibility for providing adequately for others. Individuals look forward to a rewarding and productive career, but their new interdependencies may constrain choices away from work as a calling and toward work that provides an adequate financial income. There are paradoxes about pursuing ideals in the midst of "real" life. Even as they feel drawn toward ideals of changing the world and making a difference with their one not-so-wild but still precious life,[10] they also feel the compelling pull of the cares and concerns of family engagements, work obligations, and the need to be a responsible adult. And there are paradoxes of maintaining aspirations to make something out of one's life while also realizing that some dreams will never become real. I explore some of the primary vocational experiences of this life stage within the context of what I see as the core paradoxes of middle adulthood.

Vocational Experiences and the Paradoxes of Middle Adulthood

The Joys and Losses of Middle Adulthood

Middle adulthood is a time of joys and losses. These joys and losses often come in matched pairs in which opportunities contend with opportunity costs (e.g., the job not taken); freedoms contend with responsibilities (e.g., growing income and growing financial obligations); and successes in one life domain contending with potential losses in others (e.g., struggles with work-life balance). Middle adults have, at least in principle, extensive freedoms. They are legally autonomous to make a wide range of decisions.

They are in their peak years of financial productivity. They have the cognitive and emotional capacity to undertake and pursue big goals, even to follow their dreams—get married, build a career, create a family. They own their own computers, cars, and houses. And yet, as I have noted, middle adults also face new responsibilities, obligations, and challenges.

In the case of building a career, challenges may include the fears that one will not be able to find a good job, much less the right one, disappointments over lost promotions and work opportunities, insidious job demands that lead to overinvestments in work and underinvestments in family, facing the hard reality that one may never be passionate about work, and feeling compelled to care for children and home at the cost of career advancement. At least in Western societies, a career is something of a necessity. When adults meet for the first time, one of the opening questions is "What do you do for work?" Work matters a lot, and occupational roles comprise a significant part of the identity of many middle adults, but they often find it hard to find a job that both fits them well and will provide for themselves and their families.

My discussion here presupposes certain economic and social conditions. What about middle adults who cannot make ends meet or whose social status precludes certain educational or occupational opportunities? Is vocation something available only to those with sufficient economic means or those who find social conditions conducive to their pursuits? I certainly hope not, but some people face special challenges: single parents living below the poverty line, socially marginalized members of ethnic minorities, middle adults with less steady employment, people with unresolvable daycare needs, or those with minimal family support systems. In John's Gospel, Jesus asserted that he came that *all* might have life and have it more abundantly, but how do people overcome the social and economic conditions that, like the thief in this passage, seem to kill and destroy their hopes for abundance (10:10)? Here I think of Artis, who earns his income by doing odd jobs and yard work for people in my neighborhood. His income is uncertain, his labor is hard, and yet he tells me his work is "Nothing but joy, God bless! Nothing but joy!" My research team and I are exploring the ways that adults navigate these special challenges and, like Artis, still find meaning in their work.

Love, intimacy, and finding that special someone are also sources of joy and loss for middle adults. More than 90 percent of middle adults want to get married, yet more than half of their marriages end within five years.[11] Committing to and staying with a life partner seems to be both attractive and profoundly daunting. Society offers little help for understanding how to create and sustain a life partnership. In fact, modern social conventions seem to view marriage as an easy-entry, easy-exit relationship, but most people get married with at least the hope that the relationship will last. As the responsibilities, obligations, and challenges of their lives build up, strains on married life can also intensify. In the midst of this, where can middle adults turn for solace and help in not just maintaining, but strengthening their marriages?

Many middle adults also want to be parents, and yet struggle with the difficulties of raising children well, not to mention the challenges of balancing parenting against the opportunities and demands of other life domains. New parents often reflect that they had no idea how daunting and glorious parenthood would be.[12] Time off from work to care for a new child can turn into a period of discernment and struggle about whether work fits into their recently transformed lives. Work-family balance is one of the most common experiences of joy and loss among middle adults.[13] Work-family conflict, the negative sides of achieving this balance, is well known.

Middle adulthood is full of "reality checks" in which dreams and aspirations run into the prosaic daily demands and disappointments. Most middle adults know the joys of both personal accomplishment and of giving deeply of themselves solely for the benefit of others. They know that while life is often full of opportunities, it is also difficult to live well. Middle adults often struggle with reconciling their internal life standards with the societal standards of success they are subject to, especially in their work lives. What does it mean to be a good person in a secular context? How can I be both successful and virtuous? How should I balance personal achievement and the common good? Such questions are of great concern to middle adults, but they have little opportunity or venues in which to explore them in thoughtful and helpful ways.

Because of these reality checks, middle adults know they cannot have it all. They know the sweetness of success, the satisfaction of a job done well, the wonder of new discovery, the pride of achieving a difficult goal, and the excitement of pursuing adventures and surviving to tell about them. But they have also learned that life requires sacrifice and loss. They have grieved over the death of loved ones, suffered painful failure, endured hardship, regretted making the wrong choices, and lamented paths not taken. In research on people who found their life's calling, from both our own studies and those of other scholars, notions of sacrifice are at the core of experiencing vocation in work.[14] People who feel called to their work usually report that sacrificing and giving deeply of themselves are essential parts of their call. There is a potential dark side to sacrifice, however. People can sacrifice so much that their well-being and competency may be diminished. As such, there seems to be both "positive" and "negative" sacrifices in relationship to adult well-being. Positive forms seem to provide evidence that a calling is not self-serving: they confirm the importance and meaningfulness of the calling; and they link people's life values with their work, as Jane Patterson's description of Jesus's discernment in the garden exemplifies.[15] Negative sacrifices involve deleterious obligations that threaten well-being and may undermine the value, meaning, or enactment of a call: to give so much that one is damaged raises questions about the veracity of the call.

Middle adulthood can often be a time to grieve the past, to reconcile oneself that what might have been—the life (or lives) one might have lived or dreamed about living—is lost forever. Middle adults must learn to live with disappointments: paths not taken, botched relationships, opportunities squandered, dreams lost. It is a time in which individuals experience a profound sense of their own finitude. For some, this leads to fuller engagement with life, a stronger commitment to make the most of the gifts one has been endowed with. For others, regrets about the past haunt their choices and limit their engagement with life. A forty-something CEO of a major corporation we interviewed, who was also a divorced father of two adult children, gave voice to his own grief:

> *I've reached the pinnacle of success in business. I built [this] company and we are one of the leaders in our industry, both in our shareholders' eyes and in our customers'. We have done very well for our investors, and our customers are the happiest in our industry. . . . We are ready to expand into new markets: it is an exciting time for us. I'm proud of all that. Yet, it cost me my wife, and I barely have a relationship with my son. My daughter seems to understand, or at least she is willing to give it another try with me. There are more and more days where I wonder if it was worth it.*

Finally, middle adulthood is a time in which many people begin to attend to the limits of their life.[16] While youth is often the time when people feel invincible, middle adulthood is the time when mortality becomes real. Middle adults in the upper end of this life segment start asking questions about what their life has added up to, whether they can be proud of the way they have lived, and whether the legacy they will leave—if they even leave one—will be good or bad. Life insurance, estate planning, investments, and retirement accounts are all about the fact that there will be an end to life and that one had better prepare properly for it. Middle adults have to deal with these difficult and often sobering issues. Even if they do not have the financial means to prepare for their later life stages, middle adults experience cultural norms that tell them they *should* plan for their future. I see these normative pressures, for example, in commercials about investing and planning for retirement that air on television. These powerful cultural signals suggest that responsible middle adults will become financially independent older adults. Here the hope for a wonderful retirement meets the challenge of figuring out how to use whatever financial resources are available to meet current needs and plan for the future.

Living the Sacred and the Secular

Living well with these joys and losses is an existential, spiritual task, which may be one reason that middle adulthood is often a time in which people seek a spiritual or religious grounding in their lives. What is new, or at least much more salient for many middle adults is the desire to integrate their spiritual yearnings into the many vocations that comprise their lives. Middle adults want to live both a sacred and a secular life. Motivated in part by a desire to impart a religious or spiritual foundation to their children, and in part by their own desire to reinvigorate their spiritual lives, middle adults often seek to re-establish or rejuvenate their religious or spiritual connections. But many do so with a new perspective. Practical theologian James Fowler suggests that some adults learn to accept the paradoxes and polarities of life, acknowledge the limits of their own logic, and begin to see that mystery is essential in their spiritual life.[17] Wade Clark Roof concurs. His study of baby boomers demonstrates that the religious concerns of most middle adults tend to emphasize a "more open, spiritual searching style" in which "religion as quest, whether for spiritual support or in search of broadened horizons, or some vital mix of the two is usually the case. . . . Or perhaps better put, contemporary spiritual quests give expression to the search for unity of mind, body, and self."[18]

What seems to be essential for many middle adults is finding a self-transcendent source of meaning. Notions of transcendence among middle adults are rooted in the desire to connect with something of deep importance, something that is fundamentally, eternally true. Many middle adults acknowledge that their own lives should contribute positively to the lives of other people, to communities of various types, and to the divine good. They realize that life is not "all about me"; they want to "give back" and contribute to the common good, and to make their life count toward "something bigger than myself," what Erik Erikson describes as a desire for "generativity." The good news, literally and figuratively, Fowler reminds us, is that theological language is inevitably constructive and metaphorical in nature. Because theological language is narrative, it tells deeper truths about faith than the words alone convey and provides "centers of value that call forth our love and devotion and therefore exert ordering power on our lives and attachments," "images and realities of power" that provide security in an often chaotic, dangerous world, "a shared master story . . . [that] is meant to give direction, courage, and hope to our lives," and a story we share with others, one that "transcends us as individuals and binds us together with others."[19]

Fowler advocates for the rich use of metaphors because of the power they have to connect abstract concepts with our everyday lives. During this life stage, theological narratives that include myths and parables, and that allow for the paradoxes, tensions, and multiplicity of adulthood, can be important for shaping and supporting horizons of significance that guide and direct vocational pursuits. Similar to Jane Patterson's reflections on Paul's emergent sense of calling, middle adults may find in this story affirmation for the "ripening of an interior sense" of vocation that emerges over time. Many middle adults find it valuable to share their experiences with others as a way of helping them process what God seems to be doing in their lives. Paul's story provides language for understanding the "changes of course, and abrupt turnarounds . . . the need to grieve and repent of earlier decisions and actions" that middle adults experience.[20]

But as Taylor and others have shown, the norms and modes of living in modern societies can make it difficult for adults to pursue transcendence.[21] The dominant societal view is that *self*-fulfillment is the preeminent goal of life. Notions about what constitutes success in major domains—especially work—are highly individualist and one-dimensional: success in work is reduced to financial indicators, success in parenting is reduced to the academic and athletic achievements of one's children, success in marriage is reduced to how happy the partners are with the relationship. Many middle adults feel a terrible flatness in the everyday, and this experience has been identified particularly with commercial, industrial, or consumer society.

They feel emptiness in the repeated, accelerating cycle of desire and fulfill-ment in consumer culture, "the cardboard quality of bright supermarkets, or neat row housing in a clean suburb."[22]

Thus, middle adults often face a quandary of trying to find transcen-dence in the midst of social conditions that stymie that search. They live in a society that has either ignored or rejected religion, and yet they still experience a powerful urge toward experiencing transcendence and con-necting with eternal meaning. The current cultural context tells them to find meaning within themselves, yet they sense that the source of timeless truths about the meaning of life lies outside themselves. Taylor argues per-suasively that the modern emphasis on using self-fulfillment as a guide to finding a calling will ultimately prove ineffective: we are created for more transcendent purposes than simply meeting our own desires. Echoing Patterson's reflections about the bewilderment of the faithful person, the challenge to integrate spirituality and vocation is complicated by a desire to be both an intelligent, thoughtful, well-educated person and a person who also believes in God. In Roof's study, trying to deal with this tension, which includes recognizing and reconciling one's own religious doubts and misgivings, is typical of the spiritual pursuits of middle adults.[23] They need help in understanding how beliefs about transcendence, especially those deeply embedded in religious principles, can be the core of finding and living out the several life vocations they experience.

Sociologist Nancy Ammerman offers additional insights into how mid-dle adults strive toward this integration of transcendence and vocation. In her study of the religious lives of adults in America, she finds that most people blend two spiritual "landscapes."[24] *Theistic* spirituality is centered on God and the practices that foster a strong, positive relationship with God. It acknowledges the many ways that God can work mysteriously in the prosaic elements of life, and so it encourages middle adults both to find the sacred in the mundane and to work with God to bring spirituality into everyday work and home life. *Extra-theistic* spirituality encompasses tran-scendence in many forms, "[deep] connections to others, the sense of awe engendered by the natural world and moments of beauty, life philosophies crafted by an individual seeking meaning, and the inner core of individual self-worth."[25] Extra-theistic spirituality acknowledges that experiencing transcendence can come from both inside and outside oneself.

Ammerman finds that most middle adults embrace both forms: they are both spiritual and religious. For middle adults, the quest to discern and live into vocation is both a spiritual and a secular pursuit. They understand—or at least they hope—that they can live a godly life and find meaning and success in their secular life pursuits. Ammerman argues that, to discover the transcendent "spiritual center" to their lives, middle adults need what she calls a "sacred tribe," a community that can "provide personal support, moral guidance, and a sense of belonging" and also one that will "listen to and cocreate . . . sacred stories."[26] While some may argue the sacred-secular is a false dichotomy, my point is that many adults experience this difference as real, and they want to find a way to navigate the challenges of bringing the sacred into the secular dimensions of their lives.

Finding these tribes can be a major challenge. Friendships can certainly be important for spiritual growth, but Ammerman's work suggests that a larger community is also required. "Church shopping" can be exhausting and discouraging, yet there are few, if any, other social institutions that foster the kinds of relationships, engagement, and support that are characteristic of church-based sacred tribes. As such, middle adults can be left out on their own, in great need of a spiritual community that can help them discern how to live the sacred in the secular, and unable to find a place in which to listen, be listened to, and co-create sacred stories that can be foundational for their lives and their callings.

The Special Case of Work

Many middle adults find that work is the most difficult part of their life in which to integrate the secular and the sacred. On the one hand, notions of work as a vocation or calling speak to an ideal of what work can and should be like at its best. When work is a calling, most adults believe, it is inseparable from one's essential or truest self.[27] To enact a calling is to express one's authentic, core self in one's work in some essential, meaningful way: perhaps when Confucius talked about those who love their work, he meant we will love work when it engages our truest, most authentic selves. But the work experiences of many middle adults tend to be more of the kind Studs Terkel describes in the epigraph to this chapter. As I noted, my own life story is one of life-depleting experiences of work and a search for an experience of work that was consistent with my religious beliefs and convictions. I resolved this by making a complete break from one career path and starting over to pursue another. A recent scientific study indicates that 65 percent of adults regard work as the top source of stress in their life.[28] The Centers for Disease Control considers work stress to be at epidemic proportions.[29] Results of a 2010 poll of working adults indicate that less than one-half of American workers are satisfied with their jobs, a twenty-two-year low.[30] Most working adults report that Saturday and Sunday are the best days of their week. The worst day? Monday.[31] But research on well-being indicates that the only thing worse for adults than a bad job is no job at all.[32]

My research team and I have been studying how people find and live into work as a calling. I am interested in this because so many people view callings as an ideal of truly meaningful work, but few adults ever seem to come close to finding one. We interviewed more than two hundred educators, humanitarian workers, pastors, and physicians to gather their life stories.[33] We found that integrating "core commitments"—our term for a person's understandings and beliefs about transcendence—is foundational for experiencing work as a calling. Integration comprises both expressing one's unique capabilities, personal characteristics, and core commitments in one's work and engaging one's work in a manner that achieves standards of excellence, ethics, and professionalism set by the larger community of workers or professionals. Integration achieves a harmony between being true to oneself and being true to one's work or profession.

Like Ammerman, we found that achieving this integration is profoundly social. Especially important were the real-life models of exemplars and the personalized coaching of wise guides, two social roles that are often filled by middle adults. We found exemplars are important for two reasons. First, they are perceived as individuals who are proficient in their work and so they are regarded as role models of excellence in a particular work role. Exemplars are masters at their work; they pursue excellence and have turned that pursuit into an art. Second, exemplars are perceived as "comfortable in their own skin" in the work they do. Exemplars are perceived as being "naturals" in their work because they are not only good at what they do, but they are also truly authentic in their work role. As such, exemplars are real, salient, living role models of individuals who are living their own calling in and through their work. They can therefore serve as guides for learning how to find a calling, and how to live into a calling once it is found. These two quotes, the first from an interview with a female pastor and the second from a physician, illustrate how exemplars helped these middle adults find a calling in their work:

We grew up in church, it was always part of our life. But pursuing a career in ministry wasn't really encouraged: I don't know if I really saw it as a possibility. I knew I could be a Sunday school teacher, sing in the choir, work with the kids, all those things when I got older, but pastors are men. I never thought someone like me could be a pastor. . . . When I saw [female pastor], it was like a bolt: suddenly everything was clear to me. All those inklings? All along, they were my call.

This family practice doctor—his waiting room was always full . . . amazing what family practice doctors did back then. . . . [I] saw how important he was in the community and there was something about that which confirmed or planted something that being in medicine really is a good thing. I looked up to him. I thought he was one of the most important people in the community because he was doing so much and he was giving it his all. He was like a Marcus Welby kind of guy, he really was.

Most people seem to find a calling by observing several, often many, exemplars and then comparing themselves to those examples. When they found an exemplar that seemed to be a lot like them, like the pastor in the quote above, they had taken an important step toward finding their calling. In addition to providing real-life examples that work can be a calling, exemplars also serve as standards or archetypes people can use to imagine what kind of work might be a calling for them. People can envision themselves in a particular work role by determining how much they are like a particular exemplar. We found that people compared their talents, personality, and passions against those possessed by a variety of exemplars. When they found a good match—that is, when they discovered they were very much like a particular exemplar—they sensed that they had likely found their potential calling. For example, a female physician tells of the importance of having a woman physician as part of her repertoire of exemplars:

I was nervous about being a mom and a doctor . . . so I remember this one woman that was our attending on internal medicine and she had two or three little kids, she would talk about them a lot, she seemed like she was very involved. She would leave a little early to go to her son's soccer game and that was the kind of stuff that I really wanted to be able to know that I could do. Sometimes it's a little scary, you think, "Oh, I'm going to be a doctor." . . . She was very influential for me, knowing that it's going to be okay, you can be a mom and you can be a doctor.

An educator describes the role of two family members in her calling experience:

> *I had an aunt who was a teacher, and I was very young when I was around her. . . . I remember the positive attitude that she had toward making a difference. My grandmother on the other side of my family taught in a one-room schoolhouse and she was one of the first students at [state university]. So those two people really made me start to think about becoming a teacher.*

One challenge, however, is finding an exemplar: we discovered that women called to ministry and men called to elementary-school education struggled to acknowledge their calling until they saw their first female pastor or male teacher. This begs the question of how someone discerns a calling if she never experiences the right exemplar. As we continue our research, answering that question is an important goal.

Even more important were wise guides. They were almost always first viewed as exemplars—role models of excellence and authenticity in a profession. As such, they are individuals who are rightly to be admired and held in high esteem. When people had opportunities to interact more regularly with an exemplar, the possibility of forming a mentoring relationship emerged. We found that these relationships required a sense of deep similarity (i.e., shared core beliefs and values, similar life experiences, common personality and personal style). This deep similarity formed the basis for the relationship to develop over time through regular, often very personal conversations. Deep similarity provided the critical foundation because people could simply internalize directly much of the wise guide's advice and many of this person's ways of doing and being. Strong emotional bonds formed, which encouraged significant self-disclosure by both guide and protégé. In turn, self-disclosure formed the foundation for the guide to provide personalized advice and direction. These relationships almost always transformed over time into strong friendships. As the one-time protégé became a master in his own right, a more collegial, peer-based relationship formed. People often spoke of these as among the most important and rewarding friendships in their lives. One pastor we interviewed captures the way wise guides help people find their way through the complexities of life:

> *He was just so supportive of everything I did . . . and he was so affirming. This is one thing that he did, he just cared about me and thought I*

*was doing a good job and he affirmed that over and over. He gave me
a lot of freedom to do things the way I wanted to, but then he would
always help me figure out why things went well, or why they did not.*

We heard many stories of how wise guides worked with protégés to
process specific experiences, such as particularly good or poor job performance, dealing with a difficult work situation, and making important job
choice decisions. Conversations with and support by such guides helped
people to recognize, understand, and accept their own calling to a particular kind of work. These guides often provided the critical insight or
special validation that people needed to not only see they had a calling,
but to live into that calling, day by day, step by step. Living into a calling
is clearly a journey, and mentors are critically important partners on that
journey.

Given the importance of exemplars and wise guides for finding vocation in work, I have wondered about their importance for finding and
living out other vocations. When my boys were in their teen years, I would
have benefited immeasurably from a fatherhood guide. I had several exemplars, among them my own father, but I also needed someone to journey
with me through the fraught experiences of fathering boys as they went
through puberty and young adulthood. I struggled with how to deal with
their challenges to my authority; I sometimes felt ill-prepared to help them
work through their problems in those rare moments when they asked for
my help; and I worried about how to help them make good choices of their
own. I should have sought out my own father more often, but I would have
also benefited from another wise parenthood guide, someone to help me
figure out what kind of parenting would work for my sons and to help me
discover the kind of father I could be and needed to be.

My point is that, in addition to serving as exemplars and wise guides,
I think middle adults can benefit from their own exemplars and guides
in learning how to find and live out the several vocations that comprise
their lives. Historically, religious communities were the primary source
for both of these important relationships, but societal changes, including
the decline in church attendance, have made it more difficult for middle
adults to find good exemplars and guides. While play groups, weekend
sports activities, and dinners-out with friends offer opportunities to com-
miserate with other middle adults, still missing for many middle adults is
the deeper wisdom that can only be gained by learning from wise, experienced masters at life.

The Elusive Search for Balance

One of the most common concerns among middle adults is trying to balance the many vocations of their lives. Attaining proper work-life balance is one of the ways this challenge is experienced by adults. At the core of concerns about balance are issues related to how one person can honor each vocation, how these different vocations can all properly, appropriately, and snugly fit into one person's life. Middle adults struggle with conflicting standards of success: in work, success is measured by productivity, salary, promotions, achievement, and sometimes just keeping a job and a paycheck; at home it is loving others, creating a nurturing home, raising children well, welcoming friends and strangers, and sometimes just keeping chaos and demanding teenagers at bay. Not only does each vocation, each domain of life, have its own standards of success, but the standards in one vocation may conflict with those in another. Success at work requires more time at the office, but being a good parent requires spending more time at home. Civic organizations and church ask for evenings and weekends, but those may be the best times to be with family and friends. Even as these different domains urge us to measure success in different ways, each person is living one single life.

The tension between work and the rest of life also arises out of conflicts between individuals and the social institutions that shape the primary contexts in which they live and work. For example, individuals want meaning, purpose, and fulfillment in their work, yet many work organizations seek to maximize financial performance (e.g., profit or shareholder value) and so treat people as assets of production—"things" that must be planned, controlled, and managed. Women often experience conflicting pressures from different social institutions. Bonnie Miller-McLemore writes about the struggles mature women face trying to be engaged in the world of work and the world of family life, describing her own experience: "I joined the long history of 'thousands of women' before me by beginning my life with the same question: Must I choose?"[34] The desires to be a perfect parent run up against the desires to be a successful worker. Couples face the challenges of living together and intertwining two work lives: who will pick up the kids, make dinner, pay the bills? In the United States, there is a notable lack of supportive social structures and policies for combining work and family. Sixty days of unpaid leave for family "emergencies" are not enough to deal with the realities that many families face.[35]

Indeed, many middle adults experience the negative spillover when work impacts family (e.g., work calls during family dinner time, extended business travel, late nights or weekends in the office), and they also often feel that family impinges on their work responsibilities (e.g., staying home with a sick child who cannot go to school, fitting in physician and dentist appointments, being home for a repair person). Research also shows that there can be positive spillover between work and non-work life. A physician we interviewed shared this story:

> *My daughter always enjoyed going to the hospital with me, even late at night. She seemed to enjoy the work—after all, she did became a doctor—but what was most important for us was all the special times we had because of those hospital calls. She would wait in the nurses' station for me, and then we would go to the cafeteria for something to eat. Some of our best conversations during her teen years happened in that cafeteria. So, yeah, sometimes work caused problems at home, but it also created some wonderful opportunities.*

As I have noted, richer, more beneficial images of and social support for integrating love and work are often missing for middle adults. They need good exemplars of people who have "successfully" made it through the challenges of middle adulthood. What they do not need are people who "had it all," but rather people who led real, complex lives and who navigated and negotiated, and succeeded and failed their way through the joys and sorrows of middle adulthood.

Middle adults also need a better standard than work-life "balance." Jack Fortin argues that notions of "balance" are culturally created ideas, and he explores an alternative cultural perspective, one informed by Christian beliefs and ideals: the centered life.[36] The ideal of a perfectly ordered life, where each vocation and responsibility gets just the right amount of attention, and there is plenty of time, energy, and resources for all of life's demands, is a fiction. To paraphrase a well-known bumper sticker, "stuff happens" and when it does, it brings change, sometimes for the better and sometimes for the worse. Any balance achieved will be temporary, but even striving for that balance can cause adults to feel they are failing when things get thrown out of equilibrium. For middle adults, finding a better rhythm, or at least a less chaotic, just-getting-through-the-day experience to life, requires exploring more deeply the hopes and fears, opportunities and challenges, and joys and sorrows of all of their vocations. To-do lists and better time management are not enough. To be sure, setting one's own standards of success is important, but the twin challenges for middle adults are defining these standards and actually using them to guide their lives. Miller-McLemore argues that an emphasis on productivity and being "successful" creates a distorted ideal of work, one that can encourage over-investments in work and underinvestments at home. She urges churches to be a primary source of support—a "holding environment" that encourages deep explorations of vocation for adults that centers rather than balances their lives.

Power, Wisdom, and the Potential to Do Good and Evil

Middle adults are the most powerful of all age groups. They lead most of the businesses, governments, economies, civic and religious organizations, social service agencies, militaries, schools and universities, sports teams, and artistic groups around the world. It is largely middle adults who organize, fund, lead, and administer the communities, neighborhoods, cities and towns, and groups that are centrally important in the lives of every other age group. Middle adults create most of the new inventions, make most of the scientific discoveries, provide most of the healthcare, cook most of the meals, preach most of the sermons, teach most of the classes, and fix most of the cars.

Because of the power and authority they wield, middle adults also create much of the pain, suffering, and destruction experienced around the world. Their influence, authority, and control of resources make them potent and influential social agents, and they can use these extraordinary capacities for bad purposes. The scale of these abuses of power can range from more local (e.g., improper parenting of children) and communal (e.g., mismanagement of employees) levels to national and global (e.g., instigating wars). The point is that most middle adults have the capacity to perpetrate negative acts from a variety of different social positions. Compared to the selfish or miscreant behavior of children, youth, young adults, and even the elderly, the potential for evil among middle adults is enormous.

While there are child prodigies and late bloomers, most of what gets done around the world—working and procrastinating, loving and hating, discovering and concealing, achieving and failing, creating and destroying—is undertaken by middle adults. This is the case, in part, because middle adulthood comprises a wider range of years than any other life stage. But it is also the case because middle adulthood comprises the most productive and powerful years of most people's lives. People tend to hit their peak in productivity, control over resources, decision-making authority, social prestige, and power during this life stage. This is also the life stage in which most people make the biggest impact they will ever make. It is the time for changing the world, the time in which most people build whatever legacy they will leave.

Importantly, wisdom also tends to develop during this life stage. Wisdom is one of the most important gifts that middle adults can use for the benefit of other people and organizations, and it is also invaluable for helping them use their power well.[37] At least as scholars view it, wisdom involves understanding that life comprises many complex and difficult problems, a recognition that one's knowledge is finite and one's perspective limited, and the willingness and capacity to formulate sound (i.e., virtuous and efficacious) judgments in the face of life's uncertainties. For millennia, wisdom has been seen as the antidote to both selfishness and limited knowledge, and as the sure guide for the proper use of power. Empathy and concern for others are as central to wisdom as are knowledge and experience.[38] Societies expect middle adults to be wise, powerful, and benevolent.

But developing wisdom takes work. Building the capacity to *enact* wisdom takes time, concerted effort, self-reflection, and intentionality. Scholars who study wisdom argue that something very much like Ammerman's spiritual tribes is crucially important for developing both the foundations and capacities to enact it.[39] Wisdom grows in community, and so middle adults need elders to serve as role models and guides to provide the foundations for wisdom, and they need peers to help them figure out how to be a wise person and how to act wisely in the roles and contexts that comprise their life.

Communal Dynamics

As I have emphasized, middle adulthood is the time of multiple callings or, at least, a time when multiple domains of life—work, family, religious involvements, civic engagements—require significant investments of personal resources. Consistent with Jane Patterson's initial reflection about the metaphor of the family of God and the relational nature of callings,[40] all of these vocations are deeply social in nature. Among middle adults, conceptions of living well are informed by the quality and character of relationships, so caring for others becomes a paramount vocational concern.[41] Increasingly, middle adults are the "sandwich generation" because they care for both their own children and older family members.[42]

Social connections with work organizations represent a second, centrally important community for most middle adults. Relationships with co-workers—bosses, peers, customers, clients, beneficiaries, vendors, and suppliers—are among the most prevalent and impactful social interactions in middle adulthood. As I have noted, the growing body of research on work-family dynamics provides compelling evidence that there is significant spillover back and forth between individuals' work and family life. When things are good in one of these domains, things go better in the other; when conditions are poor in one area, they tend to have a negative impact on the other.

Many middle adults also pursue vocational commitments through their engagement in civic, religious, and social service organizations, often volunteering their time and other personal resources to help advance social missions they find compelling and important. Because these engagements are often based on personal values and beliefs, they can represent purposeful and fulfilling life activities and, therefore, they may be experienced as a calling. Unlike work, these mission-based involvements can be experienced as "pure pursuits," unsullied by monetary remuneration and other demands of the world of work. Some adults who cannot find a calling in their work compensate by finding an alternative calling outside work.[43] Others find callings by contributing to the common good through civic, religious, philanthropic, or volunteer commitments. These people share a "common fire" to make the world a better place.[44]

Generativity, the desire to positively influence future generations, is a new communal dynamic that emerges during this stage. For Erikson generativity is a concern for guiding and providing for the next generation, and he proposed that it is the major developmental task of this life stage.[45] It may be a way of experiencing transcendence, of connecting and contributing to something of lasting, eternal value. Engaging in productive work that is also socially valued is one important way that middle adults seek to express transcendence. This may be why the yearning to find work that is a calling is still so prevalent in this life stage. Middle adults strive toward generativity beyond their work by, for example, developing unity with a life mate, raising children to be independent, responsible adults, and fostering loving relationships with others inside and outside their work contexts.[46] In fact, raising children is perhaps the most common manifestation of generativity. Beyond one's own children, middle adults are the largest sources of donations to philanthropies, churches, universities, museums, arts organizations, and the like.[47] New movements such as "Conscious Capitalism"[48] and the rise of "B-corporations"[49] are ways of pursuing generativity in business. Generativity often carries forward into the next life stage and can be one important way that middle adults create continuity across their lifespan.

Ending of Middle Adulthood

Middle adulthood often ends with several rather dramatic reversals. It began with the pursuit of meaningful work, and for many it ends with an often abrupt cessation of that work. It began with commitments to a life partner, and it all too often ends with a sudden termination of that intimate partnership, through either death or divorce. It began with starting a family and raising children, and it ends with an "empty nest" as those children suddenly leave home and the demands of active parenthood decline. For many middle adults, the very things that were at the center of their sense of self—"my work, my spouse, my children"—undergo dramatic changes and, therefore, so do their identities and sense of calling.

Many men, and an increasing number of women, find that retirement from work brings a sudden loss of several foundational elements of their identity. They can no longer claim a social role; they are "just retired," apparently now individuals with nothing important to do and no meaningful place to contribute their best personal resources.[50] Retirement brings conflicting feelings: relief to be free of the stresses and constraints of work, but also a sense of loss that the positive aspects of working life are now gone. Middle adults wonder what will fill the gaps in meaning, purpose, and identity that work once provided.

Many women, and an increasing number of men, experience empty nest syndrome.[51] A life and identity that was heavily centered around being a parent, raising children, and filling a variety of important social roles (e.g., sports team coach, Sunday school teacher, classroom parent, field-trip chaperone) is uprooted as children leave home and become (more or less) independent adults. Middle adults wonder what will fill the gaps in meaning, purpose, and identity that parenting once provided.

Research suggests that perhaps the most difficult of all endings is the loss of a life partner. Whether by divorce[52] or death,[53] the dissolution of a marriage or long-term committed relationships brings a host of identity challenges and threats to well-being. An identity that was built around a sense of "we" must now adapt to being "just me." Experiences of a shared life give way to new experiences of life alone. Daily life that comprised two lives intertwined suddenly requires trying to unravel a single life from deeply ingrained patterns.

And there is often the realization that much more than half of one's life has already passed by. There is less time in the future than one has already lived in the past. Youth is clearly gone, and new concerns arise about aging, maintaining health, and living well to the end of one's life. If the golden years are ahead, what are all those years that one is leaving behind? But what if one's best years are already gone, what then can one make of the next years?

Like all transitions from one life stage to the next, the transition out of middle adulthood offers both joys and losses, and it also has its paradoxes. The difference may be, however, that middle adults know this to be true, and they look forward with both deeper wisdom and greater pragmatism. They know that aging gracefully (whatever that means) is at least partly a matter of making the right choices. Moving into middle adulthood was about building a good life, and the transition out of this life stage is about continuing that good life and passing it on.

Suggested Readings

Ammerman, Nancy Tatom. *Sacred Stories, Sacred Tribes: Finding Religion in Everyday Life*. New York: Oxford University Press, 2014.

Bellah, Robert N. *Habits of the Heart: Individualism and Commitment in American Life*. Berkeley: University of California Press, 1985.

Bronson, Po. *What Should I Do with My Life?: The True Story of People Who Answered the Ultimate Question*. New York: Ballantine, 2005.

Hahnenberg, Edward P. *Awakening Vocation: A Theology of Christian Call*. Collegeville, MN: Liturgical Press, 2010.

Ibarra, Herminia. *Working Identity: Unconventional Strategies for Your Career*. Boston: Harvard Business School Press, 2004.

Miller-McLemore, Bonnie J. *Also a Mother: Work and Family as Theological Dilemma*. Nashville, TN: Abingdon, 1994.

Neafsey, John. *A Sacred Voice Is Calling: Personal Vocation and Social Conscience*. Maryknoll, NY: Orbis, 2006.

Parks Daloz, Laurent A., Sharon Daloz Parks, Cheryl H. Keen, and James P. Keen. *Common Fire: Leading Lives of Commitment in a Complex World*. Boston: Beacon, 1997.

Paul, L. A. *Transformative Experience*. New York: Oxford University Press, 2014.

Placher, William C. *Callings: Twenty Centuries of Christian Wisdom on Vocation*. Grand Rapids, MI: Eerdmans, 2005.

Taylor, Charles. *The Ethics of Authenticity*. Cambridge, MA: Harvard University Press, 1992.

Wrzesniewski, Amy. "Callings." In *Oxford Handbook of Positive Organizational Scholarship*, edited by Kim S. Cameron and Gretchen M. Spretizer, 45–55. New York: Oxford University Press, 2010.

Elders: Ultimate Values

Jane Patterson

Biblically, the term "elder" conveys not only a person of a certain age, but a wise one, someone whose age and experience make her a person who can be depended on for astute counsel. Anna and Simeon are a pair of such wise elders in the Gospel of Luke. We meet them as they are carrying out their daily vigil in the Jerusalem temple (2:25–38). Within their historical context, they might be seen as a pair of crazy radicals. Under Roman occupation, the Jewish temple was a vivid symbol to the faithful that God was their only true ruler, and that ultimately, God's sovereignty would vanquish even Rome's rule over Israel. Over the course of the first century, the temple was the scene for various acts of Roman hegemony and Jewish political theater, including Jesus's own dramatic critique of the temple as a "den of robbers," a safe hideaway for those who colluded with Rome to rob the people of their basic sustenance (Luke 19:46).

On the day we meet these two radicals, Jesus's parents are bringing their newborn baby to the temple, to make the purification offering required after childbirth (Lev. 12:6–8). Simeon is drawn into the temple by the Holy Spirit; Anna is there because she has a consistent discipline of fasting, prayer, and worship. Simeon is described as "looking forward to the consolation of Israel" (Luke 2:25), and Anna is among those "who were looking for the redemption of Jerusalem" (2:38). Under Roman occupation, Simeon's and Anna's loyalties would be suspect. What would be the consolation of Israel, if not home rule? What would be the redemption of Jerusalem, but freedom from Rome's domination? These two wise elders give voice to the hope of salvation they see in the child Jesus. Simeon blesses the young family and speaks a hard truth to Mary concerning Jesus's future role and its effect on her: "This child is destined for the falling and rising of many in Israel, and to be a sign that will be opposed so that the inner thoughts of many will be revealed—and a sword will pierce your own soul, too" (2:34–35).

Anna and Simeon embody a focused boldness in their sense of calling, a boldness that characterizes some people who, after a lifetime of responsibly making and saving money, raising their children, doing what their community expected of them, reevaluate their lives in light of what they see as truly ultimate. In this sharp light, the preoccupations of middle adulthood—making and spending money, acquiring possessions, caring for one's reputation—appear as no longer worthy of one's precious time, attention, and heart, as we see in late adulthood in the following chapter. Such people choose to devote themselves to the things they see as truly ultimate, desiring to establish a more significant legacy not subject to decay. They work, often with a prophetic energy, for social justice, for the education of the next generation, for the care of the earth. Sensing the call of their historical context, they seem to channel the radical Spirit of God. Against many of the current community norms of the Western world, where the elderly who have retired tend to be seen as people who should simply devote themselves to play, Anna and Simeon stand as a different kind of witness and call. Anna is called a "prophet." Literally, a prophet is someone who speaks forth courageously what God gives the prophet to say. She is a widow, a person "of a great age," who has known both love and loss. To such people God entrusts the vocation of imagining what our society might be, recognizing the younger people needed to engage the work, and speaking it eloquently into being.

7

Late Adulthood

Seeking Vocation Once Again

KATHLEEN A. CAHALAN

There is a kind of turning in the adult years. Something is changing in those around me; I can feel it too, in my mid-fifties, something closer on the horizon. My sister is now a grandmother; my parents are in their eighties; we cared for my elderly mother-in-law for many years before she died; my husband is hinting about retirement; we both struggle with nagging health issues; and I wonder how much longer I want to pursue work at a full pace. In previous writings on vocation, I have drawn on my own experience of calling but in writing this chapter I realize that much of what I describe I have yet to live into. Nevertheless, I do draw on many people's lives around me—family, colleagues, neighbors, and friends—to highlight the many ways in which people experience God's callings in late adulthood.

After describing the ways people enter late adulthood and its key characteristics, I examine four vocational experiences related to work, purpose, loss, and reconciliation, and two roles that impact a sense of calling in significant relationships—becoming a grandparent and being a caregiver. Themes of vocation cut across this life phase: calling as duty as well as the calling to discover the true self; callings as continuous as well as new; callings that involve choice and decision; and callings that are given and required. The general calling as well as particular callings emerge through inner experiences as well as external callings through others; callings in this life phase appear and erupt in varying and different ways, oftentimes surprising people that vocation is not over.

Entering Late Adulthood

Is leaving middle adulthood and entering late adulthood chronological, or is it a cultural construct? When Chuck retired at 58 from being a state auditor, did he enter late adulthood, or does it begin when he takes Social Security? Is the transition determined by physical and emotional changes, familial adjustments, or a lifestyle choice? In the same year Mary Lou became a grandmother she also contracted diabetes. She discerned it was time to take care of herself, lose some weight, and exercise more in order to be healthier and live to enjoy her expanding family. But to do that, she decided to cut back at work.[1] Can we call these adjustments in adult life a distinct lifespan phase? Is a sense of calling continuous, or does something new emerge?

For many theorists, chronology is not helpful when defining late adulthood. As James Fisher, professor of adult education, and Henry Simmons, a Christian educator, note in their study of older adults, "chronology is no longer the kind of measure it was earlier in life when one had a pretty clear idea of what health and functional ability would be at 30 or 40 or 50. Now, chronology only tells how many years there have been since birth. It does not give us as many clues about health, ability, functions, roles, and relationships as it had seemed to earlier in life."[2] However, age 65 remains a powerful cultural marker, marking eligibility for Social Security benefits, which is tied to the "most common gateway" into late adult life—retirement.[3]

Questions about retirement, such as when to stop full-time work, when to draw Social Security benefits, and whether to take another job, begin long before age 65 for most Americans.[4] If retirement is a key discernment, we might say entering late adulthood begins when these questions arise persistently and decisions begin to be mulled over; even if they are put off, the cultural messages and social pressure to consider when to stop full-time employment are everywhere.

In addition to work, adults may enter this phase through awareness of bodily changes, such as a lower resistance to illness, a slowing down, or the onset of chronic conditions, some temporary but others permanent. The body's needs become more persistent. Chronic conditions shift one's ability to do things that could be done at a younger age. Bodily changes awaken one's attention to aging, and the focus of life shifts in the direction of the later years.

In addition to a new awareness of work and bodily needs, relationships change; perhaps the most significant is becoming a grandparent. Today

80 percent of those 65 and older and 51 percent of those 50 to 64 have grandchildren. Almost one-third report time with grandchildren as what they value most in being older. Many people conceive of the grandparent as the oldest member in the family. But, in fact, more people are becoming great-grandparents, which shifts the experience of grandparenting in late adulthood. Some grandparents find themselves nestled between middle adult parents and great-grandparents, which are discussed in the following chapter on older adults.[5]

Other relationship changes include caregiving for an elderly parent, a spouse, an adult child, sometimes a grandchild, or a friend. Many will experience the death of a parent, a spouse, or a partner. Having children become parents, welcoming grandchildren and forging new relationships, and caring for others mark late adulthood as distinct from the middle and older adult years.

Some theorists identify the emergence of late adulthood with new meaning and purpose related to work and service. The anthropologist Mary Catherine Bateson says we shift from the first to the second part of adulthood "when you reflect that you have done much of what you hoped to do in life but it is not too late to do something more or different. The doorway to this new stage of life is not filing Social Security but thinking differently and continuing to learn."[6] As some experience it, late adulthood emerges when a person realizes that "my job won't let me do my work," and it is time to let go of the job but continue the work in some new and different way.[7] "I am never going to retire; the work is too important," said Senator Barbara Boxer in a video interview with her oldest grandson. "But I am not going to be running for the Senate in 2016."[8]

Some adults entering this phase choose a period of searching, akin to lifecycle psychologist Erik Erikson's notion of moratorium in young adulthood, as a time of trying on new identities, activities, and perspectives. In late adulthood, Bateson notes that a moratorium is a "somewhat similar interval for study or travel or experimenting with some model of retirement that proves to be temporary, trying to find a meaningful activity they are ready to engage in during this new stage of life."[9] Peter and Beth, for example, took a leave of absence from their jobs in healthcare to travel around the world for nearly a year, visiting clinics, orphanages, and hospices. When they returned home, they went back to their jobs, but the year abroad gave them a sense of what they could do with their lives in the future after full-time employment. Bateson's metaphor for late adulthood is the atrium, a new room added into one's life, a room at the center of the other rooms, which is open to the sky. While it is a time that "gives way to old age and is marked by the consciousness of mortality," it is also a time of "new beginnings" or the "revival of earlier interests."[10] Late adulthood, then, is a particular time in life when new vocational questions and possibilities arise.

Chronologically, these changes may happen at any point, as early as the forties and into the sixties or seventies. The significance of 50th and 60th birthday parties points to the fact that life is more than half over. Other than birthday and retirement parties, the late adulthood transition is made in the absence of rituals. Culturally and religiously we lack rituals that publicly acknowledge what is ending, what is beginning, and what new responsibilities one must assume.[11]

Since there is not an exact beginning or ending, identifying one's self as being in late adulthood is a matter of self-perception that comes through changes in the body, in relationships, and in one's sense of time. The transition out of middle adulthood into this new phase is one of increasing anxiety for many—it entails separating from a fairly long period of stable identity attached to particular roles into a period of uncertainty. And this uncertainty makes late adulthood ripe for vocational searching.

Characteristics of Late Adulthood

We have included a chapter on late adulthood in this book for two primary reasons: the significant increase in the number of people moving into this phase and the lengthening of the human lifespan. Older adults in the United States, those age 65 and older, will nearly double between 2012 and 2050 from 43.1 to 83.7 million. By 2050, this segment of the population will grow from 12 percent to 21 percent, compared to 1900, when those 65 and over were 4 percent of the population.[12]

In addition to more people being over 65, we are living longer, though longevity does not mean we are going to be elderly longer. As some observers note, we are going to be adults longer. Bateson argues for the need to expand Erikson's lifespan theory to include a new stage. "We have not added decades to life expectancy by simply extending old age; instead, we have opened up a new space part-way through the life course, a second and different kind of adulthood that precedes old age, and as a result every stage of life is undergoing change."[13] Bateson contends we now have two phases of adulthood: Adulthood I, a busy and productive time of life focused on child-rearing and career-building, and Adulthood II, which "may begin as early as age forty (for example, for athletes whose first careers may last only twenty years) and extend past eighty (for example, for politicians, if they reach the Senate, and many self-employed people), for many years of participation and contribution."[14]

Despite Bateson's assertions, what is often called "late adulthood" lacks strong theoretical foundation. For a time, gerontologists talked about three "ages" of the elder years: the young-old, the old-old, and the very old. But this seems inadequate for how late adulthood is being described by Bateson and others. Popular literature is flourishing on late adulthood topics with a strong emphasis on finding meaning and purpose in the second half of life, or what some authors are calling the "third age."[15] This outpouring of cultural material indicates that people are grappling with something new. Once again, theory building, in both the social sciences and theology, will have to catch up to lived-reality.

Two interpreters offer helpful descriptions of late adulthood that connect with a theology of vocation—Fisher and Simmons's qualitative research with older adults and Bateson's reinterpretation of Erikson's life-span model. From these sources we can see that late adulthood is characterized chiefly by a continuation of middle adulthood activities; shifting patterns of work; an indeterminate sense of time; and the return of questions related to identity, intimacy, and generativity.

Continuing Middle Adulthood

In *A Journey Called Aging: Challenges and Opportunities in Older Adulthood*, Fisher and Simmons construct a framework, based on interviews with people 60 and older, for understanding the dynamics of the older adult years. Their framework is intended to describe most, not all, older adults and is based on three periods and two transition phases: extended middle age, early transition, older adult lifestyle, later transition, and final period.[16] In this chapter, I focus on the first period and transition, which ends late adulthood; the other two periods and the second transition correspond with the following chapter on older adulthood.

As indicated by its name, the chief characteristic of the first period is continuity with middle age.[17] Fisher and Simmons found that the majority of people's interests, commitments, activities, and sense of identity are largely continuous with middle adulthood, even for those who retire.

While retirement marks the single biggest decision and transition, usually taking up to a year, a person's life before and after retirement remains relatively the same. They found great variation when it comes to work in the post-retirement years: some do not leave full-time work; about one-third work at a "bridge job," something part-time and flexible, allowing a phase down over time.[18] After Chuck took his state pension and tried full-time retirement for a year, he returned to part-time work during tax season in order to both use his professional skills and gain some income. Most people did not take up radically new activities, but continued activities they learned in earlier years. Homemakers, primarily women, do not experience retirement as such but continue working through this transition. Most people live out the plans they put in place for retirement.

Other studies confirm Fisher and Simmons's findings. A significant number of people working today (77 percent) say that they will work after retirement and most because they want to work, not because they have to.[19] A Pew Research Study found no significant difference by race, ethnicity, education, income, or gender and concluded that working after age 65 is becoming a widely held cultural expectation. Cultural expectations and reality can be quite different, however. Many will work to maintain their lifestyle, have access to healthcare, maintain a regular schedule, or escape boredom, but many will have to work in order to stay out of or because of poverty. According to the National Council on Aging, "retirement is not 'golden' for all older adults. Over 23 million Americans aged 60+ are economically insecure—living at or below 250% of the federal poverty level (FPL) ($29,425 per year for a single person). These older adults struggle with rising housing and healthcare bills, inadequate nutrition, lack of access to transportation, diminished savings, and job loss."[20]

Indeterminate Time and Purpose

Despite this strong theme of continuity, two additional chief characteristics emerge—a shifting sense of time and purpose. One of the new realities retirees face is what to do with time. While freedom from work is a highly prized cultural ideal, its reality is much more challenging. The lack of a structured schedule and set of responsibilities means that weekends are no longer a respite from the workweek. Each day must be filled with something to do, and, for many, working part-time or volunteering becomes a primary focus.

Deciding what to do with time is an emerging question, as are questions about how much time one has. As Fischer and Simmons note,

> The central theme of the embarkation into older adulthood for a majority of persons is that one moves from a life's work into a period of indeterminate length without a culturally sanctioned agenda, and where choices await regarding use of time and resources, purpose for living, and relationships to be nurtured. . . . Although the transition is relatively brief, no one can predict how long older adulthood will last for any individual, creating both uncertainty and difficulty in planning.[21]

This mixture of newfound freedom and uncertainty about how long one's health or finances can sustain a particular way of life makes discernment about one's choices a real challenge.

What to do with time is one challenge. How time *feels* is another. Some experience a sense of urgency, that time is limited and now is the time to live a dream. According to Fisher and Simmons, it can be "catch-up time, now time, fulfillment time." People may want to face some "unfinished business" in their life, overcome some deficit (e.g., become literate), or expand their horizons (e.g., educational and travel programs). The "bucket list" has become a popular cultural symbol for the urgency of time in late adulthood. The urgency is framed by the sense that people begin to count the time to death rather than from birth.[22]

Identity, Intimacy, and Generativity—Again

Separating from full-time work to spending time in other ways impacts one's sense of identity and purpose. Not only does one have to shift one's activities, one also has to substitute "alternative sources of need satisfaction, develop new criteria for self-evaluation, reintegrating one's values and life goals."[23] Following Erikson's epigenetic principle, Bateson describes the psychosocial crises of Adulthood II as "engagement vs. withdrawal." The basic strength is "active wisdom" (as distinct from "receptive wisdom" in old age) and the core pathology, "indifference."[24] Active wisdom is

> culled from long lives and rich experience, the most acceptable and positive trait associated with longevity, but combines it with energy and commitment in the context of a new freedom from some kinds of

day-to-day-responsibility, a freedom that challenges expectations and may even be frightening. Together these produce the *active wisdom* that older adults have to offer, which gives them the potential for altering the shape of public and family life in America.[25]

Bateson expands Erikson's idea that the central developmental challenge of each stage is reengaged in later stages. The identity crises of adolescence, the intimacy crisis of young adulthood, and the generativity crises of Adulthood I emerge in new ways. Our "health longevity" in Adulthood II, for instance, presents us with a new identity challenge: "How can this time in my life complete or balance what came before? How do these years form an aesthetic unity?"[26] Questions of intimacy arise as relationships shift (children are raised and couples adjust to being alone together; some divorce and some forge new commitments; single life requires companionship), and generativity emerges in trying to make a difference for others (caring for adult children, a spouse, grandchildren, or engagement in community efforts).[27] Thus, questions of identity (Who am I?) are strongly linked to questions of intimacy (Who is my community?) and generativity (What difference can I make?). How a person answers these questions will determine the quality of late adulthood, according to Fisher and Simmons, and contribute to its successful completion.[28]

Vocational Experiences in Late Adulthood

The key characteristics of late adulthood—continuation of middle adulthood activity, a changing sense of time, voluntary choices, and involuntary circumstances—are the context for the primary experiences of calling. The questions of calling that one faced in young adulthood—Who am I? What can I do? For and with whom?—emerge again in late adulthood, highlighting the fact that vocation is never over. However, exploring questions of identity, capacity, and community in late adulthood is distinctive.

First, each person has a life narrative composed of years of experience that pose as the answers she once gave to those questions. Late adulthood is not a blank slate—the individual has become someone, done something, and made commitments and choices. Who one is and what he can do are interpreted in light of his circumstance—he has followed, or not, certain callings. Second, the future is open but not limitless; choices must be made *within* the choices that have thus far shaped a person's life. And, third, callings arise in situations not of our own choosing but to which we must respond. When a person discerns and responds to callings in late adulthood, she does so within a life history as well as in the current circumstances and possible futures that are available to her.

In this section I examine four vocational experiences of late adulthood: meaningful work; making a difference; facing loss; and the spiritual journey of reconciling with self, God, others, and death. These experiences highlight some of the central themes of calling: discerning one's gifts, finding purpose, responding in a place not of one's choosing, and living with authenticity.

Meaningful Work

As noted, retirement, for those who have worked in full-time paid employment for many years, marks one of the most crucial vocational experiences in life. A significant calling comes to an end. For many the image of retirement as the "golden years" of recreation, a prolonged vacation, has little appeal. What, then, can a person do with the gift of time in these years? In his book *Encore: Finding Work that Matters in the Second Half of Life*, Marc Freedman, co-founder of Experience Corps and The Purpose Prize, reports that adults are "eschewing retirement in either traditional or reinvented forms, they are instead opting for work. But they are renegotiating this relationship in order to work in new ways, on new terms, and to new ends. . . . Some are taking existing skills and applying them to new needs, while others are launching entirely new vocations, or even creating new organizations and businesses as social entrepreneurs."[29]

Leaving one place of work and beginning another kind of work or changing the amount of time given to work is an opportunity to explore work as a calling. After Martin Luther's revolutionary teaching on vocation in the Protestant Reformation (discussed in Chapter 1), calling became synonymous with work in the Protestant tradition to the extent that God's purposes aligned with one's work or profession.[30] This trajectory had several unfortunate outcomes. First, Christians equated their role or position with fulfilling God's will, thereby passively accepting the status quo. Second, the connection between God and the calling to work faded and by the twentieth century dimmed entirely.

If work has been a central calling in a person's life, embracing work in late adulthood after retirement is a chance to become clearer about one's motivations and intentions to work. To what extent does my work define my identity? Have I placed too great an emphasis on work as a source of my self-worth? Is there a way in which work has become an idol in my life? Might God be calling me to a period of Sabbath before I take on more work? Continuing to work, then, requires discernment.[31]

The Protestant tradition has also understood the calling to work in relationship to the Spirit's gifts for service to the common good. Placing work in this theological context can help people reframe work as a calling whether their work is a choice or a necessity. In Paul's understanding of the Spirit's gifts, charisms are not all given at birth or given for a lifetime. The Spirit can send forth new gifts at any time in a person's life. Thus, it is not too late for God to grace a person with new gifts. What gifts do people have at this point in life and how best can they use them? But perhaps most important, certain kinds of work can ignite a calling to service in ways a person may not have experienced in young or middle adulthood.

Making a Difference

Service for the common good is a strong theme in late adulthood literature. People with time, resources, and creativity want to make a difference, embodying the kind of boldness we see in Anna and Simeon in Jane Patterson's biblical reflection on the text from Luke.[32] They want their generative years to impact not only their children and grandchildren, but a wider community and world. Many have the time to serve in ways that they did not in middle adulthood where their time went to maintaining households or managing the workplace, as discussed by Matt Bloom in the previous chapter. Bateson, for example, has an activist view of late adulthood. "I am proposing a new activism on the part of older adults that was not on behalf of older adults—though both are important—an activism on behalf of the future beyond our lifetimes, more similar to the Gray Panthers than to the AARP."[33] Bateson recognizes the power of "an entire cohort with something new to offer to the world as years of experience combined with continuing health."[34] Of course, she is referring primarily to those persons who have the financial resources to do so without being remunerated. The pressing question for them is: "What work do I have yet to do for the world?"

The Peace Corps is recruiting people 50 and older using the phrase "Hear the Call."[35] For most of its history, only 1 percent of its volunteers were over 50; more recently, 6 percent are over 50 (of the total of 7,733 members).[36] Churches are also getting retirees involved in service. For example, NOMADs, a ministry of the Global Ministries of the United Methodist Church, seeks people who are "looking for retirement with a purpose, enjoy traveling in an RV, want to share their Christian faith, enjoy using their skills in service to others."[37] As part of his founding of Encore, an organization focused on meaningful work after retirement, Marc Freedman has created The Purpose Prize for people over age 60 "who combine passion and experience for social good."[38] He notes that the baby boomers are going to work for many reasons but that "the real force driving people to find *meaningful* work is not economic or social, but personal. It's that inner voice calling for something as simple as a change of pace, as ambitious as changing the world, as profound as reclaiming a dream deferred before it is denied."[39]

But churches should also be communities that recognize that not all people in this phase have numerous options for service, travel, and opportunity. Some, as discussed below, will be restrained by the demands of caregiving, have health issues, or have to continue working in jobs that are not fulfilling. The spokespersons of the new activism almost entirely ignore the poor, those over 60 without the economic means to remake their lives. But churches can be communities that affirm and acknowledge the gifts for service among the poor, and they can offer those without choices a way of thinking about their lives as a calling. In other words, the poor are not viewed as mere recipients of the new activists' callings to service, but rather, in a Christian theology of vocation, everyone is called, and the Spirit blesses all with gifts for service. How can the church challenge those with much, as well as those with little, to see their work as service to the common good?

Making Sense of Losses

As strong as the cultural messages are about making late adulthood a time of social activism and self-fulfillment, it is also a time of real loss, loss that cuts across socioeconomic groups, race, and gender. Loss is experienced in multiple ways: role and relationship loss (through retirement or death), functional loss (permanent bodily changes),[40] material loss (relocating one's home or place of work), and systemic loss (communities formed at work, neighborhood, and family).[41] Pastor and writer Janice Jean Springer was diagnosed with Parkinson's disease, and as her body changed she faced multiple losses—her self-image, spiritual grounding, and being able to trust her body all vanished as she has struggled with the disease. But, she writes, "perhaps the most painful loss of all: I've lost my illusions. I've lost the illusion that I am exempt from the losses and limits that besiege other people."[42]

Of course, it is not the first set of losses in a person's life. By this point, losses have accumulated. Loss has a memory. Losses in late adulthood can trigger the grief attached to previous losses and anticipate future losses, even the ultimate loss of one's own life.

How is calling related to loss? In my book *The Stories We Live*, I explore the calling of loss through the preposition "from." I write, "God calls us ultimately *from* our losses. It might sound strange to say that God calls us to grieve, but it seems that grieving is the only way to get *from* here *to* there." The point of grieving is not to forget what was lost, but to move away from the strength the loss holds in our hearts and to form new attachments. In late adulthood this emotional and relational work presents a difficult challenge since these losses are closely aligned with the commitments one made in younger and middle adulthood. Grief presents the challenge of reconstructing identity, roles, and relationships, and the capacity to do so will be strongly impacted by one's physical and emotional health and social networks.

Reconciling with Self, Others, God, and Death

If there is a calling to a new social activism in late adulthood, there is also the calling to the pilgrimage within. The theologian of spirituality Belden Lane writes, "Only a few years away from retirement, I sensed I was being called more deeply into the practice of the wild."[43] This meant leaving behind a successful calling as a university professor, teacher, and scholar, but Lane experienced a call to deepen his lifelong calling to spiritual practice, in his case, in the wilderness. "My hope was to trade the mind of the scholar for the heart of a vagabond poet. I'd always walked the edge between the two but yearned now for a deeper plunge into the other side."[44] Lane chose to respond to the call of the inner journey, but Springer had no choice. Over time, she relinquished the fight with Parkinson's and embraced the changes and limits it brought to her life as a spiritual practice. "Parkinson's is the hermitage where I slow down, pay attention, and concentrate on what is needful in the moment."[45]

Late adulthood is a time to reconcile with one's self, with others, with God, and with one's death. These tasks are also part of older adulthood, but they begin in late adulthood when people may have more time and emotional strength to face some of the hard realities of their lives. The calling is to introspection, searching one's life story, and engaging in life review.[46] Fisher and Simmons note that it can be a time when adults "attack the unfinished business accumulated through life, to overcome deficits, to mend fences and renew relationships."[47]

Both religious and secular literature is replete with the message that one's calling is found in the discovery of the true self, which is often found in the late adult years.[48] Parker Palmer, in his well-known book *Let Your Life Speak,* which was written when he was 60, tells the story of how living through a false self, which he constructed in his early and middle adult years, led to depression and poor health. Finding his true self was akin to a pilgrimage through those years and not until he reached later adulthood was he able to live fully who he knew himself to be.[49]

The idea of a true self and a false self has deep roots in Christian thought, primarily in Paul's admonition that "you have stripped off the old self with its practices and have clothed yourselves with the new self" (Col. 3:9–10). God may be inviting persons in late adulthood to shed the false self that is built up through work, marriage, and relationships. There may be parts of people's lives they are not proud of, actions taken that bring shame and guilt, or stories they hope remain hidden. Late adulthood is a pivotal time to grapple with a truer self because people may have the emotional energy and strength to engage the hard work of forgiveness and, in some cases, reconciliation with others, capacities which may become diminished in older age. God's overwhelming love and mercy may be just the grace people need at this point in their lives to accept and find some peace about the life they have lived thus far, which clears the way for hearing God's call about what is next.

Christian spiritual writers are also giving attention to the spiritual life in late adulthood, a period in which growth can occur in different ways than in young adulthood. The Catholic Franciscan priest Richard Rohr describes two halves of life as developmental rather than chronological. The first half consists of "building a strong container," an identity, purpose, and direction for one's life commitments and work, and the second half emerges through an important "falling."[50] According to Rohr, the falling that must occur is some form of "necessary suffering," a transgression, a failure, a stumbling stone, something that "we must fall into" in the sense that it is "more done to you than anything you do yourself."[51] The crucial notion here is that the kind of spiritual growth that needs to happen in late adulthood will not initially feel as if it is chosen.

The crucial turning, according to Rohr, is clarifying, purifying, and reimagining "the task within the task," that is, the intentions and motives for what one does.[52] The second half of life is living out our true self, the blueprint of ourselves that was created at our conception. The task in late adulthood is integrative—not rejecting the first half of life, but discerning what to keep and what to let go of. Rohr frames the vocational question in this way: "How can I honor the legitimate needs of the first half of life, while creating space, vision, time, and grace for the second? *The holding of this tension is the very shape of wisdom.*"[53] The falling, then, is "falling upward," learning that the secret of life is that "*the way up is the way down. Or, if you prefer, the way down is the way up.*"[54]

Falling upward links the rhythm of late adult life to the Paschal Mystery—the dying and rising to new life that marks the Christian life. Some in late adulthood may hear the calling to a deeper dying of the self. The first half of life, according to Catholic spiritual theologians Francis Nemeck and Marie Theresa Coombs, is lived (faithfully) by the claim "*I must increase so that Christ may increase,*" but the second half of the spiritual journey is relinquishing the self that we have constructed and shifts to the words of John the Baptist in John's Gospel, "*I must decrease so that Christ may increase*" (3:30).[55] By living more deeply into the mystery of God, as Jane Patterson demonstrates from the Mary and Martha story,[56] some are able to draw their lives away from the self-made self and more fully toward the imitation of Christ.[57] But the calling may be to stillness and listening even in the midst of the demands of community.

Framing the spiritual journey in terms of two halves of life may not fit or appeal to all in late adulthood.[58] What it points to, though, is that persons can experience a new way of relating to God in late adulthood as they undergo multiple changes. Such a journey opens the possibility of awakening to a new understanding of God, one that is no longer small, punitive, or tribal. It may be the calling to be in relationship to the God beyond God. This is the essential mystery of vocation to which Jesus submits in the darkness of Gethsemane: to surrender into unknowing and to trust that God still lies beyond.

Reconciling with death and dying is also part of late adulthood. Death becomes a vocational experience when mortality, one's own and others', is confronted. Death becomes more frequent in one's network of family, friends, and acquaintances. The generation ahead is closer to death as parents, aunts, uncles, and friends are buried. Persons in late adulthood gradually become aware that they are "the next generation" as the likelihood of their own dying grows nearer.

While death may not be imminent, questions about one's dying do arise: "What does my death mean in light of my calling now? How do I want to die and what choices can I make now to prepare for a good death?" Death may place an urgency on a sense of calling: "How can I change my life once and for all, to be more generous, loving, and mindful of others?" Death reminds us that callings are temporal and do not last forever: "What do I need to do to prepare for my own dying?"[59]

Communal Dynamics in Late Adulthood

Adults in later adulthood can and do experience a profound sense of calling in and through relationships. In fact, social connection and meaningful community support are crucial to late adulthood well-being, in receiving emotional and physical support as well as in giving to others, building up a community, and making a difference. As Fisher and Simmons point out, without the purpose of full-time employment for many people, "relationships may take on more importance."[60] Just as family relationships shift, friendship is an important calling in late adulthood since friends can accompany one another in grief and serious illness as well as explore new opportunities through study and travel. As Lyon notes, crucial to emotional health in later adulthood is "the ability to use current relationships and memories of earlier life events as sources of soothing and emotional vitality."[61] I will highlight two emerging roles—grandparent and caregiver—that mark new responsibilities for many persons in late adulthood.

Grandparenting

As Bateson notes, we have the first four-generation society in history. Most societies have had three generations, the third generation marked by old age, withdrawal from adult roles, and shifting contributions to the well-being of the family. Today's grandparents are different from those in the past, she writes.

Now, however, older adults, many of whom are grandparents but who have an unprecedented level of health and energy, time and resources, fit into society in new ways, often much like younger adults. And for the first time in history there are large numbers of *great*-grandparents, who look and act somewhat, but not precisely, the way grandparents used to.[62]

Furthermore, given the changing configuration of families, grandparents will be called into new relationships with stepchildren and stepgrandchildren and grandchildren from same-sex unions.[63] Surprisingly, this relationship is not explored extensively in either social science or theological literature.[64]

The grandparent-grandchild relationship is conditioned by many factors, the temporal context being a primary one. The "relationships, like individuals, are not static, but dynamic; they change and are reconceptualized over time as grandchildren mature and grandparents age."[65] Grandparents who are in their fifties, for instance, tend to be more active with children in terms of play, socializing, and travel, as compared to grandparents in their eighties. The type of relationship grandparents have with teens also varies by their age (one study found younger adolescent children value grandparents more than older adolescents), and young adults, as one study found, renegotiate relationships with grandparents as they enter adulthood, many reporting that grandparents are important, valued, and influential and that the relationship has more of a "reciprocal exchange of social and instrumental behaviors," in which the young adult can give more to a grandparent.[66]

The calling to become a grandparent is not one that can be chosen,[67] but when a person becomes a grandparent she can choose how to respond to this new role. The calling emerges in the context of the relationships, figuring out how to respond to both her adult child who is now a parent and to a new life who has joined the family. What kind of grandmother do I want to be—similar to my own or different? What is God calling me to in this new set of relationships? What is in the best interest of my child, of my child's spouse or partner? Of my grandchild? What am I able to do? What are my gifts for being a grandparent?

The call to be a grandparent can be embraced in a variety of ways.[68] First is the call to love. Grandparents provide a "natural safety net, a second ring of protection to guarantee" the nurturing of children.[69] Because grandparents have the chance to love unconditionally without the burden of parental responsibility,[70] they offer children much-needed emotional support. Second is the call to be a storyteller. Grandparents can be the link to the family's past and its genealogy. One woman remembers her grandmother "taking me on trips through her memories."[71] Most grandparents, living through historical change, are a link to "what it was like to live when" in different social and cultural situations. The telling and retelling of family stories is key to Erikson's notion of "cogwheeling."[72] By telling stories of their past, grandparents are able to integrate and find new meaning in "unfinished components in themselves,"[73] thus enhancing their own well-being. But storytelling also teaches, models, and nurtures grandchildren by forming a bond, a sense of identity, and attachment to the family history.

A third calling is to be a teacher and mentor. Grandparents can both draw out gifts, skills, and abilities from grandchildren and share their own gifts and skills, passing on the wisdom they have learned from work, family, and community life. For those who do not have biological grandchildren, volunteer opportunities in schools, daycares, or churches give them a chance to "be a grandparent" to children outside their family, engendering a sense of generativity to the larger community. A fourth calling is witnessing how to age with dignity and honor, which includes respecting the potential and limits of one's body and mind, remaining faithful in the face of adversities, and keeping a sense of humor.

The call to grandparenting is more than love, storytelling, mentoring, and teaching, however. In both animals and humans, older members of the group contribute to what evolutionary psychologists call "inclusive fitness," that is, the survival of the group and the passing on of its genetic makeup. Bateson notes, "The presence of grandparents—particularly maternal grandmothers—reduces infant and child mortality . . . increases the likelihood that children will grow up to pass on their genes, presumably the same genes that kept their grandparents healthy and supportive."[74] Furthermore, grandparents provide stability and safety during parental divorce, serious illness or death, and substance abuse.

The quality of the grandparent-grandchild relationship is dependent on many factors. One is the extent to which parents, and other family members, are committed to "kinkeeping," providing the necessary means by which the generations stay connected, which can be impacted by how close one lives to grandchildren (e.g., visits, holidays, communication, hospitality).[75] Another is gender, with same-sex ties being among the strongest, especially between grandmothers and granddaughters.[76] Age also is a key factor, with older grandparents less able to be actively involved in younger persons' lives, though they can maintain strong emotional ties. "A sick bed may be one's call to be a 'sabbath' grandparent—one who, like God, rested after the work was done. But the love in their heart can still be directed toward those who come into their presence."[77] Finally, while three-generation families living in the same home are common among immigrant groups, there is no clear pattern—some families maintain traditional bonds and others move apart due to language, economic, and social differences. Class may be more of a factor; having fewer economic resources presses many poor families into "obligatory rather than voluntary support."[78]

Increasing numbers of grandparents find themselves parenting their grandchildren, which makes them vocationally "off time" with their peers.[79] The task of taking on the parenting role involves what religious educator Anne Wimberly calls "intercessory hope," the "act of standing with and for their grandchildren in the parents' stead in order to make possible their grandchildren's worthwhile present and future life."[80] Their intercession begins with a consciousness of some suffering or tragedy that they cannot overlook, that calls on them to "open the door and make room for their grandchildren," thereby committing themselves to their care. But this calling is not easy, as Wimberly reports. In her research on families, many grandparents who were parenting children reported loneliness, fear about their health, and anger, sadness, and guilt about the parents' situations. But necessity and choice of becoming a parent to one's grandchildren is also filled with hope. "There is also a sense in which the call to carry out intercessory hope along the grandparents' journey of second-parenting holds within it a special opportunity to leave a legacy."[81] The faith community can honor them with a sense of calling. Wimberly notes that they are models for "what it means to strive for a context of meaning in the midst of adversity and challenge, when a sense of meaning is lost or called into question," and "what it means to grasp the Story of God that unfolds into a future that is not known but that is worthy of pressing toward."[82]

Caregiving

Grandparents becoming parents to grandchildren is one of the many ways that people take up the tasks, and calling, of caregiving. Like grandparenting, caregiving is not something generally chosen, but when circumstances dictate, as in the story of Ruth and Naomi, caring for another person becomes a place one can experience God's call to service. Caregiving is not an easy calling for many, and may in fact not be experienced as a calling. The challenges of caring for a child, a spouse, or an elderly parent (or extended family member), day-in and day-out, is a rigorous path filled with burdens and joys. As theologian Edward Hahnenberg notes, "suffering interrupts," and God's call may come through the suffering of others. The place where a person can hear God's call is sometimes at the foot of the cross.[83]

Researchers, policymakers, and church leaders recognize that caregiving is a widespread phenomenon.[84] A recent report, *Caregiving in the U.S.*, states that 39 percent of adults are caregivers, and of these, 60 percent are women. Their average age is 49, in fact, earlier than late adulthood, which means caregiving impacts the full range of adult life.[85] Older caregivers, within the range of late adulthood as discussed here, are more likely to care for a spouse; are less likely to be employed; and take on the tasks of negotiating with healthcare professionals, managing finances, and advocating for their care recipient. Forty-six percent of them reported that care places a high burden of stress on their lives.[86] Half said they had no choice in taking on their responsibilities; they report high stress and strain from caregiving, often because the care recipient has more needs, they feel less prepared, and they have fewer resources.[87]

A sense of calling provides a much-needed framework for caregivers. According to social scientist Jennifer F. Dobbins, "Much of the stress comes not from what they do, but rather from the meanings they ascribe to what they do."[88] According to Dobbins, that meaning is found within relationships, which are "constantly being reconfigured and renegotiated." A person is a caregiver but she is also a spouse, daughter, relative, parent, or friend. "Family caregiving never takes place in a vacuum but is rather woven in the rich matrix of activities, events, roles, and relationships that make up our lives."[89] The relational dimensions of caregiving are played out across multiple relationships that influence each other, not just the caregiver-recipient dyad that many researchers and practitioners (and probably ministers) focus on. Caregivers are in a relationship with other important people (the recipient as well as other family members and the network of support), other caregivers through support groups and online resources, and themselves.[90] Caregivers make meaning through sharing their experiences with others, Dobbins reports from her research on online support groups. "Caregivers bring their life experiences online, take their revised life stories offline, and then return with new stories based on their latest real-life experience."[91]

The Protestant theologian Karl Barth, borrowing from Dietrich Bonhoeffer, reframed Luther's understanding of vocation as a "place of responsibility" by noting that the divine summons comes to us right where we are. Many caregivers, even in the midst of their struggles and burdens, note that they could not do otherwise. Faith, for Barth, is the primary calling; the general calling to respond to the gospel comes first. General calling, as noted in chapter 1, may provide a larger framework that can give caregivers and care recipients a sense that God's call to discipleship comes regardless but that their particular situation is precisely where God's call can be experienced. Being connected to a community that names and supports callings, caregivers may find language, meaning, and direction in the place of their calling.

Ending Late Adulthood

The transition from extended middle age to older adult lifestyle in Fisher and Simmons's framework is "always life changing, often involuntary," characterized by both seriousness and uncertainty. The most common experiences that end the first period and introduce the first transition are changes in health from which there is not a complete recovery, death of a spouse or divorce, a major move, or the recognition that one needs more help. The ending of late adulthood occurs when middle-age activities, such as employment and physical activities such as hiking or biking, or travel, come to an end. The key indicators are the "presence of change and need for accommodation, uncertainty about the present and future, and the inability to sustain a middle-age lifestyle."[92]

Health changes can be sudden, as with a stroke or cancer diagnosis, or gradual, in the case of a worsening chronic condition such as arthritis or diabetes. Changes in health mean one's activities change and probably lessen, and a person may need therapy and care for a period of time. Difficult questions emerge: How long will I be sick? Will I recover? If I don't, what capacities will I have? After a serious health crisis, adults between late and older adulthood must adjust to a "new normal."

These changes are mostly involuntary, though some adults do voluntarily downsize their household, give up activities, and make plans for their later years. Most people, however, face this transition without choice. According to Fisher and Simmons, it is "qualitatively different and potentially more significant and tumultuous than any of life's previous transitions because of degrees of intensity—it is liminal and a threshold must be crossed."[93] It matters, then, whether a person encounters and can sustain a sense of calling, a deep connection to God and other people, that gives life purpose, direction, and meaning as late adulthood ends and a new time in life emerges.

Suggested Readings

Bateson, Mary Catherine. *Composing a Further Life: The Age of Active Wisdom.* New York: Knopf, 2010.

Demick, Jack, and Carrie Andreoletti, eds. *Handbook of Adult Development.* New York: Springer, 2003.

Gutowski, Carolyn. *Grandparents Are Forever.* Mahwah, NJ: Paulist, 1994.

Fisher, James C., and Henry C. Simmons. *A Journey Called Aging: Challenges and Opportunities in Older Adulthood.* New York: Routledge, 2006.

Freedman, Marc. *Encore: Finding Work that Matters in the Second Half of Life.* New York: PublicAffairs, 2007.

Lyon, K. Brynolf. "Faith and Development in Late Adulthood." In *Human Development and Faith,* edited by Felicity B. Kelcourse, 269–84. St. Louis, MO: Chalice, 2004.

Josselson, Ruthellen, Amia Lieblich, and Dan P. McAdams, eds. *The Meaning of Others: Narrative Studies of Relationships.* Washington, DC: American Psychological Association, 2007.

Palmer, Parker. *Let Your Life Speak: Listening for the Voice of Vocation.* San Francisco: Jossey-Bass, 2000.

Rohr, Richard. *Falling Upward: A Spirituality of the Two Halves of Life.* San Francisco: Jossey-Bass, 2011.

Wimberly, Anne E. Streaty. "From Intercessory Hope to Mutual Intercession: Grandparents Raising Grandchildren and the Church's Response." *Family Ministry* 14, no. 3 (Fall 2000): 19–27.

Wolfteich, Claire. *Navigating New Terrain: Work and Women's Spiritual Lives.* Mahwah, NJ: Paulist, 2002.

Blessing the Next Generation

Jane Patterson

One of the most surprising things the Bible has to say about death occurs in the very beginning, when the first man and woman are exiled from Eden. God muses that the human beings have become in some way like gods, having eaten from the tree of the knowledge of good and evil, so God sets cherubim and a flaming sword to guard the way back to Eden, lest the people "take also from the tree of life, and eat, and live forever" (Gen. 3:24). While the need to prevent Adam and Eve from eating of the tree of life happens at the time of their banishment from paradise, the way in which the caution is expressed sounds as though it's obvious that it would not be a good thing for humans to live forever, that death is appropriate to our place in the creation. The psalms speak frequently of the lifespan of human beings as being like that of the grass: tender and beautiful when it springs up, but vulnerable and short-lived, especially in comparison to the nature of God:

> As for mortals, their days are like grass;
>   they flourish like a flower of the field;
> for the wind passes over it, and it is gone,
>   and its place knows it no more.
> But the steadfast love of the LORD is from everlasting to everlasting
>   on those who fear him,
>   and his righteousness to children's children,
> to those who keep his covenant
>   and remember to do his commandments.
>   (Ps. 103:15–18)

Here, human life participates in what endures not by its own strength, but on account of being embedded in God's steadfast love, generation after generation, particularly as people relate consistently to God through covenantal living. This psalm encapsulates the virtue of the human lifespan, biblically speaking: though short, human life can mediate a love that is not subject to death when we live as a channel for the love that God holds for the whole creation, as expressed in the covenant. Joyce Mercer's story of Liz in the following chapter exemplifies an older adult who remains an open channel for God's love to those around her.

We see in the accounts of the last days of the patriarchs that impending death brings its own vocational tasks and responsibilities, chiefly the responsibility to bless the next generation. The stories of Jacob and Esau at the approach of Isaac's death (Genesis 27) and of Joseph and his brothers at the time of Jacob's death (Genesis 49) offer a contrast in family dynamics that can sometimes be seen even today when families approach the death of their matriarch or patriarch. Isaac's impending death opens up fault-lines in the family, fault-lines that had always existed, but had perhaps not been so visible until his final blessing was at stake. From the beginning, Jacob had been the favorite of his mother Rebecca, while Esau had taken after his father Isaac. Esau was seconds older than his twin brother, Jacob, so the primary blessing would ordinarily have been his as a birthright. At the urging of his mother, Jacob tricks his brother and deceives his blind father, in effect stealing his brother's blessing. In one of several heartrending passages in the story, the stunned Esau says to Isaac, "Have you only one blessing, father? Bless me also, father!" (Gen. 27:38). The drama turns on the understanding that there is only one blessing that Isaac can give and that a choice must be made between the two sons. The parents' preferences for a particular son, the natural differences between the two boys, and the sense that there could be only one blessing all work together to create havoc in the family until the brothers finally meet again many years later, and Esau initiates a generous reconciliation.

The next generation begins with even more chaos in the family. Once again, the parents' choosing of favorites among the children creates division and competition that comes to a climax when Joseph's elder brothers play a trick on him that goes horribly wrong. When Joseph is sold into slavery in Egypt, the remaining eleven brothers have to live with the unending grief and decline of their father as an ongoing reminder of the guilty secret they are ashamed to share. But this story comes to a different conclusion when Joseph, who has done well in life, makes the surprising decision to forgive his brothers rather than seek justice for their childhood crime. In doing so,

Joseph imitates his uncle Esau more than his father Jacob. But before Jacob dies, he has a chance to bless not only a chosen son, but each and all of his sons in an extended prophecy that concludes, "All these are the twelve tribes of Israel, and this is what their father said to them when he blessed them, blessing each one of them with a suitable blessing" (Gen. 49:28).

These contrasting stories of the deaths of Isaac and Jacob raise the ways in which a significant death in a family can be a time of destruction or recon-ciliation. Issues of vocation arise on both sides of the deathbed. The one dying has a chance to consider his invisible but substantial legacy of blessing, while those who stand in attendance have the chance to mend old hurts or to pull apart the fabric of the family. The end of the story of Jacob's death describes all that was felt to be a good ending to a life well lived: "When Jacob ended his charge to his sons, he drew up his feet into the bed, breathed his last, and was gathered to his people" (Gen. 49:33). The physical and the spiritual meet in Jacob's end, as he gives his last and most important gift to his sons, makes the last movements he is able to with his body, and then joins the unseen but significant company of all who have gone before him.

8

Older Adulthood

Vocation at Life's End

JOYCE ANN MERCER

O God, from my youth you have taught me,
and I still proclaim your wondrous deeds.
So even to old age and gray hairs,
O God, do not forsake me,
until I proclaim your might
to all the generations to come.

(Ps. 71:17–18, NRSV)

What does vocation in older adulthood look like? When I ask this question of people in faith communities, their responses usually indicate that while they are loathe to suggest that older adults are not called by God, at the same time it is almost impossible to imagine what vocation means or what forms it might take in older adulthood. Perhaps such imagining is particularly difficult in the context of North American fast-paced, agenda-driven life, where many struggle to recognize God's calling apart from specific forms of activity. And yet throughout the ages, the Christian tradition clings to the notion that God claims us and invites us to participate in the life of God in the world as the very people we are, in the very ages and conditions in which we live at a given time. The words of the psalmist, above, make clear this conviction that God's involvement with God's people extends from the days of youth "even to old age and gray hairs."

For older adulthood the idea that God continues to call people into the last years of life means affirming that whether or not we can walk by our own power, reason clearly with our minds, articulate spoken language in ways that others can comprehend, or hear and see clearly through our senses, our lives are of value and importance, useful in the purposes of God. In this chapter, "older adulthood" refers to the portion of the lifespan beyond late adulthood, when life appears less like an extension of one's middle adult years than like a culmination period, in which increasingly the body wears out, the mind may show evidence of less clarity, and one's focus is less on activity than at other times of life. Perhaps a better name for this stage would be "oldest adulthood," the span of years generally beginning at some point in the ninth decade of life and ending in death.

Awakening to Vocation in Older Adulthood

At the age of 88, Liz lives independently in the same fashionable downtown high-rise condominium she has occupied for almost thirty years. It takes a little longer for her to answer the door than it used to because she now uses a motorized scooter to get around, the result of progressive neuropathy in her feet that has made walking a chore for a number of years. Although many of the physical challenges of aging bring difficulties for her ("I can't just get up and go whenever I want to. And everything takes longer"), she seems unfazed. Liz has weathered her share of tragedy and struggle over the years—breast cancer in her fifties and the murder of her sister years before that—and has accompanied countless others through difficulties in her role as a Presbyterian minister.

Moving slowly and methodically, her eyes twinkle as she ushers me into her home, filled with her books and collections of sacred art and pottery. She loves to have visitors who come to stay with her. Liz's special charism is hospitality. She continues to welcome people in, even though she now gets help with house cleaning and assistance setting things up in the kitchen for ease of preparation once the groceries are delivered. As always there are fresh flowers on the table and a place set to receive a guest. A few years ago, she would have prepared a dinner party for twelve; now she makes a restaurant reservation in the neighborhood, navigating there on her motorized scooter. "I can't do all that anymore, but thankfully there are other ways."

Nearly two decades ago, new love came into Liz's life when she got to know Jim. When he moved into the apartment upstairs from hers, the two became constant companions. Jim shares with Liz a love of art, music, the church, and life in the city. The two of them enjoy concerts and art galleries, cooking, and entertaining friends. It has been a relationship of deep joy shared with others. But a few months ago, Jim suffered a bad fall in his apartment, and during the rehabilitation cognitive confusion set in. He is now in a nearby care facility. Liz spends Saturdays with him. Liz and Jim had planned to live out their older adulthood by staying in their own homes and sharing an in-home caregiver with two other couples who lived in the same building. Jim's fall and cognitive decline put an end to those plans. Liz remains upbeat about her life even as she shares her sadness and loss: "Of course, it's a big disappointment. But we're old, and when you get older you can't always do things exactly as you planned. It's the reality. We've had lots of good times along the way." Aware of her privilege and the blessings of resources to help her manage the changes and losses of old age, Liz carries on, making modifications as needed to a well-practiced, grace-filled way of life.[1]

For Liz at 88 years old, vocation particularly manifests itself in the loving service of companioning Jim, in offering hospitality, albeit in modified forms dictated by the bodily limits of old age, in prayer and worship, and in preparatory practices toward dying well—in a sense, bestowing "blessings" on others as Isaac and Jacob did. But what about Jim? In younger years Jim shared his artistic gifts with others, as a curator of sacred art and a church musician. In what ways can we speak meaningfully about the vocation of older adults like Jim whose declining physical and cognitive status narrows their worlds and closes them in so that they appear unable to give? The task of understanding vocation in older adulthood is complicated by the vast differences exhibited among people within this life stage. Liz and Jim both are visibly identifiable to others and to themselves as old people. At the same time, they are variably positioned within older adulthood based on differing physical and cognitive statuses that govern their engagements with the world around them. Jim's situation presses the question of whether vocation remains a meaningful concept in the extremes of this life stage.

In distinction to the life stage named "late adulthood" in Kathleen Cahalan's chapter, older adulthood appears significantly removed from the middle adulthood life situation of which late adulthood constitutes an extension. A combination of factors signals a person's move into older adulthood: generally, a chronological age beyond 75 or 80 years; significant limitation on mobility and the need to use assistive devices for mobility;

the need for assistance with some or all activities of daily living such as bathing, dressing, and cooking; and the constancy of death among one's age cohort. As Cahalan points out, the end of late adulthood comes when adults move from primarily being caregivers to being care-receivers. Older adulthood, then, is often marked by a continuation and deepening of the losses named in late adulthood: loss of family and friends to death, loss of one's health or physical capacities, and loss of independence. John's Gospel captures well these experiences marking older adulthood: "Very truly, I tell you, when you were younger, you used to fasten your own belt and to go wherever you wished. But when you grow old, you will stretch out your hands, and someone else will fasten a belt around you and take you where you do not wish to go" (21:18, NRSV).

Do older adults, especially those sometimes referred to as the "frail elderly," have a vocation? The authors of this volume would be quick to assert that vocation is not a possession, not something we "have," so much as it is a gift from God into which we live across the ages of our lifespan. Still, such questions about what vocation means in older adulthood are not inquiries around which theologians typically expend much effort. When there is theological reflection on older adults, with a few notable exceptions,[2] it tends toward predictable (and even sappy) stereotypes of wisdom-figures or revered sages on pedestals, bearing little resemblance to the actual life experience of many older adults. Such tropes stand in contrast to the biblical picture Jane Patterson uncovers in this volume of an elder as a wisdom figure whose long years equip him to give counsel and to bless the next generations.[3] First-person reports from older adults themselves suggest that if today's older adults are on pedestals, those pedestals must be located in broom closets and basements where they are invisible and ignored. The gap between the ideal view of older adults in Christian tradition and the actuality of real people's lives in contemporary North America brings into question the credibility of theological claims that older adults continue to experience a calling. Currently, churches and their theologians suffer from a distinct inability to articulate the shape of vocation in the waning years of life.

The inability to speak meaningfully about the calling of older adults comes, in part, from a too-easy collapse of the notion of divine calling with work or career. This collapse seems to situate older adulthood beyond the boundaries of vocation, placing people of advanced years in a life space that somehow seems "finished with vocation" because they are not "productive" or contributing in ways typically recognized as love and service. Just as we may discount the vocations of children and youth as future events for which they currently are merely in training, the calling of older adults can seem like a past-tense phenomenon—something that applied to them back when they could walk, or something completed in that part of adult life before older adulthood.

But if vocation is about God's call to persons (and communities) claiming them across the whole of their lives, surely God calls older adults amid all their differences within the time of older adulthood, to vocations of service and love, too. Absent the features that play such a critical role in the preceding years of middle and even late adulthood, we instead find older adult vocation particularly emphasizing *who* we are as creatures of God, *how* we are in relationship (with God, with others), and *what* capacities we evoke in others, rather than what we produce or accomplish. In this sense, older adulthood, and especially the situation of frail older adults, provides the test case par excellence, along with infants and young children, for the sturdiness and credibility of theological claims about vocation: if, in fact, vocation is not merely about paid labor and productivity, but instead centers around the multiple ways we are gifted, claimed, and engaged to participate in God's life, then we should be able to articulate how God's call takes shape in older adulthood.[4]

When and how does vocation in older adulthood begin? While this life period sometimes is identified as beginning in a person's eighties, chronological time does not offer a particularly consistent clue about entrance into older adulthood and its callings. In comparison with other periods in the human lifespan, old age potentially occupies a large expanse of years and encompasses an equally broad diversity of conditions. Such breadth and diversity has caused gerontologists to configure time differently in relation to older adulthood. Instead of seeing it as a single stage with transitions in and out of it, gerontologists and lifecycle theorists pose schemas depicting older adulthood as made up of multiple phases and transitions within the larger period of life's late years.

Erikson's "Ninth Stage"

Erik Erikson was among those concerned with charting the human life course who had trouble accounting for the diversity in older adulthood. Perhaps this lacunae is a byproduct of the fact that, in contrast to other times in the lifecycle, when scholars write about older adulthood they generally write about a life space they have yet to experience firsthand. In the last years before his own death at the age of 91, Erikson made critical notes in his copy of his book *The Life Cycle Completed*. After his death, his wife Joan used these notes to rectify what Erikson had recognized as an inadequacy in his eight stages of human development by adding chapters to create a "ninth stage":

> Old age in one's eighties and nineties brings with it new demands, reevaluations, and daily difficulties. These concerns can only be adequately discussed, and confronted, by designating a new ninth stage to clarify the challenges. We must now see and understand the final life cycle stages through late-eighty- and ninety-year-old eyes. . . . Despair, which haunts the eighth stage, is a close companion in the ninth because it is almost impossible to know what emergencies and losses of physical ability are imminent.[5]

Joan Erikson goes on to note that in Erikson's developmental framework, expressions of the tensions in the other eight stages generally lead with the syntonic element focused on growth and expansion (e.g., "trust"), followed by the dystonic element second (e.g., "mistrust"), which is thereby de-emphasized. In the case of old age, however, "we should recognize the fact that circumstances may place the dystonic in a more dominant position. Old age is inevitably such a circumstance."[6] This new ninth stage involves an integrative review of the previous eight stages through the lens of the particular challenges of older adulthood. For this purpose, Joan Erikson rewrites the descriptions of each point along the lifespan to put the dystonic descriptor first, "in order to underscore its prominence and potency."[7]

The result reads like a Niebuhrian-realist version of human development, in which the optimism of earlier appropriations of the well-known developmental framework is replaced by a strong sense of old age's troublesome features. The tensions in Erikson's developmental tasks get sorted out not in favor of the developmental triumph, but rather with a frank exploration of how the dystonic element in each earlier developmental phase shows up in a person's eighties and nineties. Speaking of autonomy in the developmental moment generally characterized by "autonomy vs. shame and doubt," for example, Joan Erikson writes: "Something of this doubt returns to elders as they no longer trust in their autonomy over their bodies and life choices. . . . Autonomy. Remember how it feels, how it always felt, to want everything your way. I suspect this drive continues to our last breath. When you were young, all the elders were stronger and more powerful; now the powerful are younger than you. . . . Shame and doubt challenge cherished autonomy."[8]

Perhaps the most significant revision to Erikson's lifespan theory brought about by its address through 90-year-old eyes is in the reassessment of the eighth stage, typically referred to as "integrity vs. despair and disgust," with "wisdom" as its subsequent virtue. Joan Erikson recalls that the eighth stage involves a retrospective accounting of one's life. But,

> as Erik has reminded us, "Despair expresses the feeling that the time is now short, too short for the attempt to start another life and to try out alternate roads." In one's eighties and nineties one may no longer have the luxury of such retrospective despair. Loss of capacities and disintegration may demand almost all of one's attention. One's focus may become thoroughly circumscribed by concerns of daily functioning so that it is enough just to get through a day intact, however satisfied or dissatisfied one feels about one's previous life history.[9]

The addition of a ninth stage to Erikson's lifespan schema underscores the reality that life and vocation in older adulthood are distinctive from other elder-years. Awakening to God's call in older adulthood takes form amid stark realities of decline with which persons inhabiting other parts of the lifespan do not wish to, and cannot, identify. Reimagining vocation in light of old age requires the recognition that such a calling must be able to integrate two distinct elements: being *called from* as well as being *called to* lives of love and service. I will say more about the aspect of older adulthood's vocation that involves being called from the demands and challenges of this life in this chapter's final section on dying as a feature of human vocation.

Fisher's Five-Part Framework

Like the Eriksons, James Fisher was unsatisfied with maps of adulthood containing only one location for older adults. Fisher, a specialist in adult education and development, outlines a schema positioning older adulthood in its multiplicity, beginning in a period in which a person does not even appear to be old due to this phase's continuity with middle age.[10] Cahalan uses Fisher's developmental framework in her chapter on late adulthood, which is identified by retirement and transitions out of the intensive work of parenting and paid employment.

Fisher holds that this more stable period of what we are calling late adulthood is followed by an early transition period, generally ushered in with turbulence occasioned by an illness, death of a spouse, or accident that forecloses the continuation of one's middle adulthood way of life. Perhaps the onset of cancer and its subsequent treatments disallow employment or childcare for grandchildren. Or difficulty bouncing back from an injury sustained in a fall brings new limitations on walking to the post office or preparing a dinner for friends. Perhaps adult children determine that their parent can no longer safely drive a car.

A "revised lifestyle" stage ensues from the transition to what we are calling older adulthood, identified by adaptations to circumstances brought on by loss, relocation, declining health, or diminished cognitive capacity. Fisher suggests that revising one's lifestyle to fit one's new situation becomes the point at which persons lay claim to the identity of old age, internalizing their affiliation with this age group. That is, certain realities, such as the need to use a walker to navigate safely across a room, disallow persons from continuing to categorize themselves as "not old." In fact, one of the awakening tasks to older adulthood is recognizing themselves as inhabiting a different life space than previously occupied because of changes in the body. Then comes a "later transition" defined by decreasing mobility and continuing health decline. In the last stable period that follows this transition, older adults live into the limits and possibilities posed to them by their situations, toward their dying to this life.

Fisher's template helps to clarify the entry point into older adulthood, which—if a person continues to live into the eighth or ninth decades (or beyond)—inevitably will take shape amid limitations wrought by bodily decline, experiences of loss, altered relationships and roles, and an increasing awareness of the shortness of time. At first glance, these realities marking the entrance to old age do not appear to be the raw materials out of which to reimagine vocation. Most descriptions of vocation have a forward-pressing, positive tone associated with growth, while these descriptions of aging speak of decline, debility, and even suffering. But if vocation across the lifespan unfolds around daily living with our choices and situations at all ages, then exploring those aspects of vocation brought to the foreground by the varied, sometimes unpleasant realities expressed in older adulthood can contribute to our larger understanding of how God calls us throughout our lives. As critical gerontologist Martha Holstein puts

it, "the goal should be the valuing of the whole of life in all its manifesta-
tions, not only when it is physically strong."[11] Reimagining vocation for
older adulthood means asking the (practical theological) question of what
theological perspectives arise out of the lived experiences and practices
associated with being old.

Characteristics of Older Adulthood

The Eriksons' and Fisher's perspectives, alongside the stories of Liz, Jim,
and other older adults I know through my research on aging, bring to the
foreground two characteristics important for vocation in this period of life.
First, *bodies* demand primacy of place in determining everyday realities and
are often experienced as limiting factors. Second, *time* becomes reconfigured, in both its functions and its meanings, to highlight presence (i.e., how
one wants to live and be in relation with others amid the reality of having
fewer remaining days) and the present (i.e., the importance of the here and
now). Awareness of the inevitability of death reshapes what time means.

The Body's Demands

In older adulthood the body claims center stage in determining almost
everything. Throughout her sixties and early seventies, Liz's health was
generally good even with her history of cancer. She maintained a level of
activity such that even though she was retired from full-time work, the
basic parameters of her life still resembled those of her pre-retirement,
middle-age life. Liz attended church meetings, led women's retreats,
enjoyed going to concerts with friends, and even fell in love. All of this
happened because, in some sense, her body allowed it. Gerontologists
note that as a result of medical advances, improved nutrition, and lifestyle changes (at least among the more affluent), North Americans can
expect to live more of their years in relatively good health. For increasing
numbers of older adults, 72 (or something even older) is the "new 60," as
the chronological age that marks the shift of life stage from middle to late
adulthood continues to stretch into the later years, as Cahalan underscores
in her chapter in this volume.[12]

But at some point, aging bodies become insistent in their demands.
In her seventies, Liz's body's demands gradually increased as weakness

and neuropathy made mobility difficult. As one 73-year-old man put it, "As long as I was golfing, I was 'just retired.' I didn't identify myself as old. When I had my prostate cancer surgery, that day I became officially old in my own mind." For many older people in the United States, losing the ability to drive a car marks the entry into this life phase and characterizes it as a time of increasing dependency on others.

Perhaps at no other life stage save adolescence does the body occupy such a premier place in defining the contours of life. But unlike adolescence in which bodies pulse with energy and vitality, the bodies of older adults generally speak the language of decline, leaning toward diminishment and death rather than growth. Skin thins, dries, and loses elasticity, and in combination with decreasing muscle tone, forms deep, crevasse-like wrinkles and sagging. Hearing and visual acuity diminish. Movement slows and becomes more difficult. Incontinence of bladder or bowels brings particular indignities. The so-called diseases of old age speed up the body's distress. The fact that such bodily changes force others to peer into the horizon of mortality may account for some of the repulsion expressed in social norms demanding that old women in particular cover their flesh.[13] Just as once-fecund bodies signified vitality in the exposure of their flesh, now in old age weakened, drooping flesh signifies a mortality from which many recoil in horror. Coming to terms with physical decay, letting go of attachments to culturally formed notions of physical beauty, grieving the body's losses of function, and learning how to die all constitute the central tasks of vocation in this life stage.

Gerontologists note that as the span of years after retirement but before significant losses of physical capacities is expanding, older adults, statistically speaking, can expect to spend relatively fewer of their last years in a state of acute health crisis. George Vaillant, a researcher with the Harvard Longevity Project, terms this the "compression of morbidity."[14] The span of time given over to the process of dying takes up less of the older adult years. God's calling in older adulthood therefore may involve a relatively long span of time spent living within the limits of aging bodies, followed by a relatively short span devoted to actively dying. Accordingly, for some older adults, loving God and loving the neighbor during this life phase become a work of endurance.

Socioeconomic and class status, race and ethnicity, and gender shape what it means when the normative direction of changes in one's body is toward weakening and decline. Holstein, writing on the changing cultural context of aging, argues that ageism involves "a persistent and generally unacknowledged prejudice against the old that functions through systems of inequality that privilege the young at the expense of the old."[15] Such prejudice intersects with socially constructed power relations such as gender inequality, racism, and classism, to make the difficulties of old age even more problematic for people who live on the margins. For example, in the United States about one-third of older women live below the poverty line, but among older black and Latina women this increases to 58 percent and 47 percent, respectively.[16] The impact of "cumulative disadvantage" across the lifespan—limited access to healthcare, jobs that take a toll on the body and health, poor diet, less education—shows up in the bodily experience of older adults.[17] Thus the factors in older adults' experience of health and well-being may relate as much to social realities and a lifetime of privilege (or its absence) as to the particular quality of healthcare available to them.

Not all of the body-centered experiences of older adulthood are about decline and decay, however. Witness the delight and beauty of the great-grandfather who sees in his 4-year-old great-grandson the outline of his own features. The great-grandfather permits this little one who is his physical legacy to try to "rub out the wrinkles" on his hands and forehead, as child-sized hands of the great-grandson explore the wizened flesh of his grandfather's neck in an unknowing glimpse of his own future appearance. Or picture the couple living together in a long-term care facility, twin hospital beds pulled together so that each night he can lovingly spread lotion to bring comfort to the now-fragile body of his beloved as he has across the many decades of their life together. These too are experiences of the centrality of bodies in older adulthood.

Older adulthood's amplified awareness of bodies, their limits and possibilities, underscores God's creation of human beings for vocation as the very embodied creatures we are, and not in spite of our bodies. Even when aging bodies seem to offer more hindrances than aid to our participation in God's reconciling love, in this life we do not have the option for *ad extra* vocation, the living out of God's calling beyond the body. The life stage of older adulthood has a way of bringing to the foreground the necessity of honoring our bodies even as our bodies evidence our mortality. Christians have not always been comfortable with the idea that God's call for us to receive others in relationship takes place in and through our bodies. Bodies matter in God's call and in our responses, a facet of vocation that older adulthood brings to the foreground.

In a different way, the heightened body consciousness that older adulthood thrusts into the foreground operates to critique cultural overvaluing of independence and autonomy—of bodies that do not need others. Chaplain Beth Jackson-Jordan recounts the story of a frail elderly woman confined to her bed in a nursing home, who found purpose and meaning in being a good listener to nurses' aides, housekeepers, and others who moved in and out of her room each day to provide care.[18] Such a shift disrupts the dichotomy between dependence and independence, replacing it with interdependence that does not rely on equality of physical capacity. God's call in older adulthood invites even those with frail bodies and minds to serve the neighbor, as caregiver and care-receiver are graced by one another's presence. Spiritual director and counselor Kathleen Fischer expresses it beautifully when she writes,

> There are dimensions of the Gospel, aspects of love, courage, faith, and fidelity, which only the old can sacramentalize for the human community. From the perspective of faith, the later years provide the most intense and vivid revelation of the paradox at the heart of the Christian Gospel: that in losing our lives we somehow find them; that loss can be gain, and weakness, strength; that death is the path to life.[19]

Fischer's and Jackson-Jordan's words may reflect what younger people wish to interpret about the spirituality of older adulthood, more so than the concrete, lived experience of this time for many older adults. Still, Jackson-Jordan's example from the nursing home, together with my experience of watching Liz care for Jim, testify to the possibility that some older adults experience their calling as she describes it.

A Different Kind of Time

Bodies are not the only existential aspects to change in older adulthood. Time itself gets reshaped by the reality that time has now become short, even more acutely than in time's initial whispering of short passage during late adulthood. This period of life is specifically characterized by the knowledge, first awakened in late adulthood but now present with urgency, that death is closer than birth, and that the available days of life extending into the future are outnumbered by those in the past. The chance to create "long dreams" is foreclosed. Some greet this reconfiguring of time with anxiety, reading it through the lens of fear of mortality. For others, however, such a changed perspective on time brings with it a new openness to "live each day to its fullest," as one older adult put it, or to "get on with my bucket list of things I want to do before I die," as another quipped.

Liz has always surrounded herself with people of all different ages. There is a basket of well-loved puppets in the hallway for children; a selection of newspapers for adults to enjoy over morning coffee; teens can choose from recent DVDs to watch. Divorced in her forties with no children, Liz enjoys annual reunions with her extended family that includes multiple generations of children. After years of gathering at a beach resort, the family now comes to her because, as she says, "traveling is so difficult when you are afraid of falling." Liz retired from her job as an associate pastor on the staff of a large, downtown church where she remains an active participant in the church's worship and life. Once active in her denomination's regional committees and governance, she now says, "I don't need to do that anymore." She also gave up driving several years ago, but keeps a car in the underground garage for the use of visitors. Part of our ritual of catching up with each other after a long absence involves her filling me in on those who have died. She faces into her own mortality rather directly. "Do you want to be on my funeral committee?" she asked. She has lined up the preacher and musicians for the occasion. "You can help plan the service and the party." When I agreed, she added my name to a short list of friends posted by her phone in an envelope of instructions for "what to do and whom to contact when I die."

I think of Liz's invitation for me to join her funeral committee as an open acknowledgment of death's closeness, an awareness of time's scarcity. In such ways, the meanings accorded to time take a new turn. A deeper awareness of *now* and its urgency can lead to a new embrace of life and a revaluing of the present moment. Or it can lead to denial, a refusal to acknowledge the shorting of time and the waning of opportunities to live now. As Holstein contends, "To act as if we can evade chronic illness is to reinforce already powerful cultural fears about bodily suffering and old age, fears that further marginalize the people who live with debilitating conditions . . . while blinding us to their hopes, dreams, and struggles."[20]

Dis-identification with old age can take highly problematic forms, as is the case with my father who needs help in his daily living activities to be safe, but nevertheless clings fiercely to the illusion of self-sufficiency and independence in ways that create risks. Because he is unwilling to release the burden of a now-impossible independence for the grace of interdependence, his struggles with physical and cognitive challenges take away from his ability to fully enjoy relationships and activities that are in his life.

As retired seminary professor Milton Crum notes, at some point a shift will occur, in spite of a person's best efforts to stave off the reality of aging. While our culture promotes taking responsibility for one's well-being in ways that may contribute to the lengthening of our years, Crum, quoting Richard Posner, asserts that aging is somehow viewed by younger people as "our fault rather than as inevitable."[21] Some older adults appear resigned to these realities; others accept them as the expected course of life, however difficult they may be. Either way, an important piece of the inner work of this life stage is the ability to situate self-esteem in sources other than societal standards of beauty, vitality, and productivity. As Liz navigates these waters, I notice how important the maintenance of intergenerational community is for self-esteem and for "owning" her age. Because she continually experiences her aged self in encounters with others of different ages, instead of in isolation, Liz seems not to shrink from recognition of her "status" as an older adult but finds herself valued as such in those relationships. Her experience stands in contrast to that of many people who express surprise on finding themselves inhabiting old bodies.[22] "These are not my hands," remark some older adults, surprised to see wrinkled skin because they think of themselves as younger than their years and conditions. From my vantage point, it is not necessarily a bad thing that older adults often think of themselves as much younger than their chronological ages. But I wonder what is lost when older people do not or cannot claim their position in the lifecycle whose chronological ages position them closer to dying than to future longevity.

The Vocational Experience of Slowing Down

We have been considering the way time's meaning changes during older adulthood. There exists still another—older adulthood is marked by slowness. Time slows, as do bodies. Injuries heal more slowly. Bodies move more slowly through space. Awareness of the danger of falls that bring serious injury, coupled with changes in posture, gait, muscle mass, and stamina, discourage quick motion. Speech also slows in older adulthood, partially the product of changes in the physiology of vocal sound production, but often also the result of cognitive deficits that slow the pathway from thought to speaking. The slowing of time and of bodies moving through time is for some people one of the awakening tasks in this life stage. For others it is an ending task, the prolegomenon to death.

How does slowed time participate in vocation? After all, slowness in older adults can be a source of frustration to caregivers, younger spouses, children, and even pastors with busy schedules. It can be hard to see vocation in the slowness. What the reality of such reconfigurations of time highlights about vocation may best be seen in what it evokes in others. Visiting an older adult with dementia may involve me in simply sitting with (or pacing with) that person over a generous expanse of time in which linguistic communication is completely absent. The only thing that "happens" (if such a word even fits) is time shared in the presence of God and one another. Such times may be contemplative or not, but they will surely be formative of the one who inhabits this slow time with the older adult. Practical theologian John Swinton, writing about dementia, makes the point well: "*To love one another, we need to be present for one another*. To be present, we need to learn to remember well and to use time differently and more faithfully. . . . We will discover that being with another is the most powerful way of ministering, not simply with and towards people with dementia, but also with and towards all people."[23]

In the course of my pastoral ministry with older adults, I have come to embrace the grace in this necessary slowing down in order to be with them. In the early months and years of this ministry, I came to recognize that I had to be willing to linger. One cannot just drop in for a quick conversation. It takes time to nurture these relationships, to connect across the years of different life stages, to become present to one another, and to hear the stories that narrate long lives. And in the course of accommodating to slowness, I have found myself stepping out of the frenetic pace of my middle adult life, embracing and being formed by slowing down in order to be with older adults. This is a different "story" about time than the usual stories I tell myself from the vantage point of the labors of parenting and work where time is framed in terms of organization ("How am I going to fit into my packed schedule the need to drive three children to different after-school activities today?"), efficiency, and productivity. I carefully choose how I will "spend" my time; I value devices and technologies that allow me to "save" time. But with older adults, time becomes re-storied, transformed from a commodity to be spent or saved, to a space of grace where relationships unfold, in ways that parallel children's vocations (as described earlier in the volume[24]).

When I visit older adults, I experience the gift of time. It so profoundly reshapes my life that I have come to think of the vocation of the older adults (especially those with Alzheimer's and other forms of dementia) as offering time-gifts to people who need to slow down. In this way, the callings of the ones receiving care are inextricably linked to the callings of the ones giving care. This dialectic is central in the vocation of older adulthood, where receiving becomes the more visible element in daily life, but where giving takes place in unobserved ways.

Who Will Be With Me? Communal Dynamics, Loss, and Loneliness

Alongside the prominence of bodies and the re-storying of time, the need for companionship and intimacy remains strong even as a new constancy of loss and grief emerges. Companionship and relationships take new forms such as great-grandparent, care-receiver, or caregiver of an infirm spouse. At the same time, loss becomes normative. The necessity of finding closure across multiple life domains where losses gut both the inner and outer worlds of older adults brings practices of *grieving* and *releasing* to the foreground.

Great-grandparenting

Time also is transformed in older adulthood through the cross-generational relationships allowed by increased longevity. While an earlier generation of great-grandparents did not live long enough to know or be known by their children's grandchildren, there is a current explosion of great-grandparents in the United States. One population expert contends that by the year 2030, 70 percent of all 8-year-olds will have at least one (and potentially more) great-grandparent.[25]

Gerontologists report an important distinction between grandparents and great-grandparents. As each generation adds an additional layer of distance in terms of the years between themselves and the youngest members of the family, their sense of responsibility to those children diminishes.[26] Anecdotal accounts by great-grandparents and the parents of their great-grandchildren confirm this finding, suggesting as well that some older adults bring a diminished investment in attaching emotionally to the youngest generation of the family. "They just don't have the energy for making another major attachment," as one mother said upon observing the difference in her parents as grandparents compared to their roles as great-grandparents. This means that although great-grandparents can and do hold significance in the lives of children in their extended families, the shape of this significance may be more tangential or symbolic, and less emotionally salient than in the case of grandparenting. Time across generations in the family changes the kinds of relationships that are possible.

The Constancy of Loss

Those in the initial phases of older adulthood often note the way that gradually the deaths of friends and loved ones become less of an exceptional occurrence and more the norm. A central characteristic of this stage of life is the inevitability and constancy of loss. The regularity of loss accelerates across subsequent years, such that people in their seventies and beyond begin to speak of "outliving all my friends" or being the only one left in their families so that "it all ends with me." With the death of age-mates comes an increasing sense that there is no one who can listen to and validate the stories of one's experiences of growing old. There is a loneliness inherent in losing the people who hold our stories with us.

Not all of the losses of this period involve death. There are losses of place, as desires to be near family or a change in health status necessitate relocation. There are losses of function, as elderly persons find themselves unable to perform some activity or task that used to be second nature to them. Some speak of the loss of dignity in the way healthcare is delivered or in the diminished privacy around personal finances. As Holstein remarks, "being old is an intimate but also very public experience."[27] Among couples, when one partner's health declines more rapidly than the other person's, there may be grief over abandoned plans to enjoy retirement travels or to spend the elder years helping to care for grandchildren together. Liz, unable to carry out the plan she and Jim had to grow old at home together, had to grieve the loss of a dream and adjust to an altered trajectory. She now visits Jim in a nearby elder care facility regularly and talks to him on the phone throughout each day.

One of the most common experiences named by older adults is loneliness. As loss becomes cumulative and social supports diminish, there is the general loneliness of having too few companions. Sometimes retirement and its aftermath awakens the relational emptiness that can characterize this life period, a state particularly common among men in late adulthood who were socialized to form relationships in and around work roles. The sense of emptiness easily turns to isolation in older adulthood when the crisis of giving up driving or needing assistive devices to walk or hear limits the ability to independently seek out companionship.

If loneliness is common, one of the most evident forms of loneliness in older adulthood is that which overtakes a person after the death of a spouse or partner. In John Bowlby's studies on attachment, he identified a phenomenon he termed "pining away," the intense yearning after the loss of an intimate relationship.[28] Spousal deaths taking place in rapid succession of one another are often interpreted as "dying from a broken heart." The specificity of spousal loss cannot be ameliorated by adding other relationships such as friends or additional companions, as if the loneliness were generic. That does not mean that a person suffering such a loss is not aided by support and friendship. Older adults who have extensive social support suffer less from depression.[29] Loneliness thus becomes one of the challenging staples of older adult life.

How might the loneliness of old age relate to vocation in this life phase? If we understand vocation not as a possession, something an individual "has," but rather as an interaction with God's purposes that takes place within a relational ecology in which one participates with others, then it seems possible to imagine loneliness in older adulthood evoking the community's capacities to provide a web of relationships in which older adults can grieve well. In turn, older adults suffering losses in the midst of the community "teach us how to grow through losses instead of being defeated by them."[30]

A distortion of such a perspective on vocation would be to assert that God "makes old people lonely" or "causes losses in their lives" for the sole purpose of giving others in the community the opportunity to exercise care. I do not suggest anything of the sort here. The sufferings attendant to physical disability, cognitive decline, and relational loss are consequences of human finitude and mortality, not the will of a capricious God. Put differently, we suffer such ignominies because as finite creatures our lives move toward death and so our bodies and minds decay. The claim that God's calling can be expressed even in such circumstances states the theological tenet found repeatedly throughout scripture, tradition, and human experience: God often works in and through even the most negative circumstances to draw the creation toward God's desired wholeness for all. As biblical scholar Jane Patterson puts it in her reflections on Genesis's account of Eve and Adam's expulsion from paradise, the account suggests that finitude is "appropriate to our place in creation" since for humans to live forever would place us on par with God. She goes on to note the normalcy of human death in God's creation, as upheld by the psalmist's declaration that mortal life is like grass, here for its time and then gone. What endures is the steadfastness of God's love among those who keep covenant with God (Ps. 103:15–18): "This psalm encapsulates the virtue of the human lifespan, biblically speaking: though short, human life can mediate a love that is not subject to death when we live as a channel for the love that God holds for the whole creation, as expressed in the covenant."[31]

Calling of individuals and of communities overlaps so that the circumstances of one come to be addressed in the vocation of the other. Similar to Erikson's epigenetic "cogwheeling" theory of human development discussed throughout this book,[32] in which the gifts of one stage of life intersect with the needs of another, an ecological understanding of vocation leaves room for the possibility that the needs of some parts of the community to receive care may activate giving on the part of others called to offer care.

Even with such an ecology, in which the presence of loving people offering care does something to mitigate the negative effects of grieving, loss remains a constant feature of old age and the cause of much of its suffering. It is not only about absence of personal relationships and intimacy. Loneliness may also be the result of the absence of activity for older adults whose earlier life-involvements and activities populated a world of meaning for them.[33] This was the case for Maggie:

> *Maggie, who is the same age as Liz, has not been able to live in her own home for the past fifteen years. Physical changes came upon her more rapidly and at an earlier age, when a "small stroke" left her with some paralysis on one side and severe limitations for walking and standing. She moved into a long-term care facility, not by her own choice but because her only son who lived in a different state became concerned about her ability to live safely on her own. As she describes it, things had been just fine until her husband suffered a sudden heart attack and died. "We were only in our sixties—he was still young!" she laments. She carries a deep anger about the death of her husband of forty years and makes no secret about blaming God for "taking him" from her.*
>
> *Beyond the stroke, Maggie's health began to decline more generally shortly after her husband's death. Maggie resides full-time on what*

is known as the "healthcare unit" of the long-term care facility. An aide assists her to shower, dress, and sit up in her recliner in the morning where she spends much of the day sitting or doing needlepoint. Maggie refuses to participate in the activities offered by the care facility. She stays alone in her room all day, every day. A fan of the symphony and the opera, she once held season subscriptions to performances at Washington, DC's Kennedy Center for the Performing Arts and sat on numerous community arts boards. "When you come in here [the nursing care facility], it's as if you never had a life or any interests before you arrived. Your whole life is erased into nothing." For Maggie, a lifetime of intense pleasure in music is reduced to the small stereo system in her room, but she rarely turns it on. "I can't get to it on my own. The aides or housekeeping staff come in and they change the station to that awful pop music, and then they leave and I am stuck with that noise." Maggie is bored, bitter, and angry about her situation. Visibly depressed, she is withdrawing into an ever-narrowing world where she makes few decisions or choices for herself. Maggie speaks infrequently. Her eyes have a hard, vacant look, and I learn from the nurse that she has begun to refuse food, taking control of one of the few elements of her life that she is able to decide. "Being old is a terrible thing," she says. "I am bored and alone. Why am I still here?"[34]

Maggie does not sense God's calling in her life and cannot imagine herself having a means to fulfill a calling should it exist. Her nearly total physical dependency makes it hard for others to associate her with the idea of God's call as well, given the action-oriented ways we often construe vocation. And yet Maggie continues to struggle with questions of vocation: Why am I here? Who am I? Whose am I? Maggie seems to epitomize the lamenting poet of Psalm 22: "My God, my God, why have you forsaken me? Why are you so far from helping me, from the words of my groaning? O my God, I cry by day, but you do not answer; and by night, but find no rest. . . . I am poured out like water, and all my bones are out of joint; my heart is like wax; it is melted within my breast; my mouth is dried up like a potsherd, and my tongue sticks to my jaws; you lay me in the dust of death" (vv. 1–2, 14–15, NRSV).

Unlike the psalmist who goes on to proclaim certainty of God's sure rescue, Maggie does not couple her lament with praise for God's faithfulness. Yet in some odd way her very anger at God over the losses of old age keeps her connected to God and to the question of how her life matters now. Maggie's question "Why am I here?" is vocational, and it is one asked by many older adults in one form or another, particularly those faced with significant limitations to their own agency. What purpose could God possibly have for my life, they wonder, when I can only lie here?

Such a question seems worthy of the attention of faith communities and theologians because it invites us to reconsider the extent to which we erroneously define vocation as something to be achieved and possessed through our own efforts. Vocation comes from God to us for the sake of the world, and there are endless forms it may take in our lives. The situation of older adulthood's limits, especially under conditions of disability, speaks a powerful counter-narrative: the call of God in older adulthood redefines usefulness and value in human life. Accordingly, in the lives of those like Maggie, being "useful" for God's purposes might be most powerfully understood not in what she herself can do, but instead through the power of her circumstances to evoke empathy, compassion, care, and attention among those in relationship with her as caregivers, family, faith community, and friends—still part of the family of God working together for God's purposes in the world. Older adults may call forth in others untested capacities of loyalty, commitment, justice, and love. This too is an important element in the purposes of God.

Put differently, the vocation of frail older adults involves the call to receive the care of others. Unlike other times in the lifespan, when God's call is more likely to solicit intentional action on the part of the respondent, God's call in older adulthood sometimes takes place in a receptive-dependent mode, a vocation of forming others in faith by evoking in them the practices, habits, and dispositions of faithful people. Receptive dependency may not be an easy position for persons schooled in U.S. cultural norms of self-sufficiency, autonomy, and individualism. The call to receive care (and in so doing, to nurture the caring capacities of others) functions to remind the rest of the faith community that we are created for relational interdependence and not for self-sufficiency. In the season of older adulthood, the oscillation between independence and dependence that constitutes interdependence tips decisively in the direction of a necessary reliance on others. Although I have spoken about older adults' vocation primarily in terms of how it implicitly nurtures the faith practices of others, God's call for older adults to receive care is also a call *for older adults themselves* to experience the care and presence of God, as Naomi experienced through Ruth's love and promise of companionship. Pastoral caregiver Beth Gaede suggests that faith communities recognize that "sometimes we receive [God's] care through other people. When we receive their care, we receive God."[35]

Endings: Older Adulthood's Final Transition into Death

Unlike other time periods within the lifespan for which the ending of one phase developmentally opens into a new life phase, older adulthood ends with the end of life. While death may come prematurely or unexpectedly in any age, old age exists uniquely within the lifespan as a space of conscious awareness of the coming end of life. Not everyone meets the reality of death with the degree of consciousness displayed by Liz in setting up her "funeral committee." Nevertheless, the nearness and reality of death is embedded in older adulthood.

What vocational elements are present in dying? Aging experts James Fisher and Henry Simmons, as well as systematic theologian Amy Plantinga Pauw, speak of "dying well" as the end-of-life practice to which faithful disciples are called.[36] Not to be confused with notions of a "good death" or an "easy death," both of which primarily reference the biological and medical experience of death, the idea of dying well carries within it notions that there are completion tasks to which persons should attend in order to leave this life most meaningfully. "Dying well" is also the language used by physician Ira Byock, writing of dying as a process rather than a singular moment. Byock contends that there are particular tasks involved in dying well, summed up in his short list of "things that matter most" that people need to be able to say to others: "please forgive me," "I forgive you," "thank you," "I love you," and "good-bye."[37] To die well, says Byock, involves attending to the closure tasks that are both relational and self-oriented. To put it in terms of vocation among older adults, the vocation of dying well involves a calling to bring meaningful closure to the one and only life one has lived.

Dying well often becomes more difficult in the face of the medicalization of death. In old age, consciousness of reaching a time and condition that cannot be fixed by further interventions from doctors ought to bring freedom from ceaseless chasing of another medical procedure to forestall the death sentence. While the hospice and palliative care movements have accomplished much in the way of pushing back against curative medical interventions that work at cross purposes with care at the end of life, many people still experience death as the failure of medicine rather than as the necessary terminus of old age.

K. Brynolf Lyon, a professor of practical theology and pastoral care, places older adulthood in the spiritual and religious context of its ending in death when he notes that the experience of old age for Christians is "contextualized by belief in resurrection. Although our life in this world ends in death, our death is not the final thing about us. God redeems our lives from final meaninglessness, and our present experience is nurtured through hope in the resurrection of our bodies in Jesus Christ."[38] Even in our dying, God's calling finds expression. As moral theologian Paul Wadell claims: "A pivotal witness that elderly persons can offer is to remind us that aging and death are not the worst things that can happen to us. The worst thing is not to grow old but to live a life bereft of meaning, goodness, and love."[39]

Most descriptions of vocation across the lifespan involve moving toward something, or taking on a new role or a task, as seen, for example, in the call to care for the new generation through parenting, or to contribute to the well-being of the human community through social activism. It may be distinctive to older adulthood that God's call in this time of life also entails a call *from* something.[40] We are called, in our dying, to let go of the things that bind us to this life. Dying to this life, we hear God calling us out of the responsibilities, burdens, and sufferings of this life, and into fullness in the divine life of the resurrection, as Jane Patterson reflects in the biblical interlude that completes this volume. The transition from old age to new life with our dying, then, integrates our embrace of God's call to relinquish earthly attachments and the call from the struggles and loves of our earthly existence.

Suggested Readings

Cruikshank, Margaret. *Learning to Be Old: Gender, Culture, and Aging.* 3rd ed. Lanham, MD: Rowman & Littlefield, 2013.

Erikson, Erik H., and Joan M. Erikson. *The Life Cycle Completed.* Extended ed. New York: Norton, 1997.

Fischer, Kathleen R. *Winter Grace: Spirituality for the Later Years.* New York: Paulist, 1985.

Fisher, James C. "A Framework for Describing Developmental Change among Older Adults." *Adult Education Quarterly* 43, no. 2 (1993): 76–89.

Fries, James F. "Aging, Natural Death, and the Compression of Morbidity." *New England Journal of Medicine* 303, no. 3 (1980): 130–35.

Gaede, Beth Ann. "What Will I Do Next? Discerning God's Callings for Retirement." *Journal of Religion, Spirituality, and Aging* 22, no. 1 (January 2010): 27–40.

Holstein, Martha. *Women in Late Life: Critical Perspectives on Gender and Age.* Diversity and Aging. Series ed. Toni Calasanti. Lanham, MD: Rowman & Littlefield, 2015.

Jackson-Jordan, Beth. "God's Call in Later Life: A Theological Reflection on Aging." *Chaplaincy Today* 17, no. 1 (Summer 2001): 18–21.

Lyon, K. Brynolf. "Faith Development in Late Adulthood." In *Human Development and Faith: Life-Cycle Stages of Body, Mind, and Soul,* edited by Felicity B. Kelcourse. St. Louis, MO: Chalice, 2004.

Scheib, Karen D. *Challenging Invisibility : Practices of Care with Older Women.* St. Louis, MO: Chalice, 2004.

Swinton, John. *Dementia: Living in the Memories of God.* Grand Rapids, MI: Eerdmans, 2012.

Vaillant, George E. *Triumphs of Experience: The Men of the Harvard Grant Study.* Cambridge, MA: Belknap Press of Harvard University Press, 2012.

Wadell, Paul J. "The Call Goes On: Discipleship and Aging." *The Christian Century* 128, no. 8 (April 19, 2011): 1112.

Resurrection and God's Vindication

JANE PATTERSON

Political oppression in Palestine under Seleucid and then Roman rule created the tragic conditions for the martyrdom of faithful Jews. In 2 Maccabees we read the story of seven brothers brutally executed for their commitment to observe the Torah in spite of its having been outlawed by the Seleucid king. Their mother encourages them throughout the terrifying ordeal by placing her faith in the God of creation, as she says:

> I do not know how you came into being in my womb. It was not I who gave you life and breath, nor I who set in order the elements within each of you. Therefore the Creator of the world, who shaped the beginning of humankind and devised the origin of all things, will in his mercy give life and breath back to you again, since you now forget yourselves for the sake of his laws. (27:22–23)

Though the passage postdates the historical situation portrayed, it predates the New Testament, where belief in resurrection comes to the fore not only after the death of Jesus, but also in his reported argumentation with the Sadducees, who did not believe in resurrection. Resurrection of those who have died for their faith is a way of speaking about how a just God can still bring justice to an unjust situation, even after the person in question has died. Resurrection is God's vindication of the righteous after their unjust death, and the vindication of God's Messiah is the primary understanding of the significance of Jesus's resurrection in the New Testament Gospels. The promise of resurrection vindicates those who have lived into God's calling against terrifying opposition.

We might express the understanding this way: that there is a way of life so filled with the will of God and the love of God and the service of God that no one on earth has the power to take away the life of such a person. The God of creation will continue to fill the person with life, even after earthly death. In 2 Maccabees, this resurrection most likely takes place in a dimension of being that is with God, but not in this world. What is different in the early Christian witness to the resurrection of Jesus, God's Messiah, is that he is manifested again *on earth* as risen Lord among and through his followers and their lives as they embody his commitment to God's justice, love, and mercy. Thus, God's plan of salvation continues through communities of people called and gathered in Christ's name and in his pattern of life. And Christ himself continues to empower them through the Spirit. Paul called this way of life "*in Christ*," a way to live the outpouring creativity of God on both sides of the boundary of death. John called it "eternal life," a life without bounds.

Christian hope in unbounded life begins here and now, in the concrete realities of daily life, lived in constant awareness of God's presence, God's call, and service to God's love for all. And this way of life extends after the wearing out of the body and the "putting on" of a new form of embodiment that is imperishable (1 Cor. 15:53). While early Christians held that the human person must always be embodied in some way, they saw the resurrection body as different from our earthly body as a wheat seed is from the stalk that it engenders (1 Cor. 15:35–41; John 12:24).

The New Testament writings on resurrection leave a lot of room for mystery, while at the same time rooting our hope deeply in the soil of God's consistent power to create, even in the face of death. The image of the grain of wheat disintegrating to give way to the vibrant plant calls all of us to trust ultimately that the God of creation is powerfully at work in everything. In the small deaths of our plans or hopes, and in the ultimate wearing out of our human body, the God of creation is always the most powerful force acting on, through, and with us.

Notes

Notes to Chapter 1: Introduction

1. For an examination of vocation among college students, see Tim Clydesdale, *The Purposeful Graduate: Why Colleges Must Talk to Students about Vocation* (Chicago: University of Chicago Press, 2015), and David S. Cunningham, *At This Time and in This Place: Vocation and Higher Education* (New York: Oxford University Press, 2015).

2. I temporarily bracket the question of defining the term "vocation" here and return to it in the following chapter.

3. The Collegeville Institute Seminars has hosted two seminars on vocation: the Seminar on Vocation across the Lifespan and the Seminar on Faith and Vocation in the Professions. We also hosted the authors of *Calling in Today's World: Voices from Eight Faith Perspectives*, ed. Kathleen A. Cahalan and Douglas J. Schuurman (Grand Rapids, MI: Eerdmans, 2016). Information available at Collegeville Institute Seminars, accessed December 15, 2016, http://collegevilleinstitute.org/the-seminars/.

4. Fanucci developed two small-group resources: *Called to Life*, accessed December 14, 2016, www.called-to-life.com, and *Called to Work*, accessed December 14, 2016, www.called-to-work.com.

5. We have changed the names of people from our research to honor confidentiality.

6. Matt Bloom and Amy Colbert, "Work as a Calling: Integrating Personal and Professional Identities" (unpublished manuscript, 2015), 53.

7. Gregg Levoy, *Callings: Finding and Following an Authentic Life* (New York: Random House, 1997); Diane Dreher, *Your Personal Renaissance: 12 Steps to Finding Your Life's True Calling* (Cambridge, MA: Da Capo, 2008); William Damon, *The Path to Purpose: How Young People Find Their Calling in Life* (New York: Free Press, 2008); Parker J. Palmer, *Let Your Life Speak: Listening for the Voice of Vocation* (San Francisco: Jossey-Bass, 2000).

8. See, for example, "Restaurateur Mark Barak's Home as an Elegant Scrapbook,"

accessed December 16, 2016, http://www.nytimes.com/2015/12/20/realestate/restau
rateur-mark-barak.html?_r=0.

9. Warren mentions "calling" once, in relationship to the call to service. See Rick
Warren, *The Purpose Driven Life: What On Earth Am I Here For?* (Grand Rapids, MI:
Zondervan, 2002), 229.

10. See, for example, Charles Taylor, *A Secular Age* (Cambridge, MA: Harvard
University Press, 2007), 486.

11. Practical theology is understood in at least four ways, according to Bonnie
Miller-McLemore: "(1) an activity of believers seeking to sustain a life of reflective faith
in the everyday, (2) a curricular area in theological education focused on ministerial
practice, (3) an approach to theology used by religious leaders and by teachers and students across the curriculum, and (4) an academic discipline pursued by a smaller subset
of scholars to sustain these three enterprises." Bonnie J. Miller-McLemore, *Christian
Theology in Practice* (Grand Rapids, MI: Eerdmans, 2012), 106. The emphasis in this
book is primarily on the first and third.

12. Dan P. McAdams, *The Stories We Live By: Personal Myths and the Making of the
Self* (New York: Guilford, 1997), 11; emphasis original.

13. Douglas Schuurman, *Vocation: Discerning Our Callings in Life* (Grand Rapids,
MI: Eerdmans, 2004), and Edward Hahnenberg, *Awakening Vocation: A Theology
of Christian Calling* (Collegeville, MN: Liturgical Press, 2010). See also William C.
Placher, ed., *Callings: Twenty Centuries of Christian Wisdom on Vocation* (Grand Rap-
ids, MI: Eerdmans, 2005), and Mark Schwehn and Dorothy Bass, eds., *Leading Lives
That Matter* (Grand Rapids, MI: Eerdmans, 2006).

14. Schuurman, *Vocation*, 1–5. Consider, for example, feminist critiques of self-
sacrificial love that viewed traditional interpretations as harmful for women's self-
understanding. Through listening to women's experience and continued reflection
on the cross, atonement, and salvation, feminists have brought fresh insights for how
women can relate to an ethic of self-sacrifice without the accompanying views of self-
destruction. See, for example, Cynthia Crysdale, *Embracing Travail: Retrieving the
Cross Today* (New York: Continuum, 1999), and Bonnie Miller-McLemore, *Also a
Mother: Work and Family as Theological Dilemma* (Nashville, TN: Abingdon, 1994).

15. Schuurman, *Vocation*, 4.

16. Quoted in Schuurman, *Vocation*, 4.

17. The social science language around the human lifespan includes many terms:
"lifecycle," "stages," "phases," "life course," and "human development" are all common.
We use many of these terms but in the end prefer "lifespan" since it captures the dynamic movement over time of human life and because of its biblical tone. See Eccles.
20:22; Ps. 90:10; Matt. 6:27; Luke 12:25.

18. John Neafsey wrote a book on calling, empathy, and social justice called *Act
Justly, Love Tenderly* (Maryknoll, NY: Orbis, 2016), and Jack Fortin is researching vocation and retirement.

19. Jack Fortin, *The Centered Life* (Minneapolis, MN: Augsburg, 2006), 94.

Notes to Chapter 2

1. "Vocation, n.," in *Oxford English Dictionary*, accessed December 14, 2016, http://www.oed.com/view/Entry/224289?redirectedFrom=vocation#eid.

2. Walter Brueggemann, "Covenanting as Human Vocation," *Interpretation* 33, no. 2 (April 1979): 125; emphasis original.

3. For a retrieval of the Protestant tradition, see Douglas Schuurman, *Vocation: Discerning Our Callings in Life* (Grand Rapids, MI: Eerdmans, 2004).

4. For an examination of vocation in the Catholic tradition, see Edward Hahnenberg, *Awakening Vocation: A Theology of Christian Calling* (Collegeville, MN: Liturgical Press, 2010), and John Neafsey, *A Sacred Voice Is Calling: Personal Vocation and Social Conscience* (Maryknoll, NY: Orbis, 2006).

5. Ruthellen Josselson, Amia Lieblich, and Dan P. McAdams, eds., *The Meaning of Others: Narrative Studies of Relationships* (Washington, DC: American Psychological Association, 2007), 5.

6. Robert Kegan, *The Evolving Self: Problem and Process in Human Development* (Cambridge, MA: Harvard University Press, 1982), 19.

7. Like several theologians in the twentieth century who sought other names for God, Karl Rahner suggested "Holy Mystery." See Elizabeth A. Johnson, *She Who Is: The Mystery of God in Feminist Theological Discourse* (New York: Crossroad, 1992), 45.

8. John D. Zizioulas, *Being as Communion: Studies in Personhood and the Church* (Crestwood, NY: St. Vladimir's Seminary Press, 1985).

9. Elizabeth A. Johnson, *Quest for the Living God: Mapping Frontiers in the Theology of God* (New York: Continuum, 2007), 216.

10. Johnson, *Quest*, 223. For a concise summary of the images of the Trinity, see 219–21.

11. Miguel H. Diaz, *On Being Human: U.S. Hispanic and Rahnerian Perspectives* (Maryknoll, NY: Orbis, 2001), 24.

12. Roberto S. Goizueta, *Caminemos con Jesús: Toward a Hispanic/Latino Theology of Accompaniment* (Maryknoll, NY: Orbis, 1995), 50; emphasis original.

13. Emilie M. Townes, *In a Blaze of Glory: Womanist Spirituality as Social Witness* (Nashville, TN: Abingdon, 1995), 48.

14. See Francois's story in the Collegeville Institute Seminars video project, *Lives Explored*, accessed December 14, 2016, http://www.lives-explored.com/.

15. See also Ken and Margaret's story, *Lives Explored*, accessed December 14, 2016, http://collegevilleinstitute.org/the-seminars/resources-for-congregations/lives -explored/.

16. For a discussion of vocation and social location, see John Neafsey, *Act Justly, Love Tenderly* (Maryknoll, NY: Orbis, 2016), 24–33.

17. Charles M. Wood, *The Question of Providence* (Louisville, KY: Westminster John Knox, 2008), 72.

18. This view has taken particular hold in present-day evangelical America. Some Christians find the idea of God's "plan for their lives" reassuring and others find the language off-putting, which makes for interesting ecumenical exchanges.

19. See Johnson, *She Who Is*, 236.

20. Johnson, *She Who Is*, 240.

21. See Elizabeth A. Johnson, *Ask the Beasts: Darwin and the God of Love* (New York: Bloomsbury Continuum, 2015).

22. Johnson, *Quest*, 193; emphasis original.

23. Wood, *The Question of Providence*, 88; emphasis original.

24. For an eschatological view of vocation and work, see Miroslav Volf, *Work in the Spirit: Toward a Theology of Work* (New York: Oxford University Press, 1991).

25. In my book *The Stories We Live: Finding God's Calling All around Us* (Grand Rapids, MI: Eerdmans, 2017), I develop a theology of vocation around eight prepositions: "by," "to," "as," "from," "through," "for," "in," and "within."

26. Katherine Turpin, *Branded: Adolescents Converting from Consumer Faith* (Cleveland, OH: Pilgrim, 2006), 23; emphasis original.

27. Townes, *In a Blaze*, 47.

28. Brueggemann, "Covenanting," 126.

29. Townes, *In a Blaze*, 47.

30. Goizueta, *Caminemos*, 47–48.

31. Erik H. Erikson, *Identity and the Life Cycle* (New York: International Universities Press, 1959), 121.

32. Schuurman, *Vocation*, 17.

33. Rabbi Amy Eilberg, "*Hineini* (Here I Am): Jewish Reflections on Calling," in *Calling in Today's World: Voices from Eight Faith Perspectives*, ed. Kathleen A. Cahalan and Douglas J. Schuurman (Grand Rapids, MI: Eerdmans, 2016), 7. Eilberg argues that the idea of particular "calling" is foreign to Jews because (1) "direct communication between God and human beings ended with the last of the literary prophets," (2) "Jewish religious life is highly communitarian," and (3) "one commonly held view of religious vocation—a call to religious leadership—is completely absent in Jewish life." See 5–6.

34. Jeremiah 29:11 is a verse that Christians often interpret as pertaining to an individual. But the context of this verse is the promise of God's plan for the whole people.

35. John Kelsay, "The Idea of Calling in Islam," in *Calling in Today's World*, 82.

36. Bonnie Miller-McLemore, "Spooning: How Bodies Shape Knowledge," in Dorothy C. Bass, Kathleen A. Cahalan, Bonnie J. Miller-McLemore, James R. Nieman, and Christian B. Scharen, *Christian Practical Wisdom: What It Is, Why It Matters* (Grand Rapids, MI: Eerdmans, 2016), 30.

37. Colleen M. Griffith, "Practice as Embodied Knowing: Epistemological and Theological Considerations," in *Invitation to Practical Theology: Catholic Voices and Visions*, ed. Claire E. Wolfteich (Mahwah, NJ: Paulist, 2014), 62.

38. Turpin, *Branded*, 15. See also Joyce Ann Mercer, "Call Forwarding: Putting Vocation in the Present Tense with Youth," Princeton Theological Seminary, Institute for Youth Ministry, 2002 Lectures, Compass Points: Navigating Vocation, 37, accessed December 14, 2016, http://www.ptsem.edu/lectures/?action=results&by=creator &qtext=creator%3a%22Mercer,+Joyce+Ann%22+sort%3atitle.

39. For a discussion of negative stereotypes of the elderly, see Carroll Saussy, *The Art of Growing Old* (Minneapolis, MN: Augsburg, 1998), 57–72.

40. See Jung Young Lee's story of leaving North Korea and living as an exile in the United States: "A Life In-Between: A Korean-American Journey," in *Journey at the Margin: Toward an Autobiographical Theology in American-Asian Perspective*, ed. Peter C. Phan and Jung Young Lee (Collegeville, MN: Liturgical Press, 1999), 23–40. It would be interesting to ask each of the book's contributors how they understood God's calling through their journeys. For example, Peter Phan writes that his vocation as a theologian was thrust on him. He interprets the story of how he reached the United States from Vietnam as accidental, serendipitous, and part of the mysterious design of divine providence (125).

41. Kegan, *The Evolving Self*, 7–8.

42. Kegan, *The Evolving Self*, 8.

43. Kegan, *The Evolving Self*, 11.

44. Kegan, *The Evolving Self*, 8.

45. Miller-McLemore, "Spooning," 29.

46. K. Brynolf Lyon, "Faith and Development in Late Adulthood," in *Human Development and Faith*, ed. Felicity B. Kelcourse (St. Louis, MO: Chalice, 2004), 270.

47. Janet Ruffing, *To Tell the Sacred Tale: Spiritual Direction and Narrative* (Mahwah, NJ: Paulist, 2011), 80.

48. Langdon Gilkey, *Naming the Whirlwind: The Renewal of God-Language* (Indianapolis, IN: Bobbs-Merrill, 1969), 356.

49. Gilkey, *Naming the Whirlwind*, 357–58.

50. Paul Lakeland, *Postmodernity: Christian Identity in a Fragmented Age* (Minneapolis, MN: Fortress, 1997), 4.

51. Paul Tillich, *The Interpretation of History*, Part One trans. N. A. Rasetzki, Parts Two, Three, and Four trans. Elsa L. Talmey (New York: Charles Scribner's Sons, 1936), 129.

52. Mercer, "Call Forwarding," 31–33; emphasis original.

53. Neafsey, *A Sacred Voice Is Calling*, 4.

54. Jane Patterson, "Resurrection and God's Vindication," 198.

55. Mercer, "Call Forwarding," 32.

56. Schuurman argues that the Bible supports an understanding of the call to be God's people (*Vocation*, 18–25) as well as particular calls (26–41).

57. Schuurman, *Vocation*, 5.

58. Taylor notes three sources of radical reflexivity and inwardness in modernity: self-responsible independence, recognized particularity, and the individualism of personal commitment. Charles Taylor, *Sources of the Self* (Cambridge, MA: Harvard University Press, 1989), 185.

59. Taylor, *Sources of the Self*, 185.

60. Brueggemann, "Covenanting," 126; emphasis original.

61. Stephen J. Pope describes these six forms of service in *A Step along the Way: Models of Christian Service* (Maryknoll, NY: Orbis, 2015).

62. See Volf, *Work in the Spirit*, 102–56, and Kathleen A. Cahalan, *Introducing the Practice of Ministry* (Collegeville, MN: Liturgical Press, 2010), 24–47.

63. John Lewis and Jane Patterson, "Called in Service: Vocation, Charism, and

Grace in the Letters of Paul and Modern Life" (unpublished manuscript, 2015), chapter 1, 6.

64. Lewis and Patterson, "Called in Service," chapter 2, 5.

65. For a pneumatological understanding of the vocation to work, see Volf, *Work in the Spirit*.

66. Michael Himes, "Working to Answer Three Key Questions," Boston College, accessed December 14, 2016, http://www.visitationmonasteryminneapolis.org/2010/02/on-discernment-three-key-questions/.

67. See Jane Patterson's biblical interlude, "Younger Adulthood: A Voice from Within," 92–94.

68. For the Catholic spiritual writers Marie Theresa Coombs and Francis Kelly Nemeck, God receives our choices and actions, but does not manipulate the course of events in our lives. Rather, "we cooperate and interact with God's activity and providence every day, but not always wholeheartedly or positively." God is responsive to us as "dynamic energy" and "movement." "God predestines us not in a programmatic way but in an open evolving manner which responds to our responses." See Marie Theresa Coombs and Francis Kelly Nemeck, *Called by God: A Theology of Vocation and Lifelong Commitment* (Collegeville, MN: Liturgical Press, 1992), 28.

69. Neafsey, *A Sacred Voice,* 72; emphasis original.

70. Schuurman, *Vocation,* 66.

71. Neafsey, *A Sacred Voice,* 7–10 and 146–60.

72. Jane Patterson, "Siblings: Am I My Brother's Keeper?" 64.

73. Pope, *A Step Along the Way,* 174.

74. See Matt Bloom, "Middle Adulthood: The Joys and Paradoxes of Vocation," 123–47.

75. Hahnenberg, *Awakening Vocation,* 195; emphasis original.

76. Hahnenberg, *Awakening Vocation,* 195.

77. Pope, *A Step Along the Way,* 234.

78. Jane Patterson, "Elders: Ultimate Values," 148–49.

79. Schuurman, *Vocation,* 62.

80. God's promise is not equilibrium but faithfulness, according to Brueggemann, which is precarious and requires a "full repertoire of hoping, listening, and answering to live joyously." See "Covenanting," 126.

81. Quoted in Hahnenberg, *Awakening Vocation,* 119.

82. Townes, *In a Blaze,* 47.

Notes to "Childhood: One Such Child"

1. I am especially aided by the insights from Joyce Ann Mercer, *Welcoming Children: A Practical Theology of Childhood* (St. Louis, MO: Chalice, 2005).

Notes to Chapter 3

1. Heidegger asks, "Why is there something instead of nothing?" in Martin Heidegger, *An Introduction to Metaphysics* (New Haven, CT: Yale University Press, 1959), 7–8.

2. Few have verified this more powerfully than child psychiatrist and field researcher Robert Coles. Among his books on children, see especially his trilogy, *The Moral Life of Children* (Boston: Atlantic Monthly, 1986); *The Political Life of Children* (Boston: Atlantic Monthly, 1986); and *The Spiritual Life of Children* (Boston: Houghton Mifflin, 1990).

3. Ann Patchett, *This Is the Story of a Happy Marriage* (New York: HarperCollins, 2013), 15, 19.

4. Patchett, *This Is the Story*, 16.

5. Gareth B. Matthews, *The Philosophy of Childhood* (Cambridge, MA: Harvard University Press, 1994), 5.

6. Kathleen A. Cahalan, "Swimming: How the Practice of *Lectio Divina* Heals and Transforms," in Dorothy C. Bass, Kathleen A. Cahalan, Bonnie J. Miller-McLemore, James R. Nieman, and Christian B. Scharen, *Christian Practical Wisdom: What It Is, Why It Matters* (Grand Rapids, MI: Eerdmans, 2016), 51.

7. Cahalan, "Swimming," 52.

8. For explorations of this construction of children, see Bonnie J. Miller-McLemore, *Let the Children Come: Reimagining Childhood from a Christian Perspective* (San Francisco: Jossey-Bass, 2003), chapter 1.

9. Daniel G. Scott and Jessica Evans, "Peak Experience Project," *International Journal of Children's Spirituality* 15, no. 2 (May 2010): 143–58.

10. For this distinction between general and specific vocation, see William C. Placher, ed., *Callings: Twenty Centuries of Christian Wisdom on Vocation* (Grand Rapids, MI: Eerdmans, 2005), 206.

11. Patrick McKinley Brennan, "Introduction," in *The Vocation of the Child*, ed. Patrick McKinley Brennan (Grand Rapids, MI: Eerdmans, 2008), 27, and William Werpehowski, "In Search of Real Children: Innocence, Absence, and Becoming a Self in Christ," in *The Vocation of the Child*, ed. Patrick McKinley Brennan (Grand Rapids, MI: Eerdmans, 2008), 54.

12. Paul Hartung, Erik J. Porfeli, and Fred W. Vonrack, "Child Vocational Development: A Review and Reconsideration," *Journal of Vocational Behavior* 66 (2005): 385.

13. Brennan, ed., *The Vocation of the Child*.

14. See Martha Ellen Stortz, "'Where or When was Your Servant Innocent?' Augustine on Childhood," in *The Child in Christian Thought*, ed. Marcia Bunge (Grand Rapids, MI: Eerdmans, 2001), 83–86, and Cristina L. H. Traina, "A Person in the Making: Thomas Aquinas on Children and Childhood," in *The Child in Christian Thought*, 111–20.

15. James W. Fowler, *Becoming Adult, Becoming Christian: Adult Development and Christian Faith* (San Francisco: Harper & Row, 1984).

16. See Bonnie J. Miller-McLemore, "Whither the Children? Childhood in Religious Education," *Journal of Religion* 86, no. 4 (October 2006): 635–57.

17. Bonnie J. Miller-McLemore, *Also a Mother: Work and Family as Theological Dilemma* (Nashville, TN: Abingdon, 1994), and *Let the Children Come*.

18. Patrick McKinley Brennan, "Acknowledgments," in *The Vocation of the Child*, xi.

19. Norbert Mette, "Learning to Live and Believe with Children," in *Little Children Suffer*, ed. Maureen Junker-Kenny and Norbert Mette (London: SCM, 1996), 100. See also Anton A. Bucher, "Children as Subjects," in *Little Children Suffer*.

20. For a general overview, see Mary Jane Kehily, ed., *An Introduction to Childhood Studies* (Berkshire: Open University Press, 2004). For an overview of childhood studies in religion, see John Wall, "Childhood Studies, Hermeneutics, and Theological Ethics," *The Journal of Religion* 86 (2006): 523–48.

21. See Jane Patterson, "Introducing Biblical Interludes: Vocation in the Family of God," 33–35.

22. David H. Jensen, *Graced Vulnerability: A Theology of Childhood* (Cleveland, OH: Pilgrim, 2005), 98. See also Bonnie J. Miller-McLemore, "Birthing and Mothering as Powerful Rites of Passage," in *In Her Own Time: Women and Developmental Issues in Pastoral Care*, ed. Jeanne Stevenson Moessner (Minneapolis, MN: Fortress, 2000), 175–89.

23. Margaret S. Mahler, Fred Pine, and Anni Bergman, *The Psychological Birth of the Human Infant* (New York: Basic, 1973); Daniel N. Stern, *The Interpersonal World of the Infant: A View from Psychoanalysis and Development* (New York: Basic, 1985); Sigmund Freud, *Three Essays on the Theory of Sexuality*, trans. James Strachey (New York: Basic, 1962 [1905]); Erik H. Erikson, *Childhood and Society* (New York: Norton, 1950).

24. D. W. Winnicott, *The Maturational Processes and the Facilitating Environment: Studies in the Theory of Emotional Development* (New York: International Universities Press, 1965); Heinz Kohut, *How Does Analysis Cure?* (Chicago: University of Chicago Press, 1984).

25. Melvin Konner, *Evolution of Childhood: Relationships, Emotion, and Mind* (Cambridge, MA: Harvard University Press, 2010), 220, 223.

26. Erik H. Erikson, *Insight and Responsibility: Lectures on the Ethical Implications of Psychoanalytic Insight* (New York: Norton, 1964), 113–14.

27. Robert Kegan, *The Evolving Self: Problem and Process in Human Development* (Cambridge, MA: Harvard University Press, 1983), 17–18.

28. Konner, *Evolution of Childhood*, 292, 295.

29. Karl Rahner, "Ideas for a Theology of Childhood," in *Theological Investigations*, vol. 8, trans. David Bourke (London: Darton, Longman & Todd, 1971), 47–48.

30. Rahner, "Ideas for a Theology of Childhood," 36, 47–48; emphasis original.

31. Rahner, "Ideas for a Theology of Childhood," 34. See also Kathleen A. Cahalan's chapter in this volume, "Callings over a Lifetime: In Relationship, through the Body, over Time, and for Community," for additional comments on Christian views of time.

32. Rahner, "Ideas for a Theology of Childhood," 36–37.

33. Rahner, "Ideas for a Theology of Childhood," 48, 50.

34. Sigmund Freud, *Introductory Lectures on Psycho-Analysis*, in *The Standard Edition of the Complete Psychological Works of Sigmund Freud*, ed. and trans. J. Strachey,

vol. 16 (London: Hogarth, 1963 [1916]), and *Beyond the Pleasure Principle*, in *The Standard Edition of the Complete Psychological Works of Sigmund Freud*, ed. and trans. J. Strachey, vol. 18 (London: Hogarth, 1955 [1920]).

35. See, for example, Ana Swanson, "Why Half of the Life You Experience Is Over by Age 7," *Wonkblog* (blog), *The Washington Post*, July 23, 2015, accessed December 14, 2016, https://www.washingtonpost.com/news/wonk/wp/2015/07/23/haunting -images-show-why-time-really-does-seem-to-go-faster-as-you-get-older/.

36. Miller-McLemore, *Also a Mother*, 154, 156.

37. Simone Weil, *Waiting for God*, trans. Emma Craufurd (New York: Harper & Row, 1973), 105.

38. See Joyce Ann Mercer's chapter, "Older Adulthood: Vocation at Life's End," 174–97.

39. Herbert Anderson and Susan B. W. Johnson, *Regarding Children: A New Respect for Childhood and Families* (Louisville, KY: Westminster John Knox, 1994), 25.

40. Konner, *Evolution of Childhood*, 214; Dieter Seiler, "*Fides Infantium*—A Conversion," in *Little Children Suffer*, 72.

41. See Jane Patterson, "Childhood: One Such Child," 36–37.

42. Anderson and Johnson, *Regarding Children*, 23, 25.

43. Konner, *Evolution of Childhood*, 126.

44. Jensen, *Graced Vulnerability*, xv; Anderson and Johnson, *Regarding Children*, 24.

45. Jensen, *Graced Vulnerability*, 31–32.

46. Jensen, *Graced Vulnerability*, 19, 22–27.

47. Jensen, *Graced Vulnerability*, 47.

48. Rahner, "Ideas for a Theology of Childhood," 39–40.

49. See Miller-McLemore, *Let the Children Come*, chapter 3.

50. Miller-McLemore, *Let the Children Come*, 80. See also Andrew Sung Park and Susan L. Nelson, eds., *The Other Side of Sin: Woundedness from the Perspective of the Sinned-Against* (Albany: State University of New York Press, 2001).

51. Rowan Williams, *Lost Icons: Reflections on Cultural Bereavement* (Edinburgh: T&T Clark, 2000), 12–14; emphasis original.

52. Williams, *Lost Icons*, 27; emphasis original.

53. Marcia J. Bunge, "'Best Practices' for Nurturing the Best Love of and by Children: A Protestant Theological Perspective on Vocations of Children and Parents," in *The Best Love of the Child: Being Loved and Being Taught to Love as the First Human Right*, ed. Timothy P. Jackson (Grand Rapids, MI: Eerdmans, 2011), 242–49.

54. Steven Mintz, *Huck's Raft: A History of American Childhood* (Cambridge, MA: Harvard University Press, 2004), viii.

55. Julie Hanlon Rubio, *A Christian Theology of Marriage and Family* (New York: Paulist, 2003), 162–63. See also my essay on chores, "Children, Chores, and Vocation: A Social and Theological Lacuna," in *The Vocation of the Child*, and a revised and updated version, "Work, Labor, and Chores: Christian Ethical Reflection on Children and Vocation," in *Children, Adults, and Shared Responsibilities: Jewish, Christian, and*

Muslim Perspectives, ed. Marcia J. Bunge (Cambridge: Cambridge University Press, 2012), 171–86.

56. Mihaly Csikszentmihalyi, *Flow: The Psychology of Optimal Experience* (New York: Harper & Row, 1990).

57. See Katherine Turpin, "Adolescence: Vocation in Performance, Passion, and Possibility," 74.

58. Hartung, Porfeli, and Vonrack, "Child Vocational Development," 390, 411.

59. See Jane Patterson, "Childhood: One Such Child," 36–37.

60. See Winnicott's essay "Playing: Creative Activity and the Search for the Self," in *Playing and Reality* (London: Routledge, 1971).

61. Konner, *Evolution of Childhood*, 500.

62. Margaret Bendroth, "Horace Bushnell's Christian Nurture," in *The Child in Christian Thought*, ed. Marcia Bunge (Grand Rapids, MI: Eerdmans, 2000), 350.

63. Horace Bushnell, *Christian Nurture* (New York: Charles Scribner's Sons, 1908, reprinted by Wipf and Stock, 2000), 339–40.

64. Bendroth, "Horace Bushnell's Christian Nurture," 350; Jensen, *Graced Vulnerability*, 56.

65. Bushnell, *Christian Nurture*, 338.

66. Elliot A. Medrich, Judith Roizen, Victor Rubin, and Stuart Buckley, *The Serious Business of Growing Up: A Study of Children's Lives Outside of School* (Berkeley: University of California Press, 1982), 135.

67. Bunge, "'Best Practices,'" 246.

68. See *Let the Children Come*, 84–88, 93–94. Few scholars have analyzed these codes with specific regard to children. For a recent study of how "Christian families challenged the prevailing imperial ideology" that shaped the "rigid social divisions of the period," see Margaret Y. MacDonald, *The Power of Children: The Construction of Christian Families in the Greco-Roman World* (Waco, TX: Baylor University Press, 2014), book abstract.

69. Bunge, "'Best Practices,'" 245.

70. Werpehowski, "In Search of Real Children," 66, emphasis original.

71. See Suzanne G. Farnham, Josepha P. Gill, R. Taylor, and Susan M. Ward, *Listening Hearts: Discerning Call in Community*, 20th anniversary ed. (Harrisburg, PA: Morehouse, 2011).

72. Patchett, *This Is the Story*, 16.

73. Informal conversation, Seminar on Vocation across the Lifespan, Collegeville Institute for Ecumenical and Cultural Research, December 12, 2013.

74. Patchett, *This Is the Story*, 300–303.

75. Scott and Evans, "Peak Experience Project," 155.

76. Hartung, Porfeli, and Vonrack, "Child Vocational Development," 390, 394, 411–12.

77. Patchett, *This Is the Story*, 299.

78. Patchett, *This Is the Story*, 288; emphasis original.

79. Bunge, "'Best Practices,'" 234–42.

80. Rubio, *A Christian Theology of Marriage and Family*, 107. See Bonnie J. Miller-

McLemore, *In the Midst of Chaos: Care of Children as Spiritual Practice* (San Francisco: Jossey-Bass, 2006), chapter 6.

81. Oddly, Bunge includes "teach adults and be models of faith" as one of children's special duties in her chapter, "The Vocation of the Child: Theological Perspectives on the Particular and Paradoxical Roles and Responsibilities of Children" (in *The Vocation of the Child*, 47), but she drops this in her later 2011 rendition ("'Best Practices'").

82. Christine E. Gudorf, "Parenting, Mutual Love, and Sacrifice," in *Women's Consciousness, Women's Conscience: A Reader in Feminist Ethics*, ed. Barbara Hilkert Andolsen, Christine E. Gudorf, and Mary D. Pellauer (San Francisco: HarperSanFrancisco, 1985), 177.

83. Dorothy C. Bass, "Camping: Quotidian Practice on the Landscape of New Creation," in *Christian Practical Wisdom*, 72.

84. Erikson, *Insight and Responsibility*, 114, 152, 219.

85. Erikson, *Insight and Responsibility*, 115.

86. Erikson, *Insight and Responsibility*, 231.

87. See Miller-McLemore, *Also a Mother*, 152–53.

88. Benjamin J. Dueholm, "Why I Kiss My Stole," *The Christian Century* 132, no. 17 (June 25, 2014): 10–11.

89. Gudorf, "Parenting, Mutual Love, and Sacrifice"; Elizabeth Ann Dryer, "Asceticism Reconsidered," *Weavings: A Journal of the Christian Spiritual Life* 3 (1988): 6–15; Soskice, "Love and Attention"; Wendy M. Wright, "Living the Already But Not Yet: The Spiritual Life of the American Catholic Family," *Warren Lecture Series in Catholic Studies*, no. 25, University of Tulsa, March 21, 1993; Miller-McLemore, *In the Midst of Chaos*, chapter 9.

90. John Paul II, *On the Family* (Washington, DC: U.S. Catholic Conference, 1981), no. 26, cited by Rubio, *A Christian Theology of Marriage and Family*, 159.

91. See Pamela D. Couture, *Seeing God, Seeing Children: A Practical Theology of Children and Poverty* (Nashville, TN: Abingdon, 2000), and Joyce Ann Mercer, *Welcoming Children: A Practical Theology of Childhood* (St. Louis, MO: Chalice, 2005), especially chapter 2 and 254–58. For the complexities surrounding Gospel accounts of Jesus's blessing of children, see Bonnie J. Miller-McLemore, "Jesus and the Little Children: An Exercise in the Use of Scripture," *Journal of Childhood and Religion* 1, no. 7 (October 2010): 1–35, accessed December 15, 2016, http://childhoodandreligion.com/wp-content/uploads/2015/03/Miller-McLemore-Oct-2010.pdf.

92. Nancy E. Bedford, "Little Moves Against Destructiveness: Theology and the Practice of Discernment," in *Practicing Theology: Beliefs and Practices in Christian Life*, ed. Miroslav Volf and Dorothy C. Bass (Grand Rapids, MI: Eerdmans, 2002), 168.

93. Jan Nieuwenhuis, "Das Kind wird Euch weiden: Perspektiven einer kinderfreudlichen Pastoral," in *Kinderpastoral*, ed. J. H. Wiener and H. Erharter (Vienna, 1982), 85, cited by Mette, "Learning to Live," 108.

94. Bedford, "Little Moves Against Destructiveness," 169.

95. Konner, *The Evolution of Childhood*, 431. See Sarah Blaffer Hrdy, *Mothers and Others: The Evolutionary Origin of Mutual Understanding* (Cambridge, MA: Harvard University Press, 2009).

96. Patricia Hill Collins, *Black Feminist Thought: Knowledge, Consciousness, and the Politics of Empowerment* (New York: Routledge, 1991), 119–20.

97. Jeanne Stevenson-Moessner, *The Spirit of Adoption: At Home in God's Family* (Louisville, KY: Westminster John Knox, 2003), 90.

98. Jane Patterson, "Siblings: Am I My Brother's Keeper?" 63–64.

99. Rahner, "Ideas for a Theology of Childhood," 41.

Notes to Chapter 4

1. Dori Grinenko Baker and Joyce Ann Mercer, *Lives to Offer: Accompany Youth on Their Vocational Quests* (Cleveland, OH: Pilgrim, 2007).

2. This is a primary tension of youth ministry named by David F. White, *Practicing Discernment with Youth* (Cleveland, OH: Pilgrim, 2005), 43. See also Katherine Turpin, *Branded: Adolescents Converting from Consumer Faith* (Cleveland, OH: Pilgrim, 2006), and Brian J. Mahan, Michael Warren, and David F. White, *Awakening Youth Discipleship: Christian Resistance in a Consumer Culture* (Eugene, OR: Cascade, 2008).

3. I gathered the stories in this chapter from adolescents and from young and middle adults looking back on their experiences of calling in adolescence, and I have changed their names.

4. Jane Patterson, "Siblings: Am I My Brother's Keeper?" 63–64.

5. Ronald Nydam, "Early Adolescence," in *Human Development and Faith*, ed. Felicity B. Kelcourse (St. Louis, MO: Chalice, 2004), 216–17.

6. For a helpful treatment of the social formation of masculinity in adolescence, see C. J. Pascoe, *Dude, You're a Fag: Masculinity and Sexuality in High School* (Berkeley: University of California Press, 2012 [2007]).

7. Psalm 139, NRSV. This biblical text is often used in denominational curricular resources on adolescent sexuality to refer to bodily transformation and sexual maturity.

8. Baker and Mercer, *Lives to Offer*, 112.

9. James W. Fowler, *Stages of Faith: The Psychology of Human Development and the Quest for Meaning* (San Francisco: HarperCollins, 1995), 72.

10. Dan P. McAdams, "Personality, Modernity, and the Storied Self: A Contemporary Framework for Studying Persons," *Psychological Inquiry* 7 (1996): 311.

11. Barbara Strauch, *The Primal Teen: What the New Discoveries about the Teenage Brain Tell Us about Our Kids* (New York: Anchor, 2004), 206.

12. Baker and Mercer, *Lives to Offer*, 155.

13. John Neafsey, *A Sacred Voice Is Calling: Personal Vocation and Social Conscience* (Maryknoll, NY: Orbis, 2006). Neafsey's nuanced discussion of the role of suffering in vocational discernment takes place in chapter 7.

14. Peter L. Benson, *Sparks: How Parents Can Help Ignite the Hidden Strengths of Teenagers* (San Francisco: Jossey-Bass, 2008), 28.

15. Mihaly Csikszentmihalyi and Jeanne Nakamura, "The Dynamics of Intrinsic Motivation: A Study of Adolescents," in *Research on Motivation in Education: Goals and Cognitions*, ed. R. Ames and C. Ames (New York: Academic, 1989), 45–71.

16. Nancy Lesko, *Act Your Age! A Cultural Construction of Adolescence* (New York: Routledge Falmer, 2001), 111.

17. Michael Nakkula and Eric Toshalis dedicate an entire chapter to the importance of experimentation in forming adolescent identity in their book for educators. Michael Nakkula and Eric Toshalis, "Risk Taking and Creativity," in *Understanding Youth: Adolescent Development for Educators* (Cambridge, MA: Harvard Education Press, 2006), 41–60.

18. Baker and Mercer, *Lives to Offer*, 164–65.

19. Lesko, *Act Your Age!* 146.

20. Lesko, *Act Your Age!* 146.

21. Nakkula and Toshalis, *Understanding Youth*, 6.

22. Nakkula and Toshalis, *Understanding Youth*, 6.

23. James W. Fowler, *Becoming Adult, Becoming Christian: Adult Development and Christian Faith* (San Francisco: Jossey-Bass, 2000), 47.

24. Evelyn L. Parker, *Trouble Don't Last Always: Emancipatory Hope Among African-American Adolescents* (Cleveland, OH: Pilgrim, 2003), 148.

25. Beverly Daniel Tatum, *Why Do All of the Black Kids Sit Together in the Cafeteria? And Other Conversations about Race,* fifth anniversary rev. ed. (New York: Basic, 2003), 74.

26. Nakkula and Toshalis, *Understanding Youth*, 7.

27. Bert Roebben, *Seeking Sense in the City: European Perspectives on Religious Education* (Münster: LIT Verlag, 2009), 13.

28. Nakkula and Toshalis, *Understanding Youth*, 34.

29. Egan develops this aspect of adolescent imagination and its uses in education in "The Romantic Self," in Kieran Egan, *The Educated Self: How Cognitive Tools Shape Understanding* (Chicago: University of Chicago Press, 1997), 71–103.

30. The idea of vocational exemplars is explored by Matt Bloom and Amy Colbert, "Work as a Calling: Integrating Personal and Professional Identities" (unpublished manuscript, 2015), 24. I discuss the importance of exemplars in young adulthood in more depth in the following chapter.

31. Jane Addams, *Twenty Years at Hull House,* One Hundredth Anniversary Edition (New York: Penguin, 1999), 46.

32. Evelyn Parker, "Theological Framework for Youth Ministry: Hope," in *Starting Right: Thinking Theologically about Youth Ministry,* ed. Kenda Creasy Dean, Chap Clark, and Dave Rahn (Grand Rapids, MI: Youth Specialties Academic, 2001), 272.

33. Strauch, *Primal Teen,* 210.

34. For an example of vocational interviews with adolescents using appreciative inquiry, see Katherine Turpin and Anne Carter Walker, *Nurturing Different Dreams: Youth Ministry across Lines of Difference* (Eugene, OR: Pickwick, 2014), 14.

35. Baker and Mercer, *Lives to Offer*, 107.

36. Nakkula and Toshalis, *Understanding Youth*, 3.

37. Baker and Mercer, *Lives to Offer*, 167.

38. Thomas Merton, *New Seeds of Contemplation* (New York: New Directions, 1972), 29.

39. Merton, *New Seeds*, 31.

40. Merton, *New Seeds*, 32; emphasis original.

Notes to Chapter 5

1. The vignettes in this chapter are composite representations of young adults except for the story of Andrea (name changed), who is a middle adult reflecting on her experience of calling as a young adult.

2. Jeffrey Jensen Arnett, *Emerging Adulthood: The Winding Road from the Late Teens through the Twenties*, 2nd ed. (New York: Oxford University Press, 2015). He discusses how emerging adulthood differs from older adolescence or young adulthood (20–24). In this chapter, I use the terms "young adulthood" and "emerging adulthood" interchangeably.

3. Sharon Daloz Parks, *Big Questions, Worthy Dreams: Mentoring Young Adults in Their Quest for Meaning, Purpose, and Faith* (San Francisco: Jossey-Bass, 2001), 8.

4. Robert Wuthnow, *After the Baby Boomers: How Twenty- and Thirty-Something Adults Are Shaping the Future of American Religion* (Princeton, NJ: Princeton University Press, 2007), 37.

5. Parks, *Big Questions, Worthy Dreams*, 35.

6. Jane Patterson, "Younger Adulthood: A Voice from Within," 93.

7. Parks, *Big Questions, Worthy Dreams*, 6.

8. For a helpful discussion on finding true self-knowledge as an initial step in vocational discernment for those entering professions, see Matt Bloom and Amy Colbert, "Work as a Calling: Integrating Personal and Professional Identities" (unpublished manuscript, 2015), 17–22.

9. Erik Erikson, *Youth: Identity and Crisis* (New York: Norton, 1994 [1968]), 128–35.

10. Robert Kegan, "The Growth and Loss of the Institutional Self," in *The Evolving Self: Problem and Process in Human Development* (Cambridge, MA: Harvard University Press, 1982), 221–54.

11. Bloom and Colbert, "Work as a Calling," 24.

12. Wuthnow, *Beyond Baby Boomers*, 28.

13. Richard Fry, "A Rising Share of Young Adults Live in Their Parents' Home," Pew Research Center, accessed December 15, 2016, http://www.pewsocialtrends.org/2013/08/01/a-rising-share-of-young-adults-live-in-their-parents-home/#overview.

14. Richard Fry and Jeffrey S. Passel, "In Post-Recession Era, Young Adults Drive Continuing Rise in Multi-Generational Living," Pew Research Center, accessed December 15, 2016, http://www.pewsocialtrends.org/2014/07/17/in-post-recession-era-young-adults-drive-continuing-rise-in-multi-generational-living/.

15. Richard Fry, "Young Adults, Student Debt and Economic Well-Being," Pew Research Center, accessed December 15, 2016, http://www.pewsocialtrends.org/2014/05/14/young-adults-student-debt-and-economic-well-being/.

16. Jennifer Grant Haworth, *Living with Purpose in Early Adulthood: A Preliminary Needs Assessment,* Internal Report, Lilly Endowment, Inc., May 2015, 4.

17. Parks, *Big Questions, Worthy Dreams,* 67.

18. Derek Thompson, "A World without Work," *The Atlantic* 361, no. 1 (July–August 2015): 51–61.

19. Steven Greenhouse, "A Part-Time Life, as Hours Shrink and Shift," *The New York Times,* accessed December 15, 2016, http://www.nytimes.com/2012/10/28/business/a -part-time-life-as-hours-shrink-and-shift-for-american-workers.html?pagewanted=1.

20. Wuthnow, *Beyond the Baby Boomers,* 1–32.

21. Rainer Maria Rilke, *Letters to a Young Poet,* rev. ed., trans. M. D. Herter Norton (New York: Norton, 1993), 13.

22. Parks, *Big Questions, Worthy Dreams,* 65.

23. Bloom and Colbert, "Work as a Calling," 47.

24. Bloom and Colbert, "Work as a Calling," 27.

25. Jane Patterson, "Younger Adulthood: A Voice from Within," 94.

26. John Neafsey, *A Sacred Voice Is Calling: Personal Vocation and Social Conscience* (Maryknoll, NY: Orbis, 2006). Neafsey's nuanced discussion of the role of suffering in vocational discernment takes place in chapter 7.

27. Carol Howard Merritt, *Tribal Church: Ministering to the Missing Generation* (Herndon, VA: Alban Institute, 2007), 93.

28. Herbert Anderson explores the pastoral dynamics of young adults leaving their families of origin in his helpful book *Leaving Home* (Louisville, KY: Westminster John Knox, 1993).

29. Parks, *Big Questions, Worthy Dreams,* 7.

30. Haworth, *Living with Purpose,* 2.

31. Madeleine L'Engle, *Two-Part Invention: The Story of a Marriage,* The Crosswicks Journals, Book 4 (San Francisco: HarperOne, 1989).

32. Merritt, *Tribal Church,* 87.

33. Merritt, *Tribal Church,* 137.

34. Merritt, *Tribal Church,* 136.

35. Michael Jinkins, foreword to Merritt, *Tribal Church,* ix.

36. Bloom and Colbert, "Work as a Calling," 32–33.

37. Both Merritt in *Tribal Church* and Nancy Ammerman in *Sacred Stories, Sacred Tribes: Finding Religion in Everyday Life* (New York: Oxford University Press, 2013) evoke the language of "tribe" as a response to the resistance to institutional religion in contemporary culture, particularly among young adults.

38. Parks, *Big Questions, Worthy Dreams,* 155.

39. Jane Patterson, "Adolescence: God Looks on the Heart," 66.

40. For an interesting personal exploration of retaining a sense of calling as a pastor in the midst of experiences of closure and denial, see "You are a pastor," a blog by Carol Howard Merritt in *The Christian Century,* accessed December 15, 2016, https://www .christiancentury.org/blogs/archive/2015-03/you-are-pastor.

41. Generativity, or the readiness to nurture and care for the next generation, was one of the strengths of adulthood named by Erik Erikson, *Insight and Responsibility*

(New York: Norton, 1994 [1964]), 130–31. See also Matt Bloom's chapter on middle adulthood in this volume.

Notes to Chapter 6

1. Studs Terkel, *Working: People Talk about What They Do All Day and How They Feel about What They Do* (New York: Pantheon, 1974).

2. Quotes in this chapter come from my research on well-being at work: http://wellbeing.nd.edu/.

3. Philosopher Laurie Paul calls these "transformative experiences." She argues that we cannot use reason alone to figure out which choice to make because our choice will change who we are: we become different people depending on which life path we choose. L. A. Paul, *Transformative Experience* (New York: Oxford University Press, 2014).

4. Jane Patterson, "Points of Decision in Adulthood," 120–21.

5. Erik H. Erikson, *Identity and the Life Cycle* (New York: Norton, 1992 [1959]); James W. Fowler, *Weaving the New Creation* (San Francisco: HarperSanFrancisco, 1991); Wade Clark Roof, *Spiritual Marketplace: Baby Boomers and the Remaking of American Religion* (Princeton, NJ: Princeton University Press, 1999); Paul T. P. Wong, ed., *The Human Quest for Meaning: Theories, Research, and Applications* (New York: Routledge, 2012).

6. C. L. Park, "Making Sense of the Meaning Literature: An Integrative Review of Meaning Making and Its Effects on Adjustment to Stressful Life Events," *Psychological Bulletin* 136 (2010): 257–301; idem, "Religion and Meaning," in *Handbook of the Psychology of Religion and Spirituality*, 2nd ed., ed. R. F. Paloutzian and C. L. Park (New York: Guilford, 2013), 357–79.

7. Charles Taylor, *Sources of the Self: The Making of Modern Identity* (Cambridge, MA: Harvard University Press, 1989); idem, *The Ethics of Authenticity* (Cambridge, MA: Harvard University Press, 1991), 35.

8. Edward Hahnenberg, *Awakening Vocation* (Collegeville, MN: Liturgical Press, 2010).

9. See Jane Patterson, "Points of Decision in Adulthood," 119–20.

10. Poet Mary Oliver's vivid description in "The Summer Day" resonates for many middle adults. Mary Oliver, "The Summer Day," in *New and Selected Poems* (Boston: Beacon, 1992), 101.

11. Emerging data suggest possible changes in this pattern. See "The Decline of Marriage and Rise of New Families," Pew Research Center, accessed December 15, 2016, http://www.pewsocialtrends.org/2010/11/18/the-decline-of-marriage-and-rise-of-new-families/.

12. Studies about the happiness of parents are equivocal. See A. Deaton and A. A. Stone, "Evaluative and Hedonic Wellbeing among Those with and without Children at Home," *Proceedings of the National Academy of Sciences* 11 (2014): 1328–33, accessed December 15, 2016, www.pnas.org/content/111/4/1328.full.pdf; C.M. Herbst and J. Ifcher,

"The Increasing Happiness of Parents," accessed December 15, 2016, https://aleteiaen .files.wordpress.com/2015/04/increasing-happiness-of-parents-draft-jpopecon-4-10 -14.pdf; see also accessed December 15, 2016, www.open.ac.uk.researchprojects.en duringlove and nymag.com/news/features/67024/.

13. T. D. Allen, E. Chao, and L. L. Meier, "Work-Family Boundary Dynamics," *Annual Review of Organizational Psychology and Organizational Behavior* 1 (2014): 99–121; E. L. Kelly, E. E. Kossek, L. B. Hammer, M. Durham, J. Bray, K. Chermack, et al., "Getting There from Here: Research on the Effects of Work-Family Initiatives on Work-Family Conflict and Business Outcomes," *Academy of Management Annals* 2, no. 1 (2008): 305–49.

14. M. Bloom and A. Colbert, "Work as a Life Calling: Integrating Personal and Professional Identities" (unpublished manuscript, 2015); P. Bronson, *What Should I Do with My Life?* (New York: Ballantine, 2005); J. S. Bunderson and J. A. Thompson, "The Call of the Wild: Zookeepers, Callings, and the Double-Edged Sword of Deeply Meaningful Work," *Administrative Science Quarterly* 54 (2009): 32–57.

15. See Jane Patterson, "Points of Decision in Adulthood," 121–22.

16. P. R. Shaver and M. Mikulincer, eds., *Meaning, Mortality, and Choice: The Social Psychology of Existential Concerns* (Washington, DC: American Psychological Association, 2012), 55–73.

17. James W. Fowler, *Stages of Faith: The Psychology of Human Development and the Quest for Meaning* (San Francisco: HarperSanFrancisco, 1981).

18. Roof, *Spiritual Marketplace*, 46.

19. Fowler, *Stages of Faith*, 99–102.

20. See Jane Patterson, "Younger Adulthood: A Voice from Within," 94.

21. Charles Taylor, *A Secular Age* (Cambridge, MA: Harvard University Press, 2007).

22. Taylor, *A Secular Age*, 309.

23. Roof, *Spiritual Marketplace*, 46–47.

24. Nancy T. Ammerman, *Sacred Stories, Sacred Tribes* (New York: Oxford University Press, 2014).

25. Ammerman, *Sacred Stories, Sacred Tribes*, 34.

26. Ammerman, *Sacred Stories, Sacred Tribes*, 34.

27. While many philosophers and theologians have explored the "true self," social scientists have more recently explored how people experience their deepest, most authentic self. See, for example, J. E. Dutton, L. M. Roberts, and J. Bednar, "Positive Identities and Organizations: An Introduction and Invitation," in *Exploring Positive Identities and Organizations: Building a Theoretical and Research Foundation*, ed. L. M. Roberts and J. E. Dutton (New York: Psychology Press, 2009), 3–20; D. P. McAdams, "The Psychology of Life Stories," *Review of General Psychology* 5 (2004): 1–23; R. J. Schlegel, J. A. Hicks, J. Arndt, and L. A. King, "Thine Own Self: True Self-Concept Accessibility and Meaning in Life," *Journal of Personality and Social Psychology* 96 (2009): 473–90.

28. "Coping with Stress at Work," American Psychological Association, accessed December 15, 2016, http://www.apa.org/helpcenter/work-stress.aspx.

29. "Stress at Work," Centers for Disease Control, accessed December 15, 2016, http://www.cdc.gov/niosh/docs/99-101/#b.

30. Julianne Pepitone, "U.S. Job Satisfaction Hits 22-Year Low," *CNN Money*, accessed December 15, 2016, http://money.cnn.com/2010/01/05/news/economy/job_satisfaction_report/.

31. Clifton Parker, "Stanford Research Explores Weekend Happiness, Unemployment Blues," Stanford News, accessed December 16, 2016, http://news.stanford.edu/news/2014/february/time-value-jobless-022014.html.

32. E. Diener and R. Biswas-Diener, *Happiness: Unlocking the Mysteries of Psychological Wealth* (New York: Wiley-Blackwell, 2008).

33. Bloom and Colbert, "Work as a Life Calling."

34. Bonnie J. Miller-McLemore, *Also a Mother: Work and Family as Theological Dilemma* (Nashville, TN: Abingdon, 1994), 113.

35. "Family Medical Leave Act," U.S. Department of Labor, accessed December 15, 2016, www.dol.gov/whd/fmla/.

36. Jack Fortin, *The Centered Life: Awakened, Called, Set Free, Nurtured* (Minneapolis, MN: Augsburg Fortress, 2006).

37. M. Ardelt and S. Jacobs, "Wisdom, Integrity, and Life Satisfaction in Very Old Age," in *Handbook of Research on Adult Learning and Development* (New York: Routledge, 2009), 732–49; P. Baltes and U. Staudinger, "Wisdom: A Metaheuristic (Pragmatic) to Orchestrate Mind and Virtue toward Excellence," *American Psychologist* 55, no. 1 (2000): 122–36.

38. J. Glück and S. Bluck, "Laypeople's Conceptions of Wisdom and Its Development: Cognitive and Integrative Views," *The Journals of Gerontology: Series B: Psychological Sciences and Social Sciences* 66, no. 3 (2011): 321–24.

39. R. J. Sternberg, ed., *Wisdom: Its Nature, Origins, and Development* (New York: Cambridge University Press, 2009).

40. Jane Patterson, "Introducing Biblical Interludes: Vocation in the Family of God," 33.

41. P. B. Baltes, U. M. Staudinger, and U. Lindenberger, "Lifespan Psychology: Theory and Application to Intellectual Functioning," *Annual Review of Psychology* 50 (1999): 471–507; Carol Gilligan, *In a Different Voice* (Cambridge, MA: Harvard University Press, 1982).

42. D. Miller, "The 'Sandwich' Generation: Adult Children of the Aging," *Social Work* 26 (1981): 419–23; see also K. Parker and E. Patten, "The Sandwich Generation: Rising Financial Burdens for Middle-Aged Americans," *Pew Research* (2013), and C. R. Pierret, "The 'Sandwich Generation': Women Caring for Parents and Children," *Monthly Labor Review* (September 2006): 3–9.

43. J. M. Berg, A. M. Grant, and V. Johnson, "When Callings Are Calling: Crafting Work and Leisure in Pursuit of Unanswered Occupational Callings," *Organization Science* 21 (2010): 973–94.

44. Laurent A. Parks Daloz, Sharon Daloz Parks, Cheryl H. Keen, and James P. Keen, *Common Fire: Leading Lives of Commitment in a Complex World* (Boston: Beacon, 1997).

217

45. Erik H. Erikson, *Identity and the Life Cycle* (New York: International Universities Press, 1959).

46. Charles L. Slater, "Generativity Versus Stagnation: An Elaboration of Erikson's Adult Stage of Human Development," *Journal of Adult Development* 10, no. 1 (2003): 53–65.

47. Carole Fleck, "Boomers Most Generous at Charitable Giving," accessed December 15, 2016, http://blog.aarp.org/2013/08/08/boomers-most-generous-at-charitable-giving/. See also, accessed December 15, 2016, www.convio.com/files/next-gen-whitepaper.pdf; www.forbes.com/sites/deborahljacobs/2013/08/08/charitable-giving-baby-boomers-donate-more-study-shows/. However, a survey by World Vision suggests that young men are *more* likely to give: accessed December 15, 2016, www.worldvision.org/press-release/world-vision-holiday-giving-survey-shows-young-men-most-likely-give-gift-charity.

48. See Conscious Capitalism, accessed December 15, 2016, www.consciouscapitalism.org.

49. See B Corps, accessed December 15, 2016, www.bcorporation.net.

50. David J. Ekerdt and Robert S. Weiss, *The Experience of Retirement* (Ithaca, NY: Cornell University Press, 2005).

51. D. Chen, X. Yang, and S. Dale Aagard, "The Empty Nest Syndrome: Ways to Enhance Quality of Life," *Educational Gerontology* 38, no. 8 (2012): 520–29; Sara Harkness, "Empty Nest Syndrome," in *Encyclopedia of Aging and Public Health*, ed. Sana Loue and Martha Sajatovic (New York: Springer, 2008), 318–19; B. Mitchell and L. Lovegreen, "The Empty Nest Syndrome in Midlife Families: A Multimethod Exploration of Parental Gender Differences and Cultural Dynamics," *Journal of Family Issues* 30, no. 12 (2009): 1651–70; E. J. Myers and L. J. Raup, "The Empty Nest Syndrome: Myth or Reality?" *Journal of Counseling & Development* 68, no. 2 (1989): 180–83.

52. See the special issue of *Psychological Inquiry* 25, no. 1 (2014); Diener and Biswas-Diener, *Happiness: Unlocking the Mysteries of Psychological Wealth*; K. Gustavson, W. Nilsen, R. Ørstavik, and E. Røysamb, "Relationship Quality, Divorce, and Well-being: Findings from a Three-Year Longitudinal Study," *The Journal of Positive Psychology* 9, no. 2 (2014): 163–74; and A. Mastekaasa, "Psychological Well-Being and Marital Dissolution: Selection Effects?" *Journal of Family Issues* 15, no. 2 (1994): 208–28.

53. C. S. Bergeman, *Aging: Genetic and Environmental Influences* (Thousand Oaks, CA: Sage, 1997); Deborah Carr, Randolph Ness, and Camille B. Wortman, eds., *Spousal Bereavement in Later Life* (New York: Springer, 2005); T. Damianakis and E. Marziali, "Older Adults' Response to the Loss of a Spouse: The Function of Spirituality in Understanding the Grieving Process," *Aging & Mental Health* 16, no. 1 (2012): 57–66; A. D. Ong, C. S. Bergeman, and S. M. Boker, "Resilience Comes of Age: Defining Features and Dynamic Conceptions," *Journal of Personality* 77, no. 6 (2009): 2–28; I. Sasson and D. Umberson, "Widowhood and Depression: New Light on Gender Differences, Selection, and Psychological Adjustment," *The Journals of Gerontology: Series B: Psychological Sciences and Social Sciences* 69, no. 1 (2014): 135–45.

Notes to Chapter 7

1. I draw upon several stories from our research in this chapter; I have changed the names of people to honor confidentiality.

2. James C. Fisher and Henry C. Simmons, *A Journey Called Aging: Challenges and Opportunities in Older Adulthood* (New York: Routledge, 2006), 60.

3. Fisher and Simmons, *A Journey Called Aging*, 41. Most people today do not enter late adulthood at 65.

4. Retirement can be defined as a time "in which one discontinues full-time employment that has provided a livelihood through the adult years and negotiates a path into a new life-world." Retirement refers to "the process of retiring and to the whole period of life after one has ceased working at what was one's highest status, paying employ." Fisher and Simmons, *A Journey Called Aging*, 39.

5. We are becoming a four-generation society. By 2030, more than 70 percent of 8-year-olds will have a great-grandparent. "Here Come the Great-Grandparents," *The New York Times*, November 2, 2006, accessed December 16, 2016, http://www.nytimes.com/2006/11/02/fashion/02parents.html?pagewanted=all&_r=0.

6. Mary Catherine Bateson, *Composing a Further Life: The Age of Active Wisdom* (New York: Knopf, 2010), 19.

7. Bateson, *Composing a Further Life*, 26.

8. Adam Nagourney, "Boxer Says She Won't Seek Re-election to Senate in California in 2016," *The New York Times*, accessed December 15, 2016, http://www.nytimes.com/2015/01/09/us/politics/senator-barbara-boxer-says-she-wont-seek-re-election-in-2016.html?hp&action=click&pgtype=Homepage&module=second-column-region&region=top-news&WT.nav=top-news&_r=0.

9. Bateson, *Composing a Further Life*, 19–20.

10. Bateson, *Composing a Further Life*, 20.

11. Retirement is an "incomplete ritual" in our society, according to Peter Jarvis. There is no structural way for adults to leave behind their former status and accept a new status and role. Quoted in Fisher and Simmons, *A Journey Called Aging*, 57. See Belden Lane's story about a ritual he performs, a death lodge, in the wilderness to mark the transition of his retirement. See Belden C. Lane, *Backpacking with the Saints: Wilderness Hiking as Spiritual Practice* (New York: Oxford University Press, 2015), 144–45.

12. This growth is due to 76 million baby boomers who began turning 65 in 2011. See "Growing Old in America: Expectations vs. Reality," Pew Research Center, accessed December 15, 2016, http://www.pewsocialtrends.org/2009/06/29/growing-old-in-america-expectations-vs-reality/; Jennifer M. Ortman, Victoria A. Velkoff, and Howard Hogan, "An Aging Nation: The Older Population in the United States," U.S. Census Bureau, May 2014.

13. Bateson, *Composing a Further Life*, 12.

14. Bateson, *Composing a Further Life*, 13–14.

15. William Sadler, *The Third Age: Six Principles for Personal Growth and Rejuvenation after Forty* (Cambridge, MA: Perseus, 2000).

16. For an overview, see Fisher and Simmons, *A Journey Called Aging*, 20.

17. Fisher and Simmons note that "everyone over fifty strives to stay middle-aged forever" and those over 65 who identify as middle aged are healthier, more active, happier, and better adjusted. *A Journey Called Aging*, 60.

18. Fisher and Simmons define a "bridge job" as a short-term job after retiring from a career in contrast to a career job that lasts ten or more years. *A Journey Called Aging*, 43.

19. "Working After Retirement: The Gap between Expectations and Reality," Pew Research Center, September 21, 2006, accessed December 15, 2016, http://www.pew socialtrends.org/2006/09/21/working-after-retirement-the-gap-between-expecta tions-and-reality/.

20. National Council on Aging, "Economic Security for Seniors Facts," accessed December 15, 2016, https://www.ncoa.org/news/resources-for-reporters/get-the -facts/economic-security-facts/.

21. Fisher and Simmons, *A Journey Called Aging*, 52–53.

22. Fisher and Simmons, *A Journey Called Aging*, 68.

23. Fisher and Simmons, *A Journey Called Aging*, 66.

24. Bateson, *Composing a Further Life*, 79.

25. Bateson, *Composing a Further Life*, 19.

26. Bateson, *Composing a Further Life*, 67.

27. Bateson, *Composing a Further Life*, 78.

28. Fisher and Simmons, *A Journey Called Aging*, 56.

29. Marc Freedman, *Encore: Finding Work that Matters in the Second Half of Life* (New York: PublicAffairs, 2007), 18–19.

30. Edward Hahnenberg, *Awakening Vocation: A Theology of Christian Calling* (Collegeville, MN: Liturgical Press, 2010), 101.

31. On discerning work and rhythms of Sabbath, see Claire Wolfteich, *Navigating New Terrain: Work and Women's Spiritual Lives* (Mahwah, NJ: Paulist, 2002), 111–34.

32. See Jane Patterson, "Elders: Ultimate Values," 148–49.

33. Bateson, *Composing a Further Life*, 55. See also Jane Fonda, "Life's Third Act," TED, December 2011, accessed December 15, 2016, https://www.ted.com/talks/jane _fonda_life_s_third_act.

34. Bateson, *Composing a Further Life*, 52.

35. Peace Corps, "Hear the Call," accessed December 15, 2016, http://www.peace corps.gov/50plus/.

36. "Seniors Doing Their Piece," Peace Corps, February 26, 2005, accessed December 15, 2016, http://www.peacecorps.gov/media/forpress/news/1019/. Professions are promoting international volunteer work for people over 55. For example, The Financial Services Volunteer Corps, a nonprofit organization in New York, recruits financial experts for brief consulting projects in developing countries and the International Senior Lawyers Project recruits volunteers for pro bono projects overseas. See "Experienced, Eager, Will Travel," *The New York Times*, April 1, 2009, accessed December 15, 2016, http://www.nytimes.com/2009/04/02/business/retirement special/02PEACE.html?ref=retirement. See also AARP Foundation Experience Corps, accessed July 20, 2015, http://www.aarp.org/experience-corps/.

37. "NOMADS Mission and Vision," accessed December 15, 2016, http://www.nomadsumc.org/missionandvision.

38. See Encore.org, accessed December 15, 2016, http://encore.org/prize/.

39. Freedman, *Encore*, 84; emphasis in original.

40. "Older adulthood, in particular, can produce an alienation from our bodies: a sense that who we are is somehow not who we see reflected in the mirror, that our self-identity is different from what our bodies seem to reflect back to us. The body can seem, to varying degrees, fundamentally or significantly 'other,' producing the challenge of integrating our experience of our bodies and our sense of self or adaptively altering the character of our investment in our bodily selves." K. Brynolf Lyon, "Faith and Development in Late Adulthood," in *Human Development and Faith*, ed. Felicity B. Kelcourse (St. Louis, MO: Chalice, 2004), 273.

41. I am drawing on the six types of loss discussed in Kenneth Mitchell and Herbert Anderson, *All Our Losses, All Our Griefs* (Philadelphia: Westminster, 1983), 36–46.

42. Janice Jean Springer, "Illness as Hermitage: How Parkinson's Became My Spiritual Practice," *The Christian Century* 132, no. 19 (September 16, 2015): 10.

43. Lane, *Backpacking*, 144.

44. Lane, *Backpacking*, 145.

45. Springer, "Illness as Hermitage," 11.

46. For information on conducting a life review, see the Legacy Project, accessed December 16, 2016, http://www.legacyproject.org/guides/guides.html.

47. Fisher and Simmons, *A Journey Called Aging*, 67.

48. In the twentieth century Thomas Merton (1915–68) made the concept popular in Catholic spirituality. See James Finley, *Merton's Palace of Nowhere: In Search of God through Awareness of the True Self* (Notre Dame, IN: Ave Maria, 1978). D. C. Winnicott introduced it into psychoanalytic thought and it is used in two widely read books on vocation: John Neafsey, *A Sacred Voice Is Calling: Personal Vocation and Social Conscience* (Maryknoll, NY: Orbis, 2006), and Parker Palmer, *Let Your Life Speak: Listening for the Voice of Vocation* (San Francisco: Jossey-Bass, 2000).

49. Palmer, *Let Your Life Speak*, 18.

50. Richard Rohr, *Falling Upward: A Spirituality of the Two Halves of Life* (San Francisco: Jossey-Bass, 2011), xiii, xx.

51. Rohr, *Falling Upward*, xx–xxi.

52. Rohr, *Falling Upward*, xiv.

53. Rohr, *Falling Upward*, 138; emphasis original.

54. Rohr, *Falling Upward*, xviii; emphasis original.

55. Francis Kelly Nemeck, OMI, and Marie Theresa Coombs, *The Spiritual Journey: Critical Thresholds and Stages of Adult Spiritual Genesis* (Wilmington, DE: Michael Glazer, 1986), 41; emphasis in original.

56. Jane Patterson, "Points of Decision in Adulthood," 120–21.

57. Francis Kelly Nemeck, OMI, and Marie Theresa Coombs, *The Spiritual Journey: Critical Thresholds and Stages of Adult Spiritual Genesis* (Wilmington, DE: Michael Glazier, 1986), 41; Jane Patterson, "Points of Decision in Adulthood," 121-22.

58. Lyon notes that people do not become more religious as they grow older. "Faith and Development," 281.

59. For a discussion of vocation in retirement and older age as serving the "kingdom on the left," see Beth Ann Gaede, "What Will I Do Next? Discerning Vocations for Retirement: A Group Process for Older Adults" (DMin thesis, Luther Seminary, 2006), 87.

60. Fisher and Simmons, *A Journey Called Aging*, 54.

61. Lyon, "Faith and Development," 275.

62. Bateson, *Composing a Further Life*, 13.

63. Lyon, "Faith and Development," 280. Lyon points out that invisible older adults in our communities include aging lesbians (single and partnered) as well as the urban poor.

64. The "grandparent-grandchild relationship is one that has been neglected in family research literature to date." See Laura Hess Brown and Paul A. Roodin, "Grandparent-Grandchild Relationships and the Life Course Perspective," in *Handbook of Adult Development,* ed. Jack Demick and Carrie Andreoletti (New York: Springer, 2003), 461. Likewise, in theological literature on aging and older adults, the topic of grandparents is rarely treated. A major project on the family devotes four pages to the topic of grandparents. See Ray Anderson, "The Tasks of Grandparents in Families," in *The Family Handbook,* ed. Herbert Anderson, Don S. Browning, Ian S. Evison, and Mary Stewart Van Leeuwen (Philadelphia: Westminster John Knox, 1998), 84–88. Similarly a volume dedicated to women and developmental issues in pastoral care does not include the topic of grandmothers. See Jeanne Stevenson-Moessner, *In Her Own Time: Women and Developmental Issues in Pastoral Care* (Minneapolis, MN: Fortress, 2000).

65. Brown and Roodin, "Grandparent-Grandchild Relationships," 464.

66. For an overview of these studies, see Brown and Roodin, "Grandparent-Grandchild Relationships," 464–75.

67. But it is one that can be mourned if an adult child is infertile.

68. The four roles, or callings, discussed here are drawn from Carolyn Gutowski, *Grandparents Are Forever* (Mahwah, NJ: Paulist, 1994).

69. Gutowski, *Grandparents*, 5.

70. Research has shown that most grandmothers see their role as voluntary and short-term, focused on social and emotional support, with a clear sense of not wanting to be parents again. See Anne E. Streaty Wimberly, "From Intercessory Hope to Mutual Intercession: Grandparents Raising Grandchildren and the Church's Response," *Family Ministry* 14, no. 3 (Fall 2000): 21.

71. Gutowski, *Grandparents*, 44.

72. See earlier discussions of cogwheeling in this volume in the opening chapters on vocation (19) and on children (56).

73. Gutowski, *Grandparents*, 53.

74. Bateson, *Composing a Further Life*, 15–16. For further evidence, see Brown and Roodin, "Grandparent-Grandchild Relationships," 462.

75. Brown and Roodin, "Grandparent-Grandchild Relationships," 467. Older grandparents can also feel disconnected, without a clear role, and powerless in con-

temporary society, not knowing what their place is in family or society, being replaced as caregivers, and viewed as out of date in terms of parenting. See Wimberly, "From Intercessory Hope," 21.

76. For research on grandfathers, see Brown and Roodin, "Grandparent-Grandchild Relationships," 476.

77. Gutowski, *Grandparents,* 106.

78. See Brown and Roodin, "Grandparent-Grandchild Relationships," 468–70.

79. Julie Hicks Patrick and Eric A. Goedereis, "The Importance of Context and the Gain-Loss Dynamic for Understanding Grandparent Caregivers," in *How Caregiving Affects Development: Psychological Implications for Child, Adolescent, and Adult Caregivers,* ed. Kim Shifren (Washington, D.C.: American Psychological Association, 2009), 172. Wimberly's statistics are from the 1990s; grandparent parents were on the rise due to the "inability, unavailability, or unwillingness of the children's parents to care for their offspring due to one or more of the following": AIDS, other illnesses, and death; abandonment; abuse; divorce; drug addiction; incarceration; teen pregnancy and unwed teen parenthood; joblessness. See Wimberly, "From Intercessory Hope," 24–25.

80. Wimberly, "From Intercessory Hope," 20.

81. Wimberly, "From Intercessory Hope," 28.

82. Wimberly, "From Intercessory Hope," 30.

83. Hahnenberg, *Awakening Vocation,* 214.

84. Rosalynn Carter quotes a colleague as saying there are only four kinds of people in the world: those who have been caregivers, those who currently are caregivers, those who will be caregivers, and those who will need caregivers. See *Helping Yourself Help Others: A Book for Caregivers* (New York: Three Rivers, 1995).

85. The majority of caregivers, one-third, are 50 to 64 years of age; 12 percent are 65 to 74 years old; and 7 percent are over 75. Nearly half of caregivers care for a parent or parent-in-law; one in 10 care for a spouse. See *Caregiving in the U.S.: Executive Summary,* The National Alliance for Caregiving and AARP Public Policy Institute, June 2015, 30–31, accessed December 15, 2016, http://www.caregiving.org/caregiving2015/.

86. *Caregiving in the U.S.,* 10.

87. *Caregiving in the U.S.,* 19.

88. Jennifer F. Dobbins, "Connections of Care: Relationships and Family Caregiver Narratives," in *The Meaning of Others: Narrative Studies of Relationships,* ed. Ruthellen Josselson, Amia Lieblich, and Dan P. McAdams (Washington, DC: American Psychological Association, 2007), 191.

89. Dobbins, "Connections of Care," 190.

90. Dobbins, "Connections of Care," 206.

91. Dobbins, "Connections of Care," 209.

92. Fisher and Simmons, *A Journey Called Aging,* 84.

93. Fisher and Simmons, *A Journey Called Aging,* 88.

Notes to Chapter 8

1. This narrative was reviewed by Liz in December 2014 in her home in Minneapolis, Minnesota. It appears here with her permission. Because her companion is not in a position to give meaningful consent, I chose the pseudonym Jim to refer to him.

2. See, for example, K. Brynolf Lyon, "Faith Development in Late Adulthood," in *Human Development and Faith: Life-Cycle Stages of Body, Mind, and Soul,* ed. Felicity B. Kelcourse (St. Louis, MO: Chalice, 2004); Karen D. Scheib, *Challenging Invisibility: Practices of Care with Older Women* (St. Louis, MO: Chalice, 2004); John Swinton, *Dementia: Living in the Memories of God* (Grand Rapids, MI: Eerdmans, 2012).

3. Jane Patterson, "Elders: Ultimate Values," 148–49.

4. In "Elders: Ultimate Values," Jane Patterson shows how the call of Simeon and Anna, two elder adults, is linked with the infant Jesus, whose calling they identify. See 148–49.

5. Erik H. Erikson and Joan M. Erikson, *The Life Cycle Completed,* extended ed. (New York: Norton, 1997), 105–6.

6. Erikson, *The Life Cycle Completed,* 106.

7. Erikson, *The Life Cycle Completed,* 106.

8. Erikson, *The Life Cycle Completed,* 106.

9. Erikson, *The Life Cycle Completed,* 113.

10. James C. Fisher, "A Framework for Describing Developmental Change among Older Adults," *Adult Education Quarterly* 43, no. 2 (1993).

11. Martha Holstein, *Women in Late Life: Critical Perspectives on Gender and Age,* Diversity and Aging, series ed. Toni Calasanti (Lanham, MD: Rowman & Littlefield, 2015), 21.

12. Martha Holstein argues that the dominant cultural script of "successful aging" that emphasizes vigorous, healthy older adults is ultimately problematic, especially for women, because it encourages women to separate themselves from negative stereotypes of old age without doing anything to change those problematic meanings. She contends that the goal to be "not old" is a losing strategy that reinforces ageism. Consequently, Holstein refutes the division of older adulthood into separate "third" and "fourth" time frames, which she views as an effort to segregate the harsher realities of old age from the rest of the aging process. See Holstein, *Women in Late Life,* 136–39. While I agree with the critical thrust of her work, I find that for purposes of thinking about the vocation of older adulthood, it is useful to make the distinction between late and older adult life.

13. Holstein suggests that the new rhetoric on aging depicting "successful aging" as the ability to maintain health and remain vigorous participates in the denial of aging since eventually everyone succumbs to physical diminishment in some form. Holstein maintains that the repulsion toward women's aging bodies is linked to fear of identification with those whose mortality is most visible. See Holstein, *Women in Late Life,* 45, 99–116.

14. George E. Vaillant, *Triumphs of Experience: The Men of the Harvard Grant Study* (Cambridge, MA: Belknap Press of Harvard University Press, 2012), 225, 228.

Vaillant cites James F. Fries as the orginator of this term. See James F. Fries, "Aging, Natural Death, and the Compression of Morbidity," *New England Journal of Medicine* 303, no. 3 (1980): 130–35.

15. Holstein, *Women in Late Life*, 63.

16. Cited in Margaret Cruikshank, *Learning to Be Old: Gender, Culture, and Aging*, 3rd ed. (Lanham, MD: Rowman & Littlefield, 2013), 148.

17. Cruikshank, *Learning to Be Old*, 118.

18. Beth Jackson-Jordan, "God's Call in Later Life: A Theological Reflection on Aging," *Chaplaincy Today* 17, no. 1 (2001): 20–21.

19. Kathleen R. Fischer, *Winter Grace: Spirituality for the Later Years* (New York: Paulist, 1998), 19.

20. Holstein, *Women in Late Life*, 21.

21. Milton Crum, "I'm Old" (unpublished manuscript, 2011), 14.

22. Of course, the fact that Liz's intergenerational community does not marginalize her due to her age has a powerful role in the maintenance of self-esteem that cannot be assumed in the experience of many older adults, particularly women. See Cruikshank, *Learning to Be Old*, and Holstein, *Women in Late Life*.

23. Swinton, *Dementia*, 229–30; emphasis original.

24. See Bonnie J. Miller-McLemore's chapter, "Childhood: The (Often Hidden yet Lively) Vocational Life of Children," 38–62.

25. Kenneth W. Wachter, cited by Stephanie Rosenblum, "Here Come the Great-Grandparents," *The New York Times*, November 2, 2006, accessed December 15, 2016, http://www.nytimes.com/2006/11/02/fashion/02parents.html?pagewanted=all.

26. Linda Drew and Merrill Silverstein, "Intergenerational Role Investments of Great-Grandparents: Consequences for Psychological Well-Being," *Ageing and Society* 24 (2004): 95–111.

27. Holstein, *Women in Late Life*, 11.

28. John Bowlby, *Attachment and Loss*, 3 vols. (New York: Basic, 1969); Bernice Levin Neugarten and Dail Ann Neugarten, *The Meanings of Age: Selected Papers of Bernice L. Neugarten* (Chicago: University of Chicago Press, 1996); Robert Stuart Weiss, *Loneliness: The Experience of Emotional and Social Isolation* (Cambridge, MA: MIT, 1974).

29. Peggy A. Thoits, "Mechanisms Linking Social Ties and Support to Physical and Mental Health," *Journal of Health and Social Behavior* 52, no. 2 (2011): 156.

30. Paul J. Wadell, "The Call Goes On: Discipleship and Aging," *The Christian Century* 128, no. 8 (April 19, 2011): 11.

31. See Jane Patterson, "Blessing the Next Generation," 171–72.

32. See 19, 56, and 166.

33. Fischer, *Winter Grace*, 30.

34. This narrative tells the story of a person with whom I had a pastoral relationship. I use a pseudonym for her and have changed other identifying information. Since the time of this chapter's initial draft, Maggie's health declined rapidly, and she died last year.

35. Beth Ann Gaede, "What Will I Do Next? Discerning God's Callings for Retirement," *Journal of Religion, Spirituality, and Aging* 22, no. 1 (2010): 38.

36. James C. Fisher and Henry C. Simmons, *A Journey Called Aging: Challenges and Opportunities in Older Adulthood* (New York: Routledge, 2006); Amy Plantinga Pauw, "Dying Well," in *Practicing Our Faith: A Way of Life for a Searching People,* ed. Dorothy Bass (San Francisco: Jossey-Bass, 1997).

37. Ira Byock, *Dying Well: The Prospect for Growth at the End of Life* (New York: Riverhead, 1997); idem, *The Four Things That Matter Most: A Book About Living* (New York: Free Press, 2004).

38. Lyon, "Faith Development in Late Adulthood," 284.

39. Wadell, "The Call Goes On," 12.

40. See Kathleen A. Cahalan, *The Stories We Live: Finding God's Calling All around Us* (Grand Rapids: Eerdmans, 2017), 47–59.

Contributors

Matt Bloom is a psychologist, teaches in the Mendoza College of Business at the University of Notre Dame, and is the principal investigator for the Well-Being at Work project (http://wellbeing.nd.edu/).

Kathleen A. Cahalan directs the Collegeville Institute Seminars, is professor of practical theology at Saint John's School of Theology and Seminary, and is co-editor of *Calling in Today's World: Voices from Eight Faith Perspectives,* with Douglas J. Schuurman (Eerdmans, 2016) and author of *The Stories We Live* (Eerdmans, 2017).

Joyce Ann Mercer is professor of practical theology and pastoral care at Yale Divinity School. She is the author of *Lives to Offer: Accompanying Youth on Their Vocational Quests* (Pilgrim, 2007) and *Welcoming Children: A Practical Theology of Childhood* (Chalice, 2005). An ordained Presbyterian minister, she participates in ministries with older adults through her local congregation.

Bonnie J. Miller-McLemore is E. Rhodes and Leona B. Carpenter Professor of Religion, Psychology, and Culture at the Divinity School and Graduate Department of Religion at Vanderbilt University. She is the author of *Also a Mother: Work and Family as Theological Dilemma* (Abingdon, 1994) and *In the Midst of Chaos: Care of Children as Spiritual Practice* (Jossey-Bass, 2006).

Jane Patterson is assistant professor of New Testament at Seminary of the Southwest in Austin, Texas, and author of *Keeping the Feast: Metaphors of Sacrifice in 1 Corinthians and Philippians* (Society of Biblical Literature, 2015).

An ordained Episcopal priest, she is co-director of a ministry called The Work-Shop that guides laity in the use of the scriptures for discerning how to live faithfully in all aspects of daily life (http://theworkshop-sa.org/).

Katherine Turpin is associate professor of religious education, Iliff School of Theology, and author of *Branded: Adolescents Converting from Consumer Faith* (Pilgrim, 2006) and co-author with Anne Carter Walker of *Nurturing Different Dreams: Youth Ministry across Lines of Difference* (Pickwick, 2014).

Index

Addams, Jane, 84
Adolescence, 65–66; brain restructuring during, 72, 97; diminishment of to a linear *chronos* trajectory, 23–24; ending adolescence, 69–70, 89–90, 97; entering adolescence, 67–70, 89; nineteenth-century view of, 74–75; and religious rituals, 74; stereotypes of, 87; as a time of discernment, 68, 76, 81, 86–87; vocational gifts from adolescents to other generations, 87–89. *See also* Adolescence, characteristics of; Adolescence, communal practices for the nurture of vocation in; Adolescence, vocational experiences in; David

Adolescence, characteristics of: bodily changes and body consciousness, 70–71; developing adult capabilities, 74–75; openness and malleability, 72–74; performance of self, 71–72

Adolescence, communal practices for the nurture of vocation in: living commitments heroically, 82–83; mentoring by adults, 81–82; opportunities for real work, 84–85; resistance to the "one true thing"

narrative, 85–87; taking adolescents seriously, 87

Adolescence, vocational experiences in: creating friendships and significant relationships, 76–77; experiences of suffering and loss, 77–78; experimentation with possible selves, 75–76; negotiating cultural narratives, 78–80; schooling, 80–81

Adoption: in Greco-Roman society, 34; New Testament metaphor of, 34–35, 43

Advocacy, 28, 29

Age/Aging, 22

Ageism, 183–84

Agency, 30

Ammerman, Nancy: *Sacred Stories, Sacred Tribes: Finding Religion in Everyday Life*, 214n37; on the "sacred tribe," 135, 143; on spirituality, 134–35

Anderson, Herbert, 47, 49; *All Our Losses, All Our Griefs* (with Mitchell), 221n41; on "immediacy," 47; *Leaving Home*, 214n28

Anderson, Ray, "The Tasks of Grandparents in Families," 222n64

Anna and Simeon, 29, 148–49, 159

Aquinas, Thomas, 41

Index

across *Lines of Difference* (with Walker), 212n34

Vaillant, George, on the "compression of morbidity," 183

Vocation: and the body of Christ, 18–20; and charisms, 26–27; and the common good, 28–29; and community, 18–20, 25–26; definition of, 12; and duty and obligation, 30–31; and embodiment, 20–22; and empathy, 27–28; as a gift from God for the sake of the world, 177, 191, 194; and God as the One-Who-Calls, 12, 14, 15–17, 31; key practices of (*see* Discernment; Prayer; Storytelling); lifespan perspective on, 1, 12–13, 16; narrow conception of as moral and spiritual aspiration, 41–42; practical theology of, 6–8; recovering the language of, 4–6; and relationship, 13–17, 19; the secular term "vocation," 40; theology of, 7; and time, 22–25, 126; using verbs and prepositions in speaking about vocation, 16–17, 203n25. *See also* Calling; Vocation, Christian communities' weaknesses regarding

Vocation, Christian communities' weaknesses regarding: discounting of or inability to talk about religious experiences, 3; failure to engage people in the practices of vocation, 3–4; inability to talk about or interpret religious experiences, 3; limited, mostly nonexistent, experiences and conceptions of God as Caller, 2–3; references to major commitments clustered in the younger adult years, 3; the term "vocation," 4, 5, 12

Volf, Miroslav, *Work in the Spirit: Toward a Theology of Work*, 203n24, 205n65

Vulnerability, 49; of children, 48–50; of God, 49; "inherited vulnerability," 49–50; of Jesus, 49

Wadell, Paul, 196

Walker, Anne Carter, *Nurturing Different Dreams: Youth Ministry across Lines of Difference* (with Turpin), 212n34

Wall, John, "Childhood Studies, Hermeneutics, and Theological Ethics," 207n20

Warren, Rick, 5; *The Purpose Driven Life: What on Earth Am I Here For?* 5, 201n9

Weil, Simone, 47

Werpehowski, William, 53

White, David, *Practicing Discernment with Youth*, 211n2

Williams, Rowan, 50

Wimberly, Anne, 167, 223n79; on "intercessory hope," 167

Winnicott, D. W.: on "holding environment," 44, 51; on the true self, 221n48

Wise guides, 138; and middle adults, 136, 138–39

Witness, 26, 29; the call of the late adult to witness how to age with dignity and honor, 166

Wolfteich, Claire, *Navigating New Terrain: Work and Women's Spiritual Lives*, 220n31

Wood, Charles, 16

Wright, Wendy, 57

Wuthnow, Robert, 98, 101, 105

Younger adulthood, 92–96; and college and graduate school, 98; cultural markers of adulthood and barriers to achieving them, 102–3; and discernment, 106–7, 115; as "emerging adults," 97; ending younger adulthood, 117–18; entering younger adulthood, 96–98; and exemplars, 83, 100–101, 106; negative labeling of younger adults, 102–3; and service-sector jobs, 98, 104–5; vocational gifts of to other generations, 115–17; and "young adult ministry," 114. *See also* Paul, Damascus road